Bureaucracy in Historical Perspective

The Scott, Foresman

Topics in Comparative History Series

Michael S. Werthman, General Editor

Other topics to be included in the series:

Law and Order
Jon Sutherland, Michael S. Werthman

Ecology
Robert Detweiler, Jon Sutherland, Michael S. Werthman

Imperialism
Richard Wires

Economic Development

Nationalism

Slavery

Social Mobility

Urban Development

Bureaucracy in Historical Perspective

Edited by
Michael T. Dalby
Michael S. Werthman

Scott, Foresman and Company
Glenview, Illinois   London

Library of Congress Catalog Card Number: 74-137138
Copyright © 1971 by Scott, Foresman and Company, Glenview, Illinois 60025.
Philippines Copyright 1971 by Scott, Foresman and Company.
All Rights Reserved.
Printed in the United States of America.
Regional Offices of Scott, Foresman are located in Dallas, Oakland, N.J.,
Palo Alto, and Tucker, Ga.

Foreword

Topics in Comparative History is a series of anthologies intended to supply instructors and students with a new tool for the study of human institutions. The theme of the series is the diversity and comparability of significant elements in history.

The series represents a departure from the theoretical foundations of other, more traditional books of readings. It is not our intention to offer yet another collection of description and analysis of dynasties, commentary on the role of specific personalities, or recital of important events and dates. Rather, this series aims at sensitizing students to the institutional dimensions of human history. Books devoted to problems, cases, or issues can be of use in the study of history, but it is not always possible to carry the lessons of such study over to other historical developments. Institutions are not abstractions. They are concrete and identifiable components of man's society—past, present, and often future. Institutions may be defined and minutely characterized so that the student can learn to detect their presence and influence in all his researches. This institutional approach can be more productive of mature judgments than the study of such amorphous themes as the Renaissance. It is the aim of the series to help train students in understanding—not memorization—of the topic, in itself one of the highest goals of college instruction.

The series employs the comparative method, by which each topic is placed in historical perspective through descriptions of its nature and development in various times and places. When the student sees an institution functioning in different societies, he becomes more aware of the variations possible in comparable institutions. This wider perspective enables him to probe more intelligently his own history, society, and culture.

The volumes in this series will also allow instructors and students to incorporate their own special interests into various courses. Either whole volumes or individual chapters can be selected to accompany and supplement general textbook sections, thus facilitating more penetrating exploration by students into topics of particular interest and freeing instructors to be more interpretive in their lectures. Selections are by writers whose knowledge of the topic and whose aptness of style guarantee the student's surest acquisition of information that will be of the greatest significance and utility in his studies.

The most enduring value of the topics in comparative history series is its concentration on institutions and not merely on issues. Even the most glamorous and seemingly significant issues come and go, but by studying man's institutions, the student gains the ability to deal with any issue in any historical or social context. Issues, problems, and cases in historical development are relatively evanescent when compared with institutions, the persistence of which makes mastery of their nature and meaning one of the basic tools of historical scholarship.

Instructional materials should mirror the richness and scope of human history, and yet must also instill self-confidence in the students attempting to assimilate such a complex subject. The comparative study of institutions which this series offers can provide techniques for perceiving the variations in institutional history. Oversimplification, mere labeling, and memorization lose their attraction. The sophistication so acquired can be a permanent contribution to the student's skills in research and analysis.

Michael S. Werthman
General Editor

Preface

Bureaucracy is an important and characteristic institution in modern society. On a political level, bureaucratic organization has facilitated the development of both representative democracy and rule by totalitarian parties. Each of these methods of government relies on the support of a rationally directed, hierarchically organized, and impartially motivated corps of bureaucrats. The people in charge depend on bureaucrats who will respond to direction and who will translate the general policy of the government into action. Similarly, bureaucratic organization has played a significant role in the economic and social changes associated with the industrial revolution. The management of a modern factory must analyze the overall task of the factory into carefully defined segments. These smaller tasks are then assumed by sections of a bureaucratically organized staff. In the social sphere, a staff member will often find his status, prestige, and even his self-confidence to be a direct function of his position in the bureaucratic structure. Bureaucratic organization demands intensive examination because of its influence on the operation and consequences of modern institutions.

The approach of this book is twofold. Each chapter is addressed to a single, significant aspect of bureaucratic organization. At the same time, the articles in each section take examples from various places and eras. Our general aim is to place bureaucracy in historical perspective, because history provides us the broadest context for studying this complex institution. Furthermore, the works of historians, sociologists, and practicing administrators have been drawn upon in order to demonstrate the wide range of interest in bureaucracy, and to show the several ways in which it has been studied. It is expected that the student will assess both the topic and the selections to form his own conclusions.

We are chiefly concerned with the administrative bureaucracy of government—or civil service—because it exhibits all the characteristics of general bureaucratic organization. Civil servants have been prominent in the institutional life of many societies in history. And civil service is also the type of bureaucracy most evident in modern life. In the United States, for example, more than twelve and a half million persons are employed in all levels of government (including the military); most of these civil servants work within a bureaucratic type of organization. Civil service bureaucracies have ever greater power and influence at their disposal. The role they play in shaping our society and our destiny is a crucial one.

Michael T. Dalby
Michael S. Werthman

Contents

1

The Role of Bureaucracy in Society

The role of civil service bureaucracy in society depends on two things: first, the distinctive characteristics of bureaucracy that set it apart from other systems in society; second, the relationship of civil service to other institutions such as politics or social mobility. The special characteristics of bureaucracy are discussed sociologically in the first two articles of this section. The observations of Weber and Blau illuminate our understanding of bureaucracy in all societies. However, because the relative position and importance of bureaucracy vary from society to society and from time to time, we shall examine the scale of possible variation by using two examples of societies in which bureaucracy has played a prominent role—Britain and China.

Max Weber (1864-1920), German sociologist and historian, is without doubt the most influential general theorist of bureaucracy. In his *Economy and Society* Weber defined the ideal type of bureaucracy. Weber's ideal type is not the average of the characteristics of bureaucracies found in different times, places, and environments. Instead, his hypothesis was intended to distinguish the features of bureaucracy, on a "pure" or abstract level, from other kinds of human organization, and to provide criteria to distinguish bureaucratic societies from his other ideal types of society: the feudal society and the patrimonial society. Thus, for example, payment of civil servants by the government in the form of a salary is a characteristic of bureaucratic organization, whereas payment in the form of rights to exploit a segment of the population is a feature of feudal society. Weber's ideal type is valuable to sociologists and, in some cases, to historians. Sometimes the ideal type is used as a standard; more often it simply stimulates the formulation of certain kinds of questions about a society that has bureaucratic features.

Peter M. Blau analyzes some of the implications of Weber's method in the selection from his *Bureaucracy in Modern Society*. He maintains in particular that the ideal type defines the elements of bureaucratic organization, but that Weber's hypotheses about the relationship between elements may well need to be modified by empirical research. Accordingly, Blau sees the development of bureaucracy in terms of the interrelationship of bureaucracy with other institutions. For instance, a bureaucracy may help to solve new problems for which it was not specifically created. But rarely is a "felt need" for bureaucracy the mother of its invention, because "if needs inevitably created ways of meeting them, human society would be a paradise." Blau's arguments reinforce the importance of recognizing variation as well as similarity in bureaucratic societies.

The role of bureaucracy in British society is extraordinary in the first instance because it began so early, in comparison with other modern European states, and also because of its remarkable continuity and efficiency. The spirit and high standards of the British bureaucracy affirm the dignity of the civil servant, in the best sense of the term. But these traditions are not derived from the security of a monopoly of state administration, in the manner of Weber's ideally monocratic structure. As Sir Ivor Jennings explains in *The Queen's Government*, urban areas and rural localities in England have never been totally subject to centralized bureaucratic authority. Nor has the selection of bureaucrats always been free from politics, for patronage remained potent through the eighteenth century. The impressive achievement of the English civil service rests on an evolved consensus of the proper division of spheres of authority, and on the rightful and honorable place of the bureaucrat as an employee of the public.

Imperial China contrasts markedly with Britain, as do the roles of the Chinese and British bureaucracies. Etienne Balazs (1905-1963), in "China as a Permanently Bureaucratic Society," deals with the nature and consequences of the centrality of bureaucracy in virtually all aspects of Chinese life. Whereas in Britain the civil service is subordinate to political authority, the bureaucracy of imperial China *was* political authority, subject only to the Emperor. A career as a bureaucrat in the West is one alternative among many, but in China, from Sung times, a career in the bureaucracy was the primary source of power, status, and wealth. The role of the bureaucracy was to coordinate society as a whole; the role of the Chinese bureaucrat ". . . was at one and the same time that of architect, engineer, teacher, administrator, and ruler." As Balazs points out, there are numerous characteristics of the Chinese bureaucracy that are similar to those of the totalitarian societies of our day, but it was the especially important central role of bureaucracy in China that made Chinese society so different from others in world history.

Max Weber

The Ideal Type
of Bureaucracy

[CHARACTERISTICS OF BUREAUCRACY_/

Modern officialdom functions in the following specific manner:

I.   There is the principle of fixed and official jurisdictional areas, which are generally ordered by rules, that is, by laws or administrative regulations.

1.   The regular activities required for the purposes of the bureaucratically governed structure are distributed in a fixed way as official duties.

2.   The authority to give the commands-required for the discharge of these duties is distributed in a stable way and is strictly delimited by rules concerning the coercive means, physical, sacerdotal, or otherwise, which may be placed at the disposal of officials.

3.   Methodical provision is made for the regular and continuous fulfillment of these duties and for the execution of the corresponding rights; only persons who have the generally regulated qualifications to serve are employed.

In public and lawful government these three elements constitute "bureaucratic authority." In private economic domination, they constitute bureaucratic "management." Bureaucracy, thus understood, is fully developed in political and ecclesiastical communities only in the modern state, and, in the private economy, only in the most advanced institutions of capitalism. Permanent and public office authority, with fixed jurisdiction, is not the historical rule but rather the exception. This is so even in large political structures such as those of the ancient Orient, the Germanic and Mongolian empires of conquest, or of many feudal structures of state. In all these cases, the ruler executes the most important measures through personal trustees, table companions, or court servants. Their commissions and authority are not precisely delimited and are temporarily called into being for each case.

II.   The principles of office hierarchy and of levels of graded authority mean a firmly ordered system of super- and subordination in which there is a supervision of the lower offices by the higher ones. Such a system offers the governed the possibility of appealing the decision of a lower office to its higher authority, in a definitely regulated manner. With the full development of the bureaucratic type,

Abridged from *From Max Weber: Essays in Sociology*, edited and translated by H. H. Gerth and C. Wright Mills, pp. 196-200, 202, 203-210, 211-212, 213-216. Copyright 1946 by Oxford University Press, Inc. Reprinted by permission.

the office hierarchy is monocratically organized. The principle of hierarchical office authority is found in all bureaucratic structures: in state and ecclesiastical
structures as well as in large party organizations and private enterprises. It does not
matter for the character of bureaucracy whether its authority is called "private" or
"public."

When the principle of jurisdictional "competency" is fully carried through,
hierarchical subordination—at least in public office—does not mean that the "higher" authority is simply authorized to take over the business of the "lower." Indeed,
the opposite is the rule. Once established and having fulfilled its task, an office
tends to continue in existence and be held by another incumbent.

III.   The management of the modern office is based upon written documents
("the files"), which are preserved in their original or draught form. There is, therefore, a staff of subaltern officials and scribes of all sorts. The body of officials
actively engaged in a "public" office, along with the respective apparatus of material implements and the files, make up a "bureau." In private enterprise, "the
bureau" is often called "the office."

In principle, the modern organization of the civil service separates the bureau
from the private domicile of the official, and, in general, bureaucracy segregates
official activity as something distinct from the sphere of private life. Public monies
and equipment are divorced from the private property of the official. This condition is everywhere the product of a long development. Nowadays, it is found in
public as well as in private enterprises; in the latter, the principle extends even to
the leading entrepreneur. In principle, the executive office is separated from the
household, business from private correspondence, and business assets from private
fortunes. The more consistently the modern type of business management has been
carried through, the more are these separations the case. The beginnings of this
process are to be found as early as the Middle Ages.

It is the peculiarity of the modern entrepreneur that he conducts himself as
the "first official" of his enterprise, in the very same way in which the ruler of a
specifically modern bureaucratic state spoke of himself as "the first servant" of the
state. The idea that the bureau activities of the state are intrinsically different in
character from the management of private economic offices is a continental European notion and, by way of contrast, is totally foreign to the American way.

IV.   Office management, at least all specialized office management—and such
management is distinctly modern—usually presupposes thorough and expert training. This increasingly holds for the modern executive and employee of private
enterprises, in the same manner as it holds for the state official.

V.   When the office is fully developed, official activity demands the full working
capacity of the official, irrespective of the fact that his obligatory time in the bureau may be firmly delimited. In the normal case, this is only the product of a long
development, in the public as well as in the private office. Formerly, in all cases,
the normal state of affairs was reversed: official business was discharged as a secondary activity.

VI.   The management of the office follows general rules, which are more or less stable, more or less exhaustive, and which can be learned. Knowledge of these rules represents a special technical learning which the officials possess. It involves jurisprudence, or administrative or business management.

The reduction of modern office management to rules is deeply embedded in its very nature. The theory of modern public administration, for instance, assumes that the authority to order certain matters by decree—which has been legally granted to public authorities—does not entitle the bureau to regulate the matter by commands given for each case, but only to regulate the matter abstractly. This stands in extreme contrast to the regulation of all relationships through individual privileges and bestowals of favor, which is absolutely dominant in patrimonialism, at least in so far as such relationships are not fixed by sacred tradition.

THE POSITION OF THE OFFICIAL

All this results in the following for the internal and external position of the official:

I.   Office holding is a "vocation." This is shown, first, in the requirement of a firmly prescribed course of training, which demands the entire capacity for work for a long period of time, and in the generally prescribed and special examinations which are prerequisites of employment. Furthermore, the position of the official is in the nature of a duty. This determines the internal structure of his relations, in the following manner: Legally and actually, office holding is not considered a source to be exploited for rents or emoluments, as was normally the case during the Middle Ages and frequently up to the threshold of recent times. Nor is office holding considered a usual exchange of services for equivalents, as is the case with free labor contracts. Entrance into an office, including one in the private economy, is considered an acceptance of a specific obligation of faithful management in return for a secure existence. It is decisive for the specific nature of modern loyalty to an office that, in the pure type, it does not establish a relationship to a *person*, like the vassal's or disciple's faith in feudal or in patrimonial relations of authority. Modern loyalty is devoted to impersonal and functional purposes. Behind the functional purposes, of course, "ideas of culture-values" usually stand. These are *ersatz* for the earthly or supra-mundane personal master: ideas such as "state," "church," "community," "party," or "enterprise" are thought of as being realized in a community; they provide an ideological halo for the master.

The political official—at least in the fully developed modern state—is not considered the personal servant of a ruler. Today, the bishop, the priest, and the preacher are in fact no longer, as in early Christian times, holders of purely personal charisma. The supra-mundane and sacred values which they offer are given to everybody who seems to be worthy of them and who asks for them. In former times, such leaders acted upon the personal command of their master; in principle, they were responsible only to him. Nowadays, in spite of the partial survival of the old theory, such religious leaders are officials in the service of a functional purpose, which in the present-day "church" has become routinized and, in turn, ideologically hallowed.

II.   The personal position of the official is patterned in the following way:

1.   Whether he is in a private office or a public bureau, the modern official always strives and usually enjoys a distinct *social esteem* as compared with the governed. His social position is guaranteed by the prescriptive rules of rank order and, for the political official, by special definitions of the criminal code against "insults of officials" and "contempt" of state and church authorities.

The actual social position of the official is normally highest where, as in old civilized countries, the following conditions prevail: a strong demand for administration by trained experts; a strong and stable social differentiation, where the official predominantly derives from socially and economically privileged strata because of the social distribution of power; or where the costliness of the required training and status conventions are binding upon him. The possession of educational certificates . . . are usually linked with qualification for office. Naturally, such certificates or patents enhance the "status element" in the social position of the official. For the rest this status factor in individual cases is explicitly and impassively acknowledged; for example, in the prescription that the acceptance or rejection of an aspirant to an official career depends upon the consent ("election") of the members of the official body. This is the case in the German army with the officer corps. Similar phenomena, which promote this guild-like closure of officialdom, are typically found in patrimonial and, particularly, in prebendal officialdoms of the past. The desire to resurrect such phenomena in changed forms is by no means infrequent among modern bureaucrats. For instance, they have played a role among the demands of the quite proletarian and expert officials during the Russian revolution.

Usually the social esteem of the officials as such is especially low where the demand for expert administration and the dominance of status conventions are weak. This is especially the case in the United States; it is often the case in new settlements by virtue of their wide fields for profit making and the great instability of their social stratification.

2.   The pure type of bureaucratic official is *appointed* by a superior authority. An official elected by the governed is not a purely bureaucratic figure. Of course, the formal existence of an election does not by itself mean that no appointment hides behind the election—in the state, especially, appointment by party chiefs. Whether or not this is the case does not depend upon legal statutes but upon the way in which the party mechanism functions. Once firmly organized, the parties can turn a formally free election into the mere acclamation of a candidate designated by the party chief. As a rule, however, a formally free election is turned into a fight, conducted according to definite rules, for votes in favor of one of two designated candidates. . . .

3.   Normally, the position of the official is held for life, at least in public bureau-

cracies; and this is increasingly the case for all similar structures. As a factual rule, *tenure for life* is presupposed, even where the giving of notice or periodic reappointment occurs. In contrast to the worker in a private enterprise, the official normally holds tenure. Legal or actual life tenure, however, is not recognized as the official's right to the possession of office, as was the case with many structures of authority in the past. Where legal guarantees against arbitrary dismissal or transfer are developed, they merely serve to guarantee a strictly objective discharge of specific office duties free from all personal considerations. In Germany, this is the case for all juridical and, increasingly, for all administrative officials. . . .

4.   The official receives the regular *pecuniary* compensation of a normally fixed *salary* and the old age security provided by a pension. The salary is not measured like a wage in terms of work done, but according to "status," that is, according to the kind of function (the "rank") and, in addition, possibly, according to the length of service. The relatively great security of the official's income, as well as the rewards of social esteem, make the office a sought-after position, especially in countries which no longer provide opportunities for colonial profits. In such countries, this situation permits relatively low salaries for officials.

5.   The official is set for a *"career"* within the hierarchical order of the public service. He moves from the lower, less important, and lower paid to the higher positions. The average official naturally desires a mechanical fixing of the conditions of promotion: if not of the offices, at least of the salary levels. He wants these conditions fixed in terms of "seniority," or possibly according to grades achieved in a developed system of expert examinations. Here and there, such examinations actually form a character *indelebilis* of the official and have lifelong effects on his career. To this is joined the desire to qualify the right to office and the increasing tendency toward status group closure and economic security. All of this makes for a tendency to consider the offices as "prebends" [sources of fixed income] of those who are qualified by educational certificates. The necessity of taking general personal and intellectual qualifications into consideration, irrespective of the often subaltern character of the educational certificate, has led to a condition in which the highest political offices, especially the positions of "ministers," are principally filled without reference to such certificates.

THE PRESUPPOSITIONS AND CAUSES OF BUREAUCRACY

The social and economic presuppositions of the modern structure of the office are as follows:

The development of the *money economy*, in so far as a pecuniary compensation of the officials is concerned, is a presupposition of bureaucracy. Today it not only prevails but is predominant. This fact is of very great importance for the whole bearing of bureaucracy, yet by itself it is by no means decisive for the existence of bureaucracy.

Historical examples of rather distinctly developed and quantitatively large bureaucracies are: (a) Egypt, during the period of the new Empire which, however, contained strong patrimonial elements; (b) the later Roman Principate, and especially the Diocletian monarchy and the Byzantine polity which developed out of it and yet retained strong feudal and patrimonial elements; (c) the Roman Catholic Church, increasingly so since the end of the thirteenth century; (d) China, from the time of Shi Hwangti until the present, but with strong patrimonial and prebendal elements; (e) in ever purer forms, the modern European states and, increasingly, all public corporations since the time of princely absolutism; (f) the large modern capitalist enterprise, the more so as it becomes greater and more complicated.

To a very great extent, partly even predominantly, cases (a) to (d) have rested upon compensation of the officials in kind. Yet they have displayed many other traits and effects characteristic of bureaucracy. The historical model of all later bureaucracies—the new Empire of Egypt—is at the same time one of the most grandiose examples of an organized subsistence economy. Yet this coincidence of bureaucracy and subsistence economy is understandable in view of the quite unique conditions that existed in Egypt. And the reservations—and they are quite considerable—which one must make in classifying this Egyptian structure as a bureaucracy are conditioned by the subsistence economy. A certain measure of a developed money economy is the normal precondition for the unchanged and continued existence, if not for the establishment, of pure bureaucratic administrations.

According to historical experience, without a money economy the bureaucratic structure can hardly avoid undergoing substantial internal changes, or indeed, turning into another type of structure. The allocation of fixed income in kind, from the magazines of the lord or from his current intake, to the officials easily means a first step toward appropriation of the sources of taxation and their exploitation as private property. This kind of allocation has been the rule in Egypt and China for thousands of years and played an important part in the later Roman monarchy as well as elsewhere. The income in kind has protected the official against the often sharp fluctuations in the purchasing power of money. Whenever the lord's prerogatives have relaxed, the taxes in kind, as a rule, have been irregular. In this case, the official has direct recourse to the tributaries of his bailiwick, whether or not he is authorized. Close at hand is the idea of securing the official against such oscillations by mortgaging or transferring the levies and therewith the power to tax, or by leasing profitable lands of the lord to the official for his own use. Every central authority which is not strictly organized is tempted to take this course either voluntarily or because the officials compel it to do so. The official may satisfy himself with the use of these levies or loans up to the level of his salary claim and then hand over the surplus. This implies strong temptation and therefore yields results chiefly unsatisfactory to the lord. Another process involves fixing the official's salary: This often occurred in the early history of German officialdom; and it happened on the largest scale in all Eastern Satrap administrations: the official hands over a stipulated amount and retains the surplus.

In such cases the official is economically in a position rather similar to that of the entrepreneurial tax farmer. Indeed, office farming, including even the leasing of offices to the highest bidder, is regularly found. On the soil of a private economy, the transformation of the statutes of villenage into tenancy relations is one of the most important among numerous examples. By tenancy arrangements the lord can transfer the trouble of changing his income-in-kind into money-income to the office tenant or to the official who is to be given a fixed sum. This was plainly the case with some Oriental regents in Antiquity. And above all, the farming out of public collection of taxes in lieu of the lord's own management of taxgathering served this purpose. From this procedure there develops the possibility for the lord to progress in the ordering of his finances into a systematic budget. This is a very important advance, for it means that a fixed estimate of the income, and correspondingly of the expenses, can take the place of a hand-to-mouth living from incalculable incomes in kind, a condition typical of all the early states of public households. On the other hand, in systematizing his budget in this way, the lord renounces the control and full exploitation of his capacity to tax for his own use. According to the measure of freedom left to the official, to the office, or to the tax farmer, the lasting capacity to pay taxes is endangered by inconsiderate exploitation. For, unlike the political overlord, the capitalist is not in the same way permanently interested in the subject's ability to pay.

The lord seeks to safeguard himself against this loss of control by regulations. The mode of tax farming or the transfer of taxes can thus vary widely, according to the distribution of power between the lord and the tenant. Either the tenant's interest in the free exploitation of capacity to pay taxes or the lord's interest in the permanence of this capacity prevails. The nature of the tax-farming system rests essentially upon the joint or the opposing influence of these motives: the elimination of oscillations in the yields, the possibility of a budget, the safeguarding of the subjects' capacity to pay by protecting them against uneconomical exploitation, and a state control of the tax farmer's yields for the sake of appropriating the maximum possible. In the Ptolemaic empire, as in Hellas and in Rome, the tax farmer was still a private capitalist. The raising of taxes, however, was bureaucratically executed and controlled by the Ptolemaic state. The tenant's profit consisted in only a share of the respective surplus over and above the tax farmer's fee, which was, in fact, only a guarantee. The tax farmer's risk consisted in the possibility of yields that were lower than this sum.

The purely economic conception of the office as a source of the official's private income can also lead to the direct purchase of offices. This occurs when the lord finds himself in a position in which he requires not only a current income but money capital—for instance, for warfare or for debt payments. The purchase of office as a regular institution has existed in modern states, in the church state as well as in that of France and England; it has existed in the cases of sinecures as well as of very serious offices; and, in the case of officers' commissions, it lagged over until the early nineteenth century. In individual cases, the economic meaning of such a purchase of office can be altered so that the purchasing sum is partly or wholly in the nature of bail deposited for faithful service, but this has not been the rule.

Every sort of assignment of usufructs [rights to the fruits of office], tributes, and services which are due to the lord himself or to the official for personal exploitation, always means a surrender of the pure type of bureaucratic organization. The official in such positions has a personal right to the possession of his office. This is the case to a still higher degree when official duty and compensation are interrelated in such a way that the official does not transfer to the lord any yields gained from the objects left to him, but handles these objects for his private ends and in turn renders to the lord services of a personal or a military, political, or ecclesiastical character.

We wish to speak of *"prebends"* and of a "prebendal" organization of office, wherever the lord assigns to the official rent payments for life, payments which are somehow fixed to objects or which are essentially *economic* usufruct from lands or other sources. They must be compensations for the fulfillment of actual or fictitious office duties; they are goods permanently set aside for the economic assurance of the office.

The transition from such prebendal organization of office to salaried officialdom is quite fluid. Very often the economic endowment of priesthoods has been "prebendal," as in Antiquity and the Middle Ages, and even up to the modern period. But in almost all periods the same form has been found in other areas. In Chinese sacerdotal law, the prebendal character of all offices forced the mourning official to resign his office. For during the ritual mourning period for the father or other household authorities, abstention from the enjoyment of possessions was prescribed. Originally this prescription was aimed at avoiding the ill will of the deceased master of the house, for the house belonged to this master and the office was considered purely as a prebend, a source for rent.

When not only economic rights but also lordly prerogatives are leased for personal execution with the stipulation of *personal* services to the lord, a further step away from salaried bureaucracy is taken. These leased prerogatives vary; for instance, with the political official, they may be in the nature of landlordism or in the nature of office authority. In both instances, and certainly in the latter, the specific nature of bureaucratic organization is completely destroyed and we enter the organizational realm of *feudal* dominion. All kinds of assignments of services and usufructs in kind as endowments for officials tend to loosen the bureaucratic mechanism, and especially to weaken hierarchic subordination. This subordination is most strictly developed in the discipline of modern officialdom. A precision similar to the precision of the contractually employed official of the modern Occident can only be attained—at least under very energetic leadership—where the subjection of the officials to the lord is personally absolute, where slaves, or employees treated like slaves, are used for administration.

The Egyptian officials were slaves of the Pharaoh, if not legally, at least in fact. The Roman latifundia [very large estates] owners liked to commission slaves with the direct management of money matters, because of the possibility of subjecting them to torture. In China, similar results have been sought by the prodigial use of the bamboo as a disciplinary instrument. The chances, however, for such direct means of coercion to function with *steadiness* are extremely unfavorable. According to experience, the relative optimum for the success and maintenance of a strict mechanization of the bureaucratic apparatus is offered by a secured money salary connected with the opportunity of a career that is not dependent upon mere accident and arbitrariness. Strict discipline and control, which at the same time has consideration for the official's sense of honor, and the development of prestige sentiments of the status group, as well as the possibility of public criticism, work in the direction of strict mechanization. With all this, the bureaucratic apparatus functions more assuredly than does any legal enslavement of functionaries. A strong status sentiment among officials not only agrees with the official's readiness to subordinate himself to the chief without any will of his own, but—just as is the case with the officer—status sentiments are the consequence of such subordination, for internally they balance the official's self-feeling. The purely impersonal character of office work, with its principled separation of the private sphere of the official from that of the office, facilitates the official's integration into the given functional conditions of a fixed mechanism based upon discipline.

Even though the full development of a money economy is not an indispensable precondition for bureaucratization, bureaucracy as a permanent structure is knit to the one presupposition of a constant income for maintaining it. Where such an income cannot be derived from private profits, as is the case with the bureaucratic organization of large modern enterprises, or from fixed land rents, as with the manor, a stable system of *taxation* is the precondition for the permanent existence of bureaucratic administration. For well-known and general reasons, only a fully developed money economy offers a secure basis for such a taxation system. The degree of administrative bureaucratization in urban communities with fully developed money economies has not infrequently been relatively greater in the contemporary, far larger states of plains. Yet as soon as these plain states have been able to develop orderly systems of tribute, bureaucracy has developed more comprehensively than in city states. Whenever the size of the city states has remained confined to moderate limits, the tendency for a plutocratic and collegial administration by notables has corresponded most adequately to their structure.

THE QUANTITATIVE DEVELOPMENT
OF ADMINISTRATIVE TASKS

The proper soil for the bureaucratization of an administration has always been the specific developments of administrative tasks. We shall first discuss the quantitative extension of such tasks. In the field of politics, the great state and the mass party are the classic soil for bureaucratization.

This does not mean that every historically known and genuine formation of great states has brought about a bureaucratic administration. The permanence of a once-existing great state, or the homogeneity of a culture borne by such a state, has not always been attached to a bureaucratic structure of state. However, both of these features have held to a great extent, for instance, in the Chinese empire. The numerous great Negro empires, and similar formations, have had only an ephemeral existence primarily because they have lacked an apparatus of officials. And the unity of the Carolingian empire disintegrated when its organization of officials disintegrated. This organization, however, was predominantly patrimonial rather than bureaucratic in nature. From a purely temporal view, however, the empire of the Caliphs and its predecessors on Asiatic soil have lasted for considerable periods of time, and their organization of office was essentially patrimonial and prebendal. Also, the Holy Roman Empire lasted for a long time in spite of the almost complete absence of bureaucracy. All these realms have represented a cultural unity of at least approximately the same strength as is usually created by bureaucratic polities.

The ancient Roman Empire disintegrated internally in spite of increasing bureaucratization and even during its very execution. This was because of the way the tax burdens were distributed by the bureaucratic state, which favored the subsistence economy. Viewed with regard to the intensity of their purely *political* unities, the temporal existences of the empires of the Caliphs, Carolingian and other medieval emperors were essentially unstable, nominal, and cohesive conglomerates. On the whole, the capacity for political action steadily diminished, and the relatively great unity of *culture* flowed from ecclesiastic structures that were in part strictly unified and, in the Occidental Middle Ages, increasingly bureaucratic in character. The unity of their cultures resulted partly from the far-going homogeneity of their social structures, which in turn was the aftermath and transformation of their former political unity. Both are phenomena of the traditional stereotyping of culture, which favors an unstable equilibrium. Both of these factors proved so strong a foundation that even grandiose attempts at expansion, such as the Crusades, could be undertaken in spite of the lack of intensive political unity; they were, one might say, performed as "private undertakings." The failure of the Crusades and their often irrational political course, however, is associated with the absence of a unified and intensive state power to back them up. And there is no doubt that the nuclei of intensive "modern" states in the Middle Ages developed concomitantly with bureaucratic structures. Furthermore, in the end these quite bureaucratic political structures undoubtedly shattered the social conglomerates, which rested essentially upon unstable equilibriums. . . .

At the beginning of the modern period, all the prerogatives of the continental states accumulated in the hands of those princes who most relentlessly took the course of administrative bureaucratization. It is obvious that technically the great modern state is absolutely dependent upon a bureaucratic basis. The larger the state, and the more it is or the more it becomes a great power state, the more unconditionally is this the case.

The United States still bears the character of a polity which, at least in the technical sense, is not fully bureaucratized. But the greater the zones of friction with the outside and the more urgent the needs for administrative unity at home become, the more this character is inevitably and gradually giving way formally to the bureaucratic structure. Moreover, the partly unbureaucratic form of the state structure of the United States is materially balanced by the more strictly bureaucratic structures of those formations which, in truth, dominate politically, namely, the parties under the leadership of professionals or experts in organization and election tactics. The increasingly bureaucratic organization of all genuine mass parties offers the most striking example of the role of sheer quantity as a leverage for the bureaucratization of a social structure. In Germany, above all, the Social Democratic party, and abroad both of the "historical" American parties are bureaucratic in the greatest possible degree.

QUALITATIVE CHANGES OF ADMINISTRATIVE TASKS

Bureaucratization is occasioned more by intensive and qualitative enlargement and internal deployment of the scope of administrative tasks than by their extensive and quantitative increase. But the direction bureaucratization takes and the reasons that occasion it vary widely.

In Egypt, the oldest country of bureaucratic state administration, the public and collective regulation of waterways for the whole country and from the top could not be avoided because of technical economic factors. This regulation created the mechanism of scribes and officials. Once established, this mechanism, even in early times, found its second realm of business in the extraordinary construction activities which were organized militarily. As mentioned before, the bureaucratic tendency has chiefly been influenced by needs arising from the creation of standing armies as determined by power politics and by the development of public finance connected with the military establishment. In the modern state, the increasing demands for administration rest on the increasing complexity of civilization and push towards bureaucratization. . . .

Among purely political factors, the increasing demand of a society, accustomed to absolute pacification, for order and protection ("police") in all fields exerts an especially persevering influence in the direction of bureaucratization. A steady road leads from modifications of the blood feud, sacerdotally, or by means of arbitration, to the present position of the policeman as the "representative of God on earth." The former means placed the guarantees for the individual's rights and security squarely upon the members of his sib [kinship group], who are obligated to assist him with oath and vengeance. Among other factors, primarily the manifold tasks of the so-called "policy of social welfare" operate in the direction of bureaucratization, for these tasks are, in part, saddled upon the state by interest groups and, in part, the state usurps them, either for reasons of power policy or for ideological motives. Of course, these tasks are to a large extent economically determined.

Among essentially technical factors, the specifically modern means of communication enter the picture as pacemakers of bureaucratization. Public land and waterways, railroads, the telegraph, etc.—they must, in part, necessarily be administered in a public and collective way; in part, such administration is technically expedient. In this respect, the contemporary means of communication frequently play a role similar to that of the canals of Mesopotamia and the regulation of the Nile in the ancient Orient. The degree to which the means of communication have been developed is a condition of decisive importance for the possibility of bureaucratic administration, although it is not the only decisive condition. Certainly in Egypt, bureaucratic centralization, on the basis of an almost pure subsistence economy, could never have reached the actual degree which it did without the natural trade route of the Nile. In order to promote bureaucratic centralization in modern Persia, the telegraph officials were officially commissioned with reporting all occurrences in the provinces to the Shah, over the heads of the local authorities. In addition, everyone received the right to remonstrate directly by telegraph. The modern Occidental state can be administered the way it actually is only because the state controls the telegraph network and has the mails and railroads at its disposal.

Railroads, in turn, are intimately connected with the development of an inter-local traffic of mass goods. This traffic is among the causal factors in the formation of the modern state. As we have already seen, this does not hold unconditionally for the past.

TECHNICAL ADVANTAGES
OF BUREAUCRATIC ORGANIZATION

The decisive reason for the advance of bureaucratic organization has always been its purely technical superiority over any other form of organization. The fully developed bureaucratic mechanism compares with other organizations exactly as does the machine with the nonmechanical modes of production.

Precision, speed, unambiguity, knowledge of the files, continuity, discretion, unity, strict subordination, reduction of friction and of material and personal costs—these are raised to the optimum point in the strictly bureaucratic administration, and especially in its monocratic form. As compared with all collegiate, honorific, and avocational forms of administration, trained bureaucracy is superior on all these points. And as far as complicated tasks are concerned, paid bureaucratic work is not only more precise but, in the last analysis, it is often cheaper than even formally unremunerated honorific service.

Honorific arrangements make administrative work an avocation and, for this reason alone, honorific service normally functions more slowly; being less bound to schemata and being more formless. Hence it is less precise and less unified than bureaucratic work because it is less dependent upon superiors and because the establishment and exploitation of the apparatus of subordinate officials and filing services are almost unavoidably less economical. Honorific service is less continuous than bureaucratic and frequently quite expensive. This is especially the case if one thinks not only of the money costs to the public treasury—costs which bureaucratic administration, in comparison with administration by notables, usually substantially increases—but also of the frequent economic losses of the governed caused by delays and lack of precision. The possibility of administration by no-tables normally and permanently exists only where official management can be satisfactorily discharged as an avocation. With the qualitative increase of tasks the administration has to face, administration by notables reaches its limits—today, even in England. Work organized by collegiate bodies causes friction and delay and requires compromises between colliding interests and views. The administration, therefore, runs less precisely and is more independent of superiors; hence, it is less unified and slower. All advances of the Prussian administrative organization have been and will in the future be advances of the bureaucratic, and especially of the monocratic, principle.

Today, it is primarily the capitalist market economy which demands that the official business of the administration be discharged precisely, unambiguously, continuously, and with as much speed as possible. Normally, the very large, mod-ern capitalist enterprises are themselves unequaled models of strict bureaucratic organization. Business management throughout rests on increasing precision, stead-iness, and, above all, the speed of operations. This, in turn, is determined by the peculiar nature of the modern means of communication, including, among other things, the news service of the press. The extraordinary increase in the speed by which public announcements, as well as economic and political facts, are trans-mitted exerts a steady and sharp pressure in the direction of speeding up the tempo of administrative reaction towards various situations. The optimum of such reac-tion time is normally attained only by a strictly bureaucratic organization.*

Bureaucratization offers above all the optimum possibility for carrying through the principle of specializing administrative functions according to purely objective considerations. Individual performances are allocated to functionaries who have specialized training and who by constant practice learn more and more. The "objective" discharge of business primarily means a discharge of business according to *calculable rules* and "without regard for persons."

"Without regard for persons" is also the watchword of the "market" and, in general, of all pursuits of naked economic interests. A consistent execution of bu-reaucratic domination means the leveling of status "honor." Hence, if the principle of the free market is not at the same time restricted, it means the universal domi-nation of the "class situation." That this consequence of bureaucratic domination has not set in everywhere, parallel to the extent of bureaucratization, is due to the differences among possible principles by which polities may meet their demands.

The second element mentioned, "calculable rules," also is of paramount im-portance for modern bureaucracy. The peculiarity of modern culture, and specifi-cally of its technical and economic basis, demands this very "calculability" of results. When fully developed, bureaucracy also stands, in a specific sense, under the principle of *sine ira ac studio*. Its specific nature, which is welcomed by capital-ism, develops the more perfectly the more the bureaucracy is "dehumanized,"

---

*Here we cannot discuss in detail how the bureaucratic apparatus may, and actually does, produce definite obstacles to the discharge of business in a manner suitable for the single case.

the more completely it succeeds in eliminating from official business love, hatred, and all purely personal, irrational, and emotional elements which escape calculation. This is the specific nature of bureaucracy and it is appraised as its special virtue.

The more complicated and specialized modern culture becomes, the more its external supporting apparatus demands the personally detached and strictly "objective" *expert*, in lieu of the master of older social structures, who was moved by personal sympathy and favor, by grace and gratitude. Bureaucracy offers the attitudes demanded by the external apparatus of modern culture in the most favorable combination.

Peter M. Blau

The Implications
of Weber's Construct

IMPLICATIONS OF THE IDEAL-TYPE CONSTRUCT

Weber dealt with bureaucracy as what he termed an "ideal type." This methodological concept does not represent an average of the attributes of all existing bureaucracies (or other social structures), but a pure type, derived by abstracting the most characteristic bureaucratic aspects of all known organizations. Since perfect bureaucratization is never fully realized, no empirical organization corresponds exactly to this scientific construct.

The criticism has been made that Weber's analysis of an imaginary ideal type does not provide understanding of concrete bureaucratic structures. But this criticism obscures the fact that the ideal-type construct is intended as a guide in empirical research, not as a substitute for it. By indicating the characteristics of bureaucracy in its pure form, it directs the researcher to those aspects of organizations that he must examine in order to determine the extent of their bureaucratization. This is the function of all conceptual schemes: to specify the factors that must be taken into consideration in investigations and to define them clearly.

The ideal type, however, is not simply a conceptual scheme. It includes not only definitions of concepts but also generalizations about the relationships between them, specifically, the hypothesis that the diverse bureaucratic characteristics increase administrative efficiency. Whereas conceptual definitions are presupposed in research and not subject to verification by research findings, hypotheses concerning relationships between factors are subject to such verification. Whether strict hierarchical authority, for example, in fact furthers efficiency is a question of empirical fact and not one of definition. But as a scientific construct, the ideal type cannot be refuted by empirical evidence. If a study of several organizations were to find that strict hierarchical authority is not related to efficiency, this would not prove that no such relationship exists in the ideal-type bureaucracy; it would show only that these organizations are not fully bureaucratized. Since generalizations about idealized states defy testing in systematic research, they have no place in science. On the other hand, if empirical evidence is taken into consideration and generalizations are modified accordingly, we deal with prevailing tendencies in bureaucratic structures and no longer with a pure type.

Two misleading implications of the ideal-type conception of bureaucracy deserve special mention. The student of social organization is concerned with the patterns of activities and interactions that reveal how social conduct is organized, and not with exceptional deviations from these patterns. The fact that one official becomes excited and shouts at his colleague, or that another arrives late at the office, is unimportant in understanding the organization, except that the rare occurrence of such events indicates that they are idiosyncratic, differing from the prevailing patterns. Weber's decision to treat only the purely formal organization of bureaucracy implies that all deviations from these formal requirements are idiosyncratic and of no interest for the student of organization. Recent empirical studies have shown this approach to be misleading. Informal relations and unofficial practices develop among the members of bureaucracies and assume an organized form without being officially sanctioned. Chester I. Barnard, one of the first to call attention to this phenomenon, held that these "informal organizations are necessary to the operations of formal organizations." These informal patterns, in contrast to exceptional occurrences, . . . are a regular part of bureaucratic organizations and therefore must be taken into account in their analysis.

Weber's approach also implies that any deviation from the formal structure is detrimental to administrative efficiency. Since the ideal type is conceived as the perfectly efficient organization, all differences from it must necessarily interfere with efficiency. There is considerable evidence that suggests the opposite conclusion; informal relations and unofficial practices often contribute to efficient operations. In any case, the significance of these unofficial patterns for operations cannot be determined in advance on theoretical grounds but only on the basis of factual investigations. Before examining such case studies of bureaucracies it is useful to explore the conditions that give rise to bureaucratization.

CONDITIONS THAT GIVE RISE
TO BUREAUCRATIZATION

To say that there is a historical trend toward bureaucracy is to state that many organizations change from less to more bureaucratic forms of administration. Yet the historical trend itself and the changes in any specific organization are different phenomena. Both are expressions of the process of bureaucratization, but since different conditions account for them, they will be discussed separately.

Historical Conditions.   One of the historical conditions that favors the development of bureaucracy is a money economy. This is not an absolute prerequisite. Bureaucracies based on compensation in kind existed, for example, in Egypt, Rome, and China. Generally, however, a money economy permits the payment of regular salaries, which, in turn, creates the combination of dependence and independence that is most conducive to the faithful performance of bureaucratic duties. Unpaid volunteers are too independent of the organization to submit unfailingly to its discipline. Slaves, on the other hand, are too dependent on their masters to have the incentive to assume responsibilities and carry them out on their own initiative. The economic dependence of the salaried employee on his job and his freedom to advance himself in his career engender the orientation toward work required for disciplined *and* responsible conduct. Consequently, there were few bureaucracies prior to the development of a monetary system and the abolition of slavery.

It has already been mentioned that sheer size encourages the development of bureaucracies, since they are mechanisms for executing large-scale administrative tasks. The large modern nation, business, or union is more likely to be bureaucratized than was its smaller counterpart in the past. More important than size as such, however, is the emergence of special administrative problems. Thus in ancient Egypt the complex job of constructing and regulating waterways throughout the country gave rise to the first known large-scale bureaucracy in history. In other countries, notably those with long frontiers requiring defense, bureaucratic methods were introduced to solve the problem of organizing an effective army and the related one of raising taxes for this purpose. England, without land frontiers, maintained only a small army in earlier centuries, which may in part account for the fact that the trend toward bureaucratization was less pronounced there than in continental nations, which had to support large armies. Weber cites the victory of the Puritans under the leadership of Cromwell over the Cavaliers, who fought more heroically but with less discipline, as an illustration of the superior effectiveness of a bureaucratized army.

The capitalistic system also has furthered the advance of bureaucracy. The rational estimation of economic risks, which is presupposed in capitalism, requires that the regular processes of the competitive market not be interrupted by external forces in unpredictable ways. Arbitrary actions of political tyrants interfere with the rational calculation of gain or loss, and so do banditry, piracy, and social upheavals. The interest of capitalism demands, therefore, not only the overthrow of tyrannical rulers but also the establishment of governments strong enough to maintain order and stability. Note that after the American Revolution such representatives of the capitalists as Alexander Hamilton advocated a strong federal government, while representatives of farmers, in the manner of Jefferson, favored a weak central government.

Capitalism then promotes effective and extensive operations of the government. It also leads to bureaucratization in other spheres. The expansion of business firms and the consequent removal of most employees from activities directly governed by the profit principle make it increasingly necessary to introduce bureaucratic methods of administration for the sake of efficiency. These giant corporations, in turn, constrain workers, who no longer can bargain individually with an employer they know personally, to organize into large unions with complex administrative machineries. Strange as it may seem, the free-enterprise system fosters the development of bureaucracy in the government, in private companies, and in unions.

These historical conditions were not causes of bureaucracy in the usual sense of the term. Evidently, a large and effective army did not cause bureaucracy; on the contrary, bureaucratic methods of operation produced an effective large army. The need for these methods, however, arose in the course of trying to build such an army without them and helped bring about a bureaucratic form of organization. The qualifying word "helped" is essential. If needs inevitably created ways of meeting them, human society would be paradise. In this world, wishes are not horses, and beggars do not ride. Social needs, just as individual ones, often persist without being met. Knowledge of the conditions that engendered a need for bureaucracy does not answer the question: What made its development actually possible under some circumstances and not under others? The Cavaliers were in need of a better fighting force, as their defeat demonstrates. Why was it not they but the Puritans who organized a disciplined army?

In *The Protestant Ethic and the Spirit of Capitalism*, Weber indirectly answers this question. He shows that the Reformation—especially Calvinism, the religious doctrine of the Puritans—apart from its spiritual significance, had the social consequence of giving rise to a this-worldly asceticism, a disciplined devotion to hard work in the pursuit of one's vocation. The Protestant has no Pope or priest to furnish spiritual guidance and absolve him for his sins, but must ultimately rely on his own conscience and faith; this encourages the emergence of self-imposed discipline. The strong condemnation of pleasure and emotions, exemplified by the Puritan "blue laws," generates the sobriety and detachment conducive to rational conduct. Moreover, in contrast to Catholicism and even Lutheranism, Calvinism does not emphasize that the existing order is God's creation but that it has been corrupted by man's sinfulness. Man's religious duty is not to adapt to this wicked world, nor to withdraw from it into a monastery, but to help transform it *pro gloriam Dei* through methodical efforts in his everyday life and regular work. The anxieties aroused by the doctrine of double predestination, according to which man cannot affect his predestined fate or even know whether he will be saved or damned, reinforced the Calvinist's tendency to adopt a rigorous discipline and immerse himself in his work as a way of relieving his anxieties.

Protestantism, therefore, has transplanted the ascetic devotion to disciplined hard work (which must be distinguished from the exertion of effort as a means for reaching specific ends) from monastic life, to which it was largely confined earlier, to the mundane affairs of economic life. Although the explicit purposes of the Reformation were other-worldly and not this-worldly, the psychological orientation it created had the unanticipated consequence of helping to revolutionize the secular world. For without this orientation toward ceaseless effort and rational conduct as intrinsic moral values, Weber argues convincingly, capitalism could not have come into existence, and neither, it should be added, could full-blown bureaucracy have developed, because it too depends on rational discipline.

Structural Conditions.   The historical conditions that led to the pervasiveness of bureaucracy today do not, of course, explain why some organizations in contemporary society are highly bureaucratized and others are not. These variations raise the problem of the conditions within a given social structure that give rise to its bureaucratization. A recent empirical study is concerned with this problem.

Alvin W. Gouldner investigated the process of bureaucratization in a gypsum plant. After the death of the old manager, the company that owned the plant appointed a man who had been in charge of one of its smaller factories as his successor. The new manager, anxious to prove himself worthy of the promotion by improving productivity, was faced with special difficulties. He was not familiar with the ways of working that had become customary in this plant, had not established informal relations with his subordinates, and did not command the allegiance of workers, who still felt loyal to his predecessor. To marshal the willing support of workers and induce them to identify with his managerial objectives, he attempted to cultivate informal relations with them; but this cannot be done overnight. In the meantime, he found it necessary to discharge his managerial responsibilities by resorting to formal procedures. In the absence of informal channels of communication to keep him informed about the work situation, the new manager instituted a system of regular operational reports for this purpose. Since he did not know the workers well enough to trust them, he closely checked on their operations and ordered his lieutenants to establish strict discipline. When some of these lieutenants, used to the more lenient ways of the former manager, failed to adopt rigorous methods of close supervision, he replaced them by outsiders who were more sympathetic with his disciplinarian approach. These innovations alienated workers and deepened the gulf between them and the manager, with the result that he had to rely increasingly on formal bureaucratic methods of administration.

> The role of the successor . . . confronted Peele with distinctive problems. He had to solve these problems if he wished to hold his job as manager. In the process of solving them, the successor was compelled to use bureaucratic methods. Peele intensified bureaucracy not merely because he wanted to, not

necessarily because he liked bureaucracy, nor because he valued it above other techniques, but also because he was constrained to do so by the tensions of his succession.

In the interest of his objective of gaining control over the operations in the plant, it was necessary for the successor to introduce bureaucratic procedures. At the same time, for workers to realize their objective of maintaining some independent control over their own work, it was necessary for them to oppose the introduction of disciplinarian measures. As noted above, the existence of a need does not explain why it is met. In this case, two conflicting needs existed side by side, with the "victor" determined by the power structure in the organization. The powerful position of the manager was responsible for his ability to meet his need by bureaucratizing operations, as indicated by the following comparison with a situation where he was not similarly successful.

This plant consisted of a gypsum mine and a wallboard factory, but the process of bureaucratic formalization was confined to the factory. Stronger informal ties and more pronounced group solidarity prevailed among miners than among factory workers, partly as a consequence of the common danger to which they were exposed in the mine. Miners were highly motivated to work hard, and they had developed their own unofficial system of assigning tasks among themselves; for instance, new miners had to do the dirty jobs. Hence there was less need in the mine for formal discipline and rules prescribing exact duties. Nevertheless, Peele attempted to formalize operating procedures there, too. The strength of their informal organization, however, made it possible for miners, in contrast to factory workers, effectively to resist these attempts. The process of bureaucratic formalization generated by succession in management is not inevitable; collective resistance can arrest it.

The miners, so to speak, had evolved an unofficial bureaucratic apparatus of their own. Their effective informal organization, by regulating their work, took the place of a more formal system of control and simultaneously gave them sufficient power to defeat endeavors to impose a formal system of discipline upon them against their will. Did efficiency suffer? Gouldner implies it did not, although he does not specifically deal with this question. In any case, the conduct of the miners calls attention, once more, to the importance of informal relations and unofficial practices in bureaucratic structures.

Sir Ivor Jennings

The Achievement
of British Bureaucracy

AGENCIES OF GOVERNMENT

Concentration on "politics" causes us to overemphasize the part played by the central administrative machine and the part played in that machine by the politicians. Because of the wisdom and efficiency of the Norman and Angevin kings, England became the first of the nation-states, with a strong central bureaucracy. There were no local potentates to compete with the King. The King's peace extended throughout England and, after Edward I, into Wales. The King's writ ran everywhere. This result was obtained, however, not by concentrating authority in the King's own hands, but by coordinating and systematizing the strong local organization of the Anglo-Saxons under the control of Norman central institutions. The shires became counties, but they were governed not by counts but by the freeholders meeting in the county court (shire moot) under the eye of the King's representative, the shire reeve or sheriff and under the control of the King's own court. From the fourteenth century they were governed even more efficiently (considering the general inefficiency of medieval government) by local men commissioned by the King as justices of the peace. These justices continued to govern the counties until they were superseded, for administrative purposes, by the county councils in 1889.

The towns did not become "free cities" independent of royal authority, like so many of the towns of Germany and Holland, but they had "liberties" under their charters involving greater or less freedom from the organization of the counties to which they belonged. Most of them had their own courts, some had separate commissions of the peace, a few even elected their own sheriffs, and all of them had councils selected by the "freemen" of the town. Even the city of London, the most independent and powerful of them all, was subject to the King's jurisdiction.

It was this combination of local autonomy and central control which made the English system of government so remarkably efficient in a world in which the breakup of the Roman Empire and the establishment of the feudal system led to a chaos of competing jurisdictions and warring local potentates. To this day the tradition remains. Though modern methods of communication have made efficient government by a central bureaucracy much easier, and though there is a growing

From *The Queen's Government* by Sir Ivor Jennings, Penguin Books Ltd., 1954, pp. 101-108. Reprinted by permission.

tendency for the Central Government to take over functions from the local authorities, the three countries of the United Kingdom, but more especially England and Wales, are still outstanding because of the strength of their local institutions. The Lancashire County Council or the Birmingham City Council does not regard itself as an instrument of Her Majesty's Government. It is governed under Acts of Parliament, it receives financial assistance from the Central Government, and often its proposals need the approval of Ministers, but it is an authority in its own right, running its affairs in its own way, and regarded by everybody as an autonomous body. We have a Ministry of Education, but it provides no schools. Certain schools receive grants direct from the Ministry, but in the main the schools are provided or assisted by the local education authorities.

This tradition of the autonomous authority operating under royal charter or commission or Act of Parliament was obviously capable of extension. Among the ancient corporations which survive to this day are the Universities of Oxford and Cambridge and the Inns of Court. Their autonomy has been extended by charter or Act of Parliament to other universities and professional organizations. When the practice of agriculture changed under the Tudors, cooperative action for land drainage became necessary and Commissioners of Sewers were appointed. As the Industrial Revolution changed the face of England, this precedent in turn was followed by the establishment of a vast network of statutory authorities, such as the turnpike trustees, the railway and canal companies, the water and drainage boards, the harbor authorities, and the gas and electricity companies. It is essential to emphasize this "gas and water socialism," for it supplied the precedent for the modern statutory corporation. There are exceptions like the Post Office, which operates the postal, telegraphic, and telephonic system, but they are exceptions. Generally speaking a public service is provided not by a Government Department but by a public corporation like the B.B.C., the Transport Commission, or the British Electricity Authority. Even public assistance is provided by a statutory body, the National Assistance Board.

To speak of these local authorities, chartered corporations and statutory boards and commissions as exercising "delegated power" is inaccurate. The powers were not conferred on some central authority and then delegated. The principle of decentralization has always been accepted because, until recently, the central administration of services under Ministerial control was thought to be neither practicable nor desirable. Britain has been a country in which even "decentralization" is an inaccurate term, because there never was centralization. The idea that Ministers must control everything is a recent development, about whose desirability there may be argument. It arises from the belief, which has never been adequately justified, that the life of a vast community of fifty million people can be "planned" by a group of politicians sitting in Cabinet and assisted by a great array of administrators and technical experts. One of the problems of the modern State is to provide an organization capable of exercising the numerous functions which the State has taken upon itself: and it may be that the tradition of leaving the parish to look after the parish pump, a tradition which arose because the pump was too far from Whitehall, supplies the answer. If nobody can pump water until he has a licence from Whitehall, there will probably be more paper than water and more officials than consumers.

Nor should it be assumed that the parish pump is unimportant. If we regard the citizen as a person in his own right and not as an anonymous unit of a nation or a class—if in other words we forget Hegel and Marx—his immediate environment is as important to him as the affairs of the nation. The multiplication of population since the Industrial Revolution and its collection in large towns, the inevitable provision of services on a large scale, the use of methods of mass production in industry, and, in short, the mechanized State, have given rise to the idea, rarely precisely formulated, that the State is an end in itself. In the last analysis the State consists of John Smith, his wife and children, and their children. As every John Smith knows, a drink of water at bedtime may cause more rumpus than the expropriation of an oil company or a war in the Balkans. Excessive concentration on one's private affairs and lack of attention to national and international affairs are to be deprecated; but it is easy for the politician and the administrator to go to the other extreme and to forget that John Smith has his own affairs. A problem is not the less important because it is a personal problem, nor a service less important because it is a local service.

Inevitably, though, national affairs occupy the center of the stage. These are in charge of an odd combination of amateur and professional administrators, the amateurs controlling the professionals.

THE CIVIL SERVICE

The average civil servant has probably forgotten why he is so called. He is an officer of one of Her Majesty's Civil Establishments, which are distinguished from Her Majesty's Naval, Military, and Air Force Establishments. He is, in other words, a civil servant because he is a civilian employee, not subject to naval, military, or Air Force discipline. The exact point at which he became a professional can never be ascertained. Technically he is, like his political chief, a servant of the Queen, dismissable at her pleasure. Even if he has what looks like a cast-iron contract—and most civil servants have no contracts at all—he cannot sue for wrongful dismissal unless he is protected by an Act of Parliament. His tenure of office is therefore as insecure as his political chief's. The fact that the politician is as changeable as the climate while the civil servant, like Tennyson's brook, goes on for ever, is simply a product of practice or convention.

The politicians of the eighteenth century did not think of themselves as politicians. They were persons of importance who were interested in affairs of State and who were requested by the monarch to undertake the responsibilities of high office. They were chosen from persons of political importance, peers or Members of Parliament, because the monarch needed a majority in Parliament, and so he chose those who had political influence. They in turn appointed the inferior officers, secretaries, assistant secretaries, clerks, writers, excisemen, dockyard officials, and so on. They could, if they pleased, appoint their relatives, friends, and political supporters. What is more, a new Minister could make a clean sweep by using the Crown's power of dismissal and filling the vacancies with his own men. This "patronage" was used for political as well as for personal purposes, and the offices which conferred the most patronage, the Treasury, the Admiralty, and the Secretary of State, were politically the most important. The First Lord of the Treasury became Prime Minister because the Treasury had the most patronage and was therefore the most influential politically.

The distribution of patronage among members of Parliament was however limited by an Act of Anne's reign which disqualified from sitting and voting in Parliament a person who was appointed to a new office, created after 1705. Other legislation, designed at first to cut down the royal influence in Parliament, notably an Act of 1741 and Burke's Economy Act of 1782, reduced the number of offices which might be held by Members of Parliament. Consequently, a distinction was drawn between offices which might be held by Members of Parliament and those which might not.

This development did not in itself make a distinction between politicians who were "transient and embarrassed phantoms" and permanent officials. No officials were permanent so long as patronage prevailed. The disappearance of patronage was due not to legislation but to administrative reforms carried out mainly under Pitt, Peel, and Gladstone. In the early stage the change was purely one of practice. A new political head made no change among the staff of his department. A further change was consequential upon Macaulay's advocacy of selection by competitive examination. On Macaulay's insistence it was applied to the Indian Civil Service, one of the largest and most fruitful branches of patronage, in 1833. The "examination wallahs" were much criticized, and the system was not applied to the United Kingdom until 1855, when the Civil Service Commission was established. The Commission was authorized to grant certificates of competence to candidates for junior posts and to hold examinations for persons nominated by the departments. The creation of a system of pensions under the Superannuation Act, 1859, encouraged the generalization of this arrangement; and since 1870 most vacancies in the public service, other than those requiring professional or technical qualifications, and excepting the "industrial workers," have been filled by examination.

The civil service is now organized into classes, recruited, mainly by examination, at the various education levels. The most important is the administrative class, which is recruited from the universities, and which is primarily responsible, under ministerial control, for the formulation and execution of the Government's policy. It says much for Victorian traditions that a service which grew out of patronage should have established and maintained a reputation for honesty as great as that of Her Majesty's judges. Its intellectual quality, too, is very high. It does not recruit quite the ablest intellectually of each generation, for they become scholars, scientists, and professional men; but it does secure nearly the best. What is more, it prefers and usually secures men and women with first classes or good

second classes whose education has been broad and general and not merely specialized. The public schools and the residential universities, whatever their defects, do
succeed in producing young men and women with character and maturing judgment who have, at least in the past, made good civil servants.

The popular newspapers make allegations about procrastination, lack of
imagination, and "red tape," but they are not entirely justified. It is true that a
decision on an important issue may take time. A business man may be able to
gamble on his "hunch" because he makes profits on the swings when he suffers
losses on the roundabouts. A civil servant must not make a mistake because he is
acting on behalf of his Minister, and neither a Minister nor a civil servant can balance his successes against his failures. It is usually necessary, therefore, for two or
more civil servants to be consulted, and this process takes time. "Red tape" is
commonly associated with financial control. The business man can risk losses provided he makes a sufficient profit over the year. The public and the House of Commons rightly insist that there shall be no losses of public funds. Financial "red
tape" has been laid down not so much by the Treasury as by the Public Accounts
Committee of the House of Commons, a body which has been meeting for nearly
a hundred years and has developed a whole volume of rules and precautions which
it expects the Treasury and the Comptroller and Auditor General to enforce
against the departments.

These restrictions affect the speed and efficiency of administration, not
through defects in the civil servants but through the very nature of public administration. They are strong reasons for not asking the civil service to do too much.
When the State engages in trade or industry it has to use the methods of trade or
industry, not the methods of the civil service. The civil servant's concern is with
policy, and in this sphere it cannot be alleged that he is lacking in imagination. On
the contrary, anybody who consistently follows a line of policy, be it foreign affairs, or colonial policy, or finance, or social welfare, must frequently be amazed
at the fertility of imagination shown by the civil service. There are few political
problems to which there are obvious solutions, for if the solutions were obvious
they would not be problems. Any outside expert who asks himself what steps he
would recommend if the responsibility for giving advice to Ministers were vested in
him frequently finds a better recommendation coming up from the civil service.
Nor is there usually much delay. In foreign affairs particularly a decision has often
to be taken on the spur of the moment.

Nor can it be alleged that the civil service is overstaffed and overpaid. It may
indeed be more truly alleged that the service is understaffed and underpaid. The
senior administrator can seldom relax. The problems keep coming before him and
he has to find solutions. If he is driving a car or washing up or playing golf his
mind is formulating the minutes which he has to write next day. The difficulty is
that so many minutes have to be written. It is impossible to make a subdivision of
labor because all the problems of government are connected with each other.
Overwork is therefore endemic in the senior ranks of the civil service and is an
inevitable part of the system. In return for this overwork the civil servant receives

a salary which is perhaps one third of what he could earn outside the public service. It is not only proper but essential for the efficiency of the service that he should retire as soon as his mind loses its elasticity, be allowed to live in modest comfort on his pension, and be honored by the Queen with a K.C.B. or a K.C.M.G.

Etienne Balazs

The Bureaucratic Society
of Imperial China

The image the West has had of China has changed from time to time, and no doubt will change again. Of course an image to some extent reflects the viewpoint of the observer, thus distorting the reality that lies behind it. First impressions, however, are usually correct, and this holds true when two civilizations first come into contact just as much as when two people meet for the first time. Upon familiarity, individual features will become more sharply defined, or some may become blurred, but the general impression of the first encounter will be found to be valid.

The first image of China formed in the West, if we discount the rationalist wisdom with which the eighteenth-century "philosophers" clothed it, was that of a mandarinate. A strange society it seemed—bizarre, even, for it lacked so many of the constituent elements of Western society at that time, such as the Church and the nobility—yet a society in which, because of the preponderant role of its "philosophers," everything was well ordered and the wheels of an omnipotent state turned without a hitch. The impressions of the first observers, to whom the rule of the all-powerful scholar-officials seemed the distinctive feature of the world—a world *sui generis*—that had newly been discovered, were fully in accord with reality.

Since the time of the first encounter, study of the scholar-officials has gone on uninterruptedly. Sometimes it has been undertaken with the conscious intention of investigating the essential features of the mandarinate, how it came into being, its history, and the conditions under which it operated; more often, even when sinologists thought they were confining their researches to Chinese language, literature, philosophy, or art, they were in fact studying the distinctive products of this one particular social stratum.

From Etienne Balazs, *Chinese Civilization and Bureaucracy*, translated by H. M. Wright and edited by Arthur F. Wright, pp. 13-19. Copyright © 1964 by Yale University. Reprinted by permission of Yale University Press.

We can understand only what we already know, and, what is more, we can become genuinely interested only in something that touches us personally. It is therefore hardly surprising that Edouard Chavannes, when he was translating the works of Ssu-ma Ch'ien in those carefree days around 1900, failed to be moved by the cry of distress in that letter—constituting also Ssu-ma Ch'ien's last will and testament—which denounced the autocratic state for the humiliations inflicted upon its subjects, and discussed with great lucidity the problem whether to commit suicide under a despotism. If Chavannes had translated this letter half a century later, its message would almost certainly have been full of meaning for the great sinologist. The fact is that we have only recently become aware of certain aspects of China that seem to be permanent features.

When I speak of "permanent features," I do not have in mind the idea of an "Eternal China," which is simply an empty cliché. To what, then, do I refer? It seems to me that there are certain aspects of the social structure of China that are permanent—namely, its bureaucratic features. These we are only now beginning to understand because we ourselves are experiencing similar tendencies common to all societies of the twentieth century, whether the pre-industrial, underdeveloped societies of Asia, or the industrialized, highly developed societies of the West. This may bring us to a better understanding of the past history of China, and that in turn may throw light upon those deep-seated and alarming tendencies—totalitarian, state-centered, bureaucratic—that are to be discerned as we move toward a unified world, everywhere pulsating with the same rhythm.

The ideas of Hegel concerning the nature of Asiatic societies have often been dismissed on the ground that he lacked a knowledge of the facts. It is indeed an easy matter to refute the Hegelian conception of a China stagnating in immobility, for with each advance in knowledge it can be seen more and more clearly that China's history was full of upheavals, abrupt transitions, and gradual changes. Yet Hegel was right, to the extent that he sensed the unchanging character of Chinese social structure, and in this he is singularly in accord with the opinion of almost all historians of China, no matter what nation or ideological camp they may belong to. The often pointless debates on the periodization of Chinese history that began in the thirties, and will no doubt last for a long time in the future, always come up against certain phenomena of an undeniably enduring nature.

You may paste on labels (Antiquity, Early or Late Middle Ages, Modern Times); you may cut it up into longer or shorter slices; but, whatever you do, you cannot conjure away the sheer length of time the Chinese Empire lasted, founded in 221 B.C. and still surviving at the beginning of the twentieth century, or deny the permanence of the imperial institutions and the perenniality of certain phenomena such as Confucianism, which endured in spite of successive metamorphoses. Explanations may differ, interpretations contradict each other, but the underlying reality persists, a majestic mountain of solid, incontrovertible fact.

Now, it seems to me that the only valid method for letting light into this solid mass of historical fact is to seek out the causes of continuity—that is, try to discover the specific and significant features of Chinese social structure. I shall have to confine myself to discussing the social structure of imperial China, for it would take me far beyond the limits of the present essay to make comparisons with earlier periods, however interesting and instructive that might be. And I can only point out the more striking of its distinctive features, since anything approaching a complete description of the social structure of imperial China would require not an essay but several large tomes.

What, then, were its most striking features?

1. In the first place, China was a large *agrarian* society, highly developed but using traditional techniques, and established on a subcontinent that lacks any marked geographical articulation. Its cells, scattered over an immense territory whose main arteries were a system of waterways, existed in an economic autarchy [system with central planning and control] that made each of them an individual unit, and isolated each unit from every other. These cells were the peasant families that composed the overwhelming majority of the population. They were self-sufficient; but without the system of economic exchanges and the organizational framework imposed from above, they would have disintegrated irremediably into their component particles, into an anarchy that would have made impossible not only the distribution, but also the production of goods, and indeed the maintenance of life itself. It was, in other words, a pre-industrial, nonmaritime society, based on a peasant subsistence economy.

2. This society was *bureaucratic* because the social pyramid—which rested on a broad peasant base, with intermediate strata consisting of a merchant class and an artisan class, both of them numerically small, lacking in autonomy, of inferior status, and regarded with scant respect—was capped and characterized by its apex: the mandarinate.

3. The class of *scholar-officials* (or mandarins), numerically infinitesimal but omnipotent by reason of their strength, influence, position, and prestige, held all the power and owned the largest amount of land. This class possessed every privilege, above all the privilege of reproducing itself, because of its monopoly of education. But the incomparable prestige enjoyed by the intelligentsia had nothing to do with such a risky and possibly ephemeral thing as the ownership of land; nor was it conferred by heredity, which after all can be interrupted; nor was it due solely to its exclusive enjoyment of the benefits of education. This unproductive elite drew its strength from the function it performed—the socially necessary, indeed indispensable, function of coordinating and supervising the productive labor of others so as to make the whole social organism work. All mediating and administrative functions were carried out by the scholar-officials. They prepared the calendar, they organized transport and exchange, they supervised the construction of roads, canals, dikes, and dams; they were in charge of all public works, especially those aimed at forestalling droughts and floods; they built up reserves against famine, and encouraged every kind of irrigation project. Their social role was at one and the same time that of architect, engineer, teacher, administrator,

and ruler. Yet these "managers" before their time were firmly against any form of specialization. There was only one profession they recognized: that of governing. A famous passage from Mencius on the difference between those who think and those who toil perfectly expresses the scholar-officials' outlook: "Great men have their proper business, and little men have their proper business . . . Some labor with their minds, and some labor with their strength. Those who labor with their minds govern others; those who labor with their strength are governed by others. Those who are governed by others support them; those who govern others are supported by them."*

4. Being specialists in the handling of men and experts in the political art of governing, *the scholar-officials were the embodiment of the state*, which was created in their image—a hierarchical, authoritarian state, paternalistic yet tyrannical; a tentacular welfare state; a totalitarian Moloch of a state. The word "totalitarian" has a modern ring to it, but it serves very well to describe the scholar-officials' state if it is understood to mean that *the state has complete control over all activities* of social life, absolute domination at all levels. The state in China was a managerial, an interventionist state—hence the enduring appeal of Taoism, which was opposed to state intervention. Nothing escaped official regimentation. Trade, mining, building, ritual, music, schools, in fact the whole of public life and a great deal of private life as well, were subjected to it.

5. There are still other reasons for speaking of a totalitarian state. In the first place, there was a *secret-police atmosphere* of mutual suspicion, in which everyone kept watch on everyone else. Then there was the *arbitrary character of justice*. In the eyes of the authorities, every accused person was assumed to be guilty. Terror was instilled by the principle of *collective responsibility* (which, contrary to what one might suppose, had no connection with the Confucianist ideal of the family), making every subject shake in his shoes, and the scholar-officials most of all, for, although they ruled the state, they were also its servants. I should like to add that this last point is only apparently contradictory. The truth is that in all totalitarian societies it is a fundamental principle that public interest comes before private interests, and that reasons of state take priority over the rights of the individual human being. The inevitable corollary is that an official in his capacity as a representative of the state is sacrosanct, but as an individual he is nothing.

A final totalitarian characteristic was the state's tendency to clamp down immediately on any form of private enterprise (and this in the long run kills not only initiative but even the slightest attempts at innovation), or, if it did not succeed in putting a stop to it in time, to take over and nationalize it. Did it not frequently happen during the course of Chinese history that the scholar-officials, although hostile to all inventions, nevertheless gathered in the fruits of other people's ingenuity? I need mention only three examples of

Mencius III A, 4; trans. James Legge, *Chinese Classics*, 2, 249-250.

inventions that met this fate: paper, invented by a eunuch; printing, used by the Buddhists as a medium for religious propaganda; and the bill of exchange, an expedient of private businessmen.

In view of its contemporary relevancy, one additional feature of the bureaucratic state may be worth mentioning here: the panicky fear of assuming responsibility. To avoid getting into trouble was the Chinese bureaucrat's main concern, and he always managed to saddle his responsibilities on to some subordinate who could serve as a scapegoat.

6.   The scholar-officials and their state found in the Confucianist doctrine an ideology that suited them perfectly. In ancient times, Confucianism had expressed the ideals of those former members of the feudal aristocracy who had formed a new social stratum of revolutionary intelligentsia, but in Han times (206 B.C.-A.D. 220), shortly after the foundation of the empire, it became a state doctrine. The virtues preached by Confucianism were exactly suited to the new hierarchical state: respect, humility, docility, obedience, submission, and subordination to elders and betters. In comparison with the usefulness of virtues such as these, ancestor worship and the cult of the family were no more than additional, though welcome, features. Moreover, the new elite found it convenient to adopt the Confucian nonreligious, rationalist outlook. Mysticism was usually a cloak for subversive tendencies, and the scholar-officials, anxious above all to maintain the position they had won, felt that it was something to be guarded against. Prudence dictated that they should remain soberly realistic and down to earth. Prudence also dictated that the new Confucianism should be conformist and traditionalist in character: strict adherence to orthodox doctrines was the surest defense against the pressures of other social groups. Thus the contradiction between the rationalism of early Confucianism and the traditionalism of its later development created a tension within the mandarinate which can be explained by the play of interests—of vital interests—within the society as a whole. The conflict of interests also explains the contradiction between, on the one hand, the claims to be a democracy (claims real enough as far as internal relations within the group of scholar-officials were concerned), and, on the other, the actual existence of an oligarchy—the contradiction, that is, between the two poles of Confucianist political doctrine.

I do not wish, however, to go into the whole question of Confucianism, which is far too complex a matter to deal with in passing. The only point I want to make is that the continuity of Confucianism depended entirely upon the continued existence of the scholar-officials' centralized, hierarchical, and bureaucratic state. Whenever this state was at bay, whenever the scholar-officials had to let other actors take the center of the stage (never for long), the Confucianists went into retirement and kept quiet, taking cover in order to prepare a triumphant return.

These, then, seem to me the features of Chinese social structure that help to explain the persistence of bureaucratic government in China.

2
Problems of Personnel

Bureaucrats wield power. Consequently, it is important to know how people are chosen to become bureaucrats. The basic criterion for selection is, theoretically, the merit of the candidate. Above all, this means his fitness to perform his future tasks responsibly. The meritocratic principle—power to those who are fit to wield it—stands in contrast to the principle of heredity, whereby power is conferred on the basis of birth and position.

Once a bureaucrat has entered the system, it seems more difficult to apply the meritocratic principle consistently to his promotion. The system of seniority allows a bureaucrat to stake out his position and hang on, regardless of his performance. A compromise usually must be struck between promotion by merit, which in theory ought to insure efficient continuity of bureaucratic operation, and promotion by seniority, which provides for the interests of the bureaucrats themselves.

If merit is adopted as the standard, someone still has to decide precisely what it means. No bureaucrat should be illiterate or incompetent, nor should he hold values that are irreconcilably in conflict with those of the society. These negative criteria allow considerable variation, however, and the specific nature of bureaucratic merit or fitness has differed from one bureaucratic state to another. For example, the perfect bureaucrat in the imperial Chinese civil service was supposed to be a superior man (*chün-tzu*). His moral sensitivity, developed because of his long exposure to the Chinese humanities, theoretically made him fit to deal with the wide range of legal, financial, and administrative problems that would be his responsibility as a district magistrate. On the other hand, a career in a complex, technical bureaucracy like that of the United States today often requires highly specialized expertise, while the value of a general liberal education is often considered irrelevant. The merit of a bureaucrat may be his ingenuity, or his willingness to follow orders; his ability to get along well with his superiors and the public, or his dexterity as an agent in conflict with other powerful forces in the state; his responsiveness to incentives, or the motivation of his idealism. Although the nature of bureaucratic merit is a subject of great interest to rulers, they are not always able to define merit by fiat. They work with approximations and compromise. They use many methods to advance their point of view: examinations to discover merit, institutes and schools to train talent and inculcate values, and incentives to encourage superior bureaucratic performance. But the simple fact that a large bureaucracy is in itself an interest group, means that accommodations must usually be made between the bureaucracy and other institutions. The nature of merit is changed by these accommodations.

E. A. Kracke, Jr., discusses the elaborate procedures used in imperial China for the recruitment and advancement of bureaucrats, in the selection from his article "The Chinese and the Art of Government." From T'ang dynasty times (A.D. 618-906) onwards, opportunities for social mobility were centered in the bureaucracy. Hence official rank was eagerly sought, despite the arduous years of study this required, and appointment to a post was considered the fulfillment of the highest social goals. Not surprisingly, most of the Chinese personnel procedures were instituted in the T'ang era. The most famous of these was the examination system, which in a more developed form excited the admiration of Voltaire, and which was abolished only in 1905. As we have seen, merit consisted ideally in moral fitness patterned on the standard of the Confucian classics. Although the vagueness of morality inevitably caused practical difficulties, both in testing for entrance and in rating for advancement, on the whole it was a powerful idealistic force in personnel policy.

In contrast to the Chinese system, merit was of little consequence in the selection of the Ottoman bureaucracy. It was applied primarily to the advancement process. The Muslim rulers of the Ottoman Empire recruited their bureaucrats from a defined class—young Christian slave boys. In "Administration of the Ottoman Empire under Suleiman (1494-1566)," E. N. Gladden explains that, once selected, future bureaucrats were subjected to rigorous training. Their advancement within the bureaucracy depended very heavily on merit demonstrated through performance. The penalties for malfeasance, moreover, were Draconian. But there were great rewards as well. In actual practice, the slave-bureaucrats acquired much of the prestige of their masters. Most of them eliminated the stigma of Christian birth by converting to Islam. According to Gladden, "Their position was so envied that it was necessary to enforce stringent rules against their recruitment from among the free Moslems who formed the bulk of the community." In this remarkable society, the rulers created and fostered merit within the system, while selection of bureaucrats on the basis of their origin in a slave class ensured the rulers a high degree of control over bureaucratic activity.

Although the meritocratic principle is the mainstay of bureaucratic organization, it can cause grave problems if its application is not modified as new conditions warrant. As Blanche D. Blank points out in "The Battle of Bureaucracy," the actual results of civil service policy in New York City often obstruct the needs of the community. Whereas American civil service laws were intended to protect bureaucrats from politicians, New York now faces an army of bureaucrats using the merit system as a weapon to protect their own interests. The extreme difficulty of dismissing incompetent bureaucrats, and the stagnation of over-elaborate testing procedures that favor incumbents, have made the merit system an obstacle to progress. Whereas incompetent Ottoman bureaucrats faced death for their failures, the most derelict New York civil servant cannot even be demoted without lengthy, exasperating review and investigation. Within New York's bureaucracy, according to Mrs. Blank, disputes over personnel matters affect the entire operation of the civil administration, because the Budget Office and the Personnel Department have become courts of last resort for conflicts involving the many bureaucratic kingdoms. This means that administrators often lose sight of their basic aims of getting good people and placing them in appropriate jobs. Department chiefs must struggle constantly simply to preserve the status quo, so as to insure the maintenance of adequate staff and operating funds.

E. A. Kracke, Jr.

Bureaucratic Recruitment and Advancement in Imperial China

Most important among administrative methods were those concerned with personnel. Since the ruler depended on professional bureaucrats alike in the formation, implementation, and enforcement of policy, his success was proportional to bureaucratic ability and morale. Personnel policies assumed a major place in state deliberations. . . . Early Chinese political thinkers evolved interesting concepts in this field; it is not too surprising that China was the first to develop many essential techniques. The primary aim was to improve the civil service proper, an élite group commonly numbering in the developed system some ten thousand or more and filling the key positions of central and local government. To obtain more and

From "The Chinese and the Art of Government," by E. A. Kracke, Jr., from *The Legacy of China*, ed. Raymond Dawson, 1964, pp. 322-329, by permission of the Clarendon Press, Oxford.

better men, the emperor Wu [reigned 140-86 B.C.] of the Han [206 B.C.-A.D. 220] founded a school at the capital which grew into a thriving university. Succeeding dynasties added local schools in all parts of the empire to train promising sons of official or commoner families at state expense.

Men were selected for government employment and advanced in office through varied methods; from the T'ang [618-906] onwards promotion and recruitment procedures were distinct. Rather primitive methods familiar elsewhere— nomination of officials' younger relatives and the sale of office—were gradually restricted and in later dynasties assumed importance only at moments of dynastic decline. In their place more constructive methods such as competitive examination, controlled sponsorship, and regular merit ratings came to play leading roles.

The earliest to develop was sponsorship. No method suited Confucian reform concepts so well as presentation of good men to the ruler by those in a position to judge their character. Tradition asserted that even in feudal times the public recommendation of such men for official position was an act of high merit, and their employment was pleasing to Heaven. By the Han at least the moral obligation assumed by the sponsor was supplemented by a legal responsibility for the acts of his protégé, and the system was widely employed to find men most highly qualified for government service. After the Han, however, recruitment through sponsorship became more and more restricted to rare instances in which exceptionally talented men had failed to seek advancement through normal channels.

In the later T'ang and the Sung [960-1279], new use was found for the idea of recommendation, in promotion within the service. Here it was valuable as a way of finding proven administrative abilities and probity, complementing the techniques of examination and merit rating (whose inherent limitations are discussed below). It also added inducements to good performance by the receiver of past or prospective recommendations. At first used chiefly to find men for special needs, sponsorship was regularized in the early eleventh century for promotions to all but the highest ranks and functions. When the candidate did well the sponsor was honored and rewarded. Exact laws governed the legal liability for sponsoring a man who later misbehaved. Penalties were graded according to the demonstrable grounds for the recommendation and the kind of crime or delinquency that occurred. All sponsors of the delinquent man suffered equally. Legislation around 1020 provided that for the most serious offenses, including venality, the punishment for sponsors should be identical with that of the man guaranteed (if the latter's penalty were death, the sponsors' would be the severest short of death). In the case of other offenses the sponsors would suffer a penalty less than that of the offender's by one degree or two degrees, or go free, according to the gravity of the offense. The number of a candidate's sponsors determined whether or how far he would be promoted. Candidates stationed away from the capital were favored by rules that allowed more recommendations annually by provincial officials. The utility of the system depended in part on a careful adjustment of penalties; when liability was too onerous few were willing to sponsor, and when too light the practice could encourage factional alliances. On the whole, sponsorship proved its worth, and continued in use while the empire lasted.

The examination system, which grew from sponsorship, was destined to oc-cupy a greater place in the history of political institutions. This system served to select men for governmental service through regular written, competitive examina-tions, open to all candidates of good character, however they came by their train-ing. The system was long in evolving. The earliest applications of examination tech-nique are obscure. At least as early as 165 B.C. men recommended for office were required to answer in writing questions set by the Han emperor Wen. The emperor Wu followed this procedure regularly, placing the candidates in exact order of demonstrated merit. Han state university students were also promoted through written tests. In the early T'ang, competitive written examination of recommended men still produced on average less than ten graduates a year. At the end of the seventh century the empress Wu, usurping power and scheming to found a new dynasty, made competitive examination a tool to recruit supporters from the large-ly untapped talent of southeast China, and during successive years the number of degrees reached six times or more the earlier average. The T'ang emperor Hsüan-tsung, retrieving the throne, improved and strengthened his government with a series of measures; and examinations grew still more important. The number of graduates diminished with T'ang decline, but Sung rule revived the trend and in the eleventh century the annual average of final degrees passed two hundred and fifty. (In addition, degrees of a lesser order were conferred on many who after persistent effort had failed to pass the final test by the age of fifty or sixty.) The graduates could now supply the greater share of civil service posts.

With growing reliance on examination came contrivance of better methods. The chief of these were in use soon after A.D. 1000. Preliminary local tests and two tests at the capital eliminated some ninety-nine percent of the contenders. Those who graduated were classed and numbered in order of ability. All would first hold rather minor offices, but examination ranking went far to determine sub-sequent promotions. Each examination paper was graded by three independent readers. Fair and objective reading was furthered by concealment of candidates' identities. A number replaced a candidate's name on his paper, which was copied out by clerks lest his handwriting be recognized.

The problems of suiting subject matter and testing method to needed apti-tudes was not so neatly solved. Debates on this were heated. Some premises were unquestioned: an official should know the principles of government and human conduct; his training should fit him to deal with widely diverse duties and situa-tions; he should be mentally acute and flexible. Classical studies served these ends by showing the foundations of morals and exemplifying historically their bearing on political problems. The Classics also provided a uniform and concise body of knowledge accessible to any scholar. The studies of law, forms of official conduct, literary composition, and later histories provided more directly applicable knowl-edge. Most minutiae of official duties were left to be learned from practical experience.

Many and ingenious written tests were devised to assess the results of these studies. The candidate proved his memory of classical writings by completing passages from which a few words were given as a clue. Or he was asked to summarize the essential meanings and implications of designated texts from the Classics, histories, formularies, or laws and ordinances, according to his specialization. Or he demonstrated his acumen by proposing solutions to problems posed by seeming conflicts of principle in classical authorities, or to current administrative dilemmas such as those of adjusting commodity supply and demand. He showed his originality and imagination by composing essays on themes presented to him. He displayed his ingenuity by composing pieces of prose or verse for which the themes, rhymes, and complex forms were assigned him.

No one kind of test was felt to be fully adequate. Simple textual familiarity with the Classics did not prove intelligence. Answers to questions on meaning might, with effort enough, be learned by rote. Questions that called for an application of knowledge to conflicts of principle or administrative quandaries might evoke original thinking, but who could grade the answers accurately and objectively? Required compositions on prescribed topics in strictly formulated literary forms might show originality and ability, and could be graded more objectively, but did the studies they encouraged produce the most practical officials? Tests of these many kinds were multiplied and tried in varying versions and combinations. A single examination might last through several day-long sessions. But when any pattern of tests was long in use, clever tutors and assiduous study of past examinations could anticipate questions and supply formulas for glib answers. The best of forms had to change. Some critics decried all forms of written test as lacking the prime requisite—detection of character.

For these reasons, no doubt, competitive examination was applied above all to recruitment. Promotion more often came through other methods. Yet in its prime the examination system brought China's ablest minds into government, and no other device promised equal results. The Mongols [reigned in China 1279-1368], who along with their foreign allies (like Marco Polo) could scarcely compete on a scholarly plane, for a time made official appointments through sponsorship. It would not do; in 1315 the old competitions returned, to continue unbroken until 1905. At first averaging only a score a year, graduate numbers grew under Ming [1368-1644] and Manchus [reigned in China 1644-1912]. But they never comprised more than half those of the Sung. This was partly compensated by granting lower offices to men who passed the local tests. More serious was the subtle dampening of original thinking. Perhaps inertia, perhaps the later dynasts' instinctive distrust of too much restiveness, took hold. During the last five centuries the famous eight-legged examination essay, treating a given theme in eight different kinds of composition, remained in vogue, and the patterns of questions varied little. Regional quotas made officialdom more representative but limited free competition. Under Mongols and Manchus the ruling races and their allies enjoyed also racial quotas and easier standards. For Chinese, the tests to hurdle on the way to a final *chin-shih* degree were multiplied beyond belief, absorbing mental energies the competitors might have used more profitably. But even so the system brought good men to run the empire, and won respect from Europeans who first met it in these latter days.

Annual merit ratings also grew from sponsorship. Han rulers required that local officials submit, with their annual reports and accounts, the names of those who served well in any capacity, that they might be promoted. Gentlemen of the court were rated on their directness, staunchness, self-abnegation, and performance in office. The T'ang brought the system of promotion by merit to the highest degree of refinement. Each year every official was checked by his superior on his possession or lack of four specified excellences and twenty-seven desirable qualities. One point could be counted for each excellence (renown for uprightness, conspicuous integrity and circumspection, laudable impartiality, or unrelaxing diligence). One point could be added if he had one of the desirable qualities appropriate to his particular office. Five points placed a man in the highest of nine merit categories. No points but fairly good conduct put him in the sixth. A record showing unjustly prejudiced actions put him in the seventh, self-interest and neglect of duty in the eighth, graft in the ninth. According to his category his salary was raised, unchanged, or reduced, and if he fell in the ninth category he was dismissed. Ratings over several years were balanced and, if other than middling, brought promotion or demotion. On paper the system could scarcely be improved. In operation, unbiased objectivity was no easier for the Chinese superior official than for his modern Western confrère who faces a similar task. The system could not be relied on exclusively, but it supplemented other techniques and gained a permanent place among personnel practices.

A government that so stressed suasion could hardly fail to emphasize morale, the first and best promoter of discipline. Fair treatment of officials and *esprit de corps* received attention early, and measures to attain these developed side by side with the techniques already described. Here only their principal features can be enumerated. Honors, titles, and decorations need hardly be mentioned. Positions were carefully classified and pay was determined by exact rules. Severe laws protected the subordinate from arbitrary exactions of his superior. Days of rest were provided at five- or ten-day periods, in addition to longer holidays and leave for family emergencies. Rules for advancement took seniority into account, along with performance in office. At seventy an official could retire on pension. Where inducement failed, penalty lay in reserve. The more humiliating punishments were applied sparingly after the Han, since they tended to damage general morale, and the superior man—the *chün-tzu*—should not need them. Where prestige was so important, threat of fine or demotion was severe, and exile or dismissal from the service was terrible indeed. Officials were bound by social pressures. Those who worked within a single administrative unit shared a joint legal responsibility. But in the end perhaps the most effective sanction was that of public reputation; good or bad, it survived the individual and brought pride or shame to his descendants.

China's political achievement, her success and the bounds of that success, certainly derived from no one political theory or concept, no one administrative device. They stemmed rather from the total energy and imagination directed into political life. Political ideas and systems grew from Chinese culture and unique Chinese experiences. In turn, they shaped the culture and its growth.

Political life both advanced and channeled social change. Prosperity and its social effects had made the expanded examinations possible; the examinations in turn opened the bureaucracy to all the ablest, and made it also representative. Apart from those families of morally tainted origin (professional entertainers, and for a time merchant families), all men could equally compete for a governmental career. Each peasant family cherished a hope of some day winning social distinction this way; folk embroideries pictured the triumphal homecoming of a son who passed the tests at the top of the list. The hope was sometimes realized. With but one office to a thousand families and more, the chance could not be great. But in the Sung and later, neither high birth nor wealth was essential for graduates. Not a few were poor, and many indeed could count no recent ancestor in office. Many more *novi homines* no doubt entered the civil service and the clerical services through other ways of recruitment. The outlook of government was affected by the bureaucrats' varied origins; their districts, where their family homes remained, benefited also. Freedom of opportunity in traditional China was not that of our modern ideal, or even of modern actualities, but few if any large, pre-modern nations could rival it.

E. N. Gladden

The Ottoman Slave-Bureaucrats

For many reasons the administrative history of the Ottoman Empire at the height of its power under the brilliant leadership of Suleiman the Magnificent (1494-1566) is of considerable interest. In the first place the great Mohammedan power ruled a considerable area within the Mediterranean sphere and at many points threatened the supremacy of the struggling civilization of the West, and the administrative methods that rendered this possible could not, in any case, be without importance. In the second place, the peculiarities of the Ottoman governmental scheme produced an administrative system, unique in many respects, which furnishes interesting parallels in administrative theory and decisive warnings of the dangers of achieving a high standard of competence at the expense of individual initiative.

The founders of the Ottoman Empire, the Turks, were at the outset a nomad-

"Administration of the Ottoman Empire under Suleiman," by E. N. Gladden, from *Public Administration*, Vol. XV, 1937, pp. 187-193. Reprinted by permission of the Royal Institute of Public Administration and the author.

ic community steeled, by their struggle against the conditions of the Asiatic steppe lands, to build up, under the stimulus of military conquest, an expanding system of overlordship, which the accompanying growth of the Mohammedan religion served to consolidate and preserve against the normal tendencies to disintegration. It is interesting to note that while the sacred law contributed the impassive power of unbreakable custom to the Empire, the active power rested with the army which remained an executive unity: so that the limits of geographical expansion were eventually reached when this army was no longer able to do more than defend one or other of the main frontiers against the attack of the two important neighboring powers, viz., Austria on the northwest and Persia on the east. The essentially missionistic zeal of the Moslem faith, on the other hand, was an important factor during the most active period of expansion, as will become apparent when the method of recruitment is considered.

GOVERNMENT AND CHURCH

Before turning to the administrative aspects of the Ottoman system it will be as well to sketch briefly the form of its governmental machinery. At the head stood the Sultan. He was the unique wielder of power and was in no way responsible to the people. Certainly his autocracy was tempered by the fundamental Turkish predilection to follow custom and antipathy to change, and although paramount in religion as well as politics, he usually led in his allegiance to the sacred law as interpreted by the most learned members of the religious schools.

The Sultan had his Cabinet, the Diwan, which, however, it became his practice to leave to the control of his Grand Vizier or prime minister. This council sat four times a week, chiefly to decide administrative and judicial questions. It included *ex-officio* members of the political side and two representatives of religion. Thus it brought into close contact the two sides of the system, the political and the religious, which were otherwise separate. The Sultan's approval was necessary at the close of each Diwan to render its decisions valid and irrevocable.

The separation of the Ottoman system into two distinct Institutions, designated by Albert H. Lybyer* as the Ruling and the Moslem Institutions respectively, is one of its outstanding characteristics. The Ruling Institution was not strictly speaking a government in the modern sense; it was an army and an administration that practically ignored the interests of the people: it was a slave system subject without appeal to the whim of the Sultan. The Moslem Institution was even less a church as we understand such; it included all Moslems outside the Ruling Institution and its leaders were learned doctors rather than priests. Politically it took the place of the modern written constitution, and the chief mufti, in interpreting the sacred law at the Sultan's request, acted as the preserver of the constitution very much in the same way as the Supreme Court in the United States today.

*The Government of the Ottoman Empire in the time of Suleiman the Magnificent.

Administratively, our interest in the Ottoman system rests entirely in the Ruling Institution. As already mentioned, this Institution was primarily an army. Its administrative functions were largely concerned with the collection of revenues and the provision for its general maintenance. In the army there were two important sections: the *Janissaries*, or infantry, famed and feared for their discipline, bravery and ruthlessness, and the *Spahis* of the Porte, or cavalry. On the administrative side were the officers of the harem, the servants of the palace, and the various officials under the Viziers (who were the leading administrative officers) and under the *Defterdars* (who were responsible for finance). These services were not clearly defined and members of the Ruling Institution were eligible for all branches.

It is convenient in discussing the form and working of an official hierarchy to consider separately the problems of recruitment, training and advancement of officers, and this method will be adopted here.

THE SERVICES: RECRUITMENT

The recruitment of the Ruling Institution was undoubtedly the most characteristic element of the Ottoman system. In the words of Lybyer, "The Ottoman system deliberately took slaves and made them ministers of state; it took boys from the sheep run and plough tail and made them courtiers and husbands of princesses; it took young men whose ancestors had borne the christian name for centuries and made them rulers in the greatest Mohammedan State, and soldiers and generals in invincible armies whose chief joy was to beat down the Cross and elevate the Crescent." Thus, it will be gathered, all members of the Ruling Institution were recruited as slaves or *kullar*, and slaves they remained until the day of their death. Yet their slavery became a mark of favor; their privileges gave them the advantages of nobility. Their position was so envied that it was necessary to enforce stringent rules against their recruitment from among the free Moslems who formed the bulk of the community. Sons of kullar were not eligible for membership of the Ruling Institution, with the exception of children of Spahis who might enter with the Sultan's permission. Grandchildren were rigidly excluded.

It has been estimated that the Ruling Institution numbered 80,000, and an annual wastage of about ten percent gives some idea of the recruitment problem. Entry was open to Christian boys, usually between the ages of 14 and 18, and recruitment was made by capture, purchase, gift or tribute. The levying of the tribute boys constituted the most systematic form of selection and produced the best officers. Every four years a body of skilled selectors traveled through the provinces from which tribute was due and chose the most suitable youths. A quota was assigned to each district. There was no appeal from the decision of the Sultan's officers. Clearly many must have feared this periodical process which might well take from parents an only son, or at successive periods a number of sons, yet the fate of the boys selected might well be envied since it opened out a whole world of opportunity beyond the dreams of those left behind.

This system was primarily designed to take the best talents from among the subject Christians of the Sultan and to add them to the Mohammedan section; for it was necessary that all those selected should become Moslems if they had any desire for advancement. Force was not used to this end; but few failed to embrace the new religion, at least in appearance, and many became its most ardent proselytes. The absence of family ties and the fact that all honor and wealth came from the Sultan, ensured a high degree of allegiance from these kullar.

TRAINING AND PROMOTION

Much care was spent upon the training of the recruits. Busbecq, a contemporary Dutch observer, in his "De Re Militari," says: "The Turks rejoice greatly when they find an exceptional man, as though they had acquired a precious object and they spare no labor or effort in cultivating him; especially if they discern that he is fit for war." The recruits were critically examined with regard to their physical appearance or intellectual promise, and assigned to two classes. Those of the greatest promise, about ten percent of the total, were assigned to the higher training. To be chosen for this group was a great advantage since it not only meant access to a literary as well as a practical education, but also ensured contacts with the great, even perhaps with the Sultan himself. But those assigned to the lower and larger group were not without hope of advancement to the higher ranges if they proved to be of sufficient merit.

Members of the first group were attached to the households of provincial governors or of high officials of the capital. The most coveted positions were those of the pages in the Sultan's palaces. The cosmopolitan nature of this school of pages is strikingly illustrated by the variety of nationalities represented therein; it is recorded that at one period these pages included Bulgarians, Hungarians, Transylvanians, Poles, Bohemians, Germans, Italians, Spaniards, French, Albanians, Slavs, Greeks, Circassians, and Russians. During their period of training the youths were taught horsemanship and the arts of war. They also learned a handicraft. The training was intensive and the discipline strict; tests were carried out at every stage and every effort was made to discover the individual's particular aptitude and to cultivate it. Pay was given, increasing each year. At the age of 25 the trainee was ready to take up a permanent post in the Ruling Institution; the majority entered the regular cavalry, became Spahis of the Porte, while some immediately received more responsible posts according to their achievements.

The rest of the recruits, the lower group, were destined to the infantry, or corps of Janissaries, which they also entered at about the same age. Their training was largely of a practical nature, though they were allowed to learn to read and write if they wished.

They spent their first two or three years in the service of richer Moslems, who were required to employ them on hard field work in order to improve their physique. They were then tested as to their knowledge of Turkish and, if satisfactory, were assigned to public works in the capital, on which the arduous nature of their labor was maintained. During this period they were expected to learn some trade useful in war. To complete their training they were attached to the messes of the Janissaries, to serve and to learn; and as vacancies arose they were given full status in the infantry of the Ottoman Empire. Certain members of the lower section of recruits were allocated to look after the gardens and palaces of the Sultan. These did not usually become Janissaries. Their avenue of advancement led through the transport, commissary and artillery services of the army or to the supervision of the imperial stables and administrative posts of a type distantly similar to the manipulative, custodial and messengerial positions in the modern State Service.

The system was designed to facilitate the advancement of the most talented. Favoritism was, of course, possible but, in the days of the Empire's greatest achievement, not common; the efficiency principle was so ingrained in the whole scheme of Moslem expansion. During that period the demand was greater than the supply. War on the one hand and territorial accession on the other ensured a steadily increasing number of higher and more responsible positions. Individuals were carefully observed and tested; the upward movement was not automatic. There were no social or economic class restrictions upon the kullar's eligibility to any position; unless we regard a natural lack of ability as the inevitable mark of the Ottoman proletarian's failure. Rewards both in wealth and dignity were considerable and increased more than proportionately at each step. At the same time the punishments increased in the same way; so that the highest officers were subject to the death penalty for the least dereliction of duty or undue assumption of power. There was no appeal from the sentence passed. The Sultan's decision was final.

ADMINISTRATION: GENERAL AND FINANCIAL

Something may now be said as to the general nature of the administrative machine. It was, as we have already indicated, inextricably interwoven with the all-pervasive military organization. Military officers became administrative officials and vice versa. For example, the Agha of the Janissaries was both general and minister of war. He came from the college of pages and was aided by his lieutenant, by a chief scribe and a bureau of clerks. He directed the enrollment of the Janissaries, the distribution of their pay, their promotions, their location, the purchase of their supplies and clothing and all the other business of the corps. In other words he not only commanded the Janissaries in the field but also controlled the organization which provided for their administrative needs, and in this latter task he was assisted by a staff consisting of executive officers and clerks.

The very nature of the clerical work of the age called for laborious methods. There were no labor-saving devices and the office routine was of the simplest form. The Turk had a strong liking for scribbling and this leaning, coupled with the demand for complicated verifications and checks, encouraged the growth of red tape and bureaucracy. In the later stages of the Empire these methods of check and cross-check became so complicated and time-destroying that instead of bringing security they defeated their own ends in complete confusion.

The organization of the financial administration in the days of Suleiman is very interesting. At the head stood the Defterdars, who controlled large geographical areas and had access to the Sultan. Between them and the Treasury Department stood a number of supernumerary officials, including the two chief bookkeepers. The Treasury Department itself consisted of 25 separate bureaus, each with its chief and a number of clerks of different grades. The total personnel amounted to more than 800. Each separate bureau dealt with a different functional field, but there was much overlapping and very little plan in the assignment of functions, since the different bureaus appear to have been set up from time to time as new needs arose. Some bureaus dealt with receipts, others with payments; some covered certain geographical areas, some dealt with classes of individuals, some dealt with specific types of transaction. The chief aim seemed to be to set off separate functions as far as possible and to leave them to special sets of officials to control. Decentralization of this sort was inherent in the practical attempts of one man to control such a vast system, and the result, with growth in complexity, was inevitably a lack of coordination and rational planning. The higher officials of the Treasury Department were selected from among the quieter and more studious members of the school of pages; the lower officials were in the early days slaves or scribes, but here Moslem-born officers began soon to displace the kullar, since the required talents were more likely to be obtainable from outside the Ruling Institution.

The system had its period of prodigious success, culminating, perhaps, within the reign of Suleiman. Some indication has been given as to the chief reasons for its great achievement. That it should share in the common mortality of human institutions is not a matter for surprise, but what, we may well ask, were the actual reasons for decline in this case? They were partly external and partly internal. The Empire ceased to expand and to continue to create an extending demand for a pressing flow of talent. The Sultan, on whom so much depended, began to lose his interest in maintaining an active standard of efficiency. He tended to delegate his functions to brilliant subordinates who would in the main think more of their own interests than of those of an institution: the lack of social ideas prevented any growth of an ideal of community service, while the need for wealth to maintain the splendor of the court led to the introduction of sale of offices, that most dangerous source of corruption which always lays in wait for any autocratic system of appointment. Lastly, the desirability of the kullar's terms of slavery, his access to wealth and honor, always acted as a tremendous attraction to those free-born Moslems who had the ambitions and often the talents to offer to the service of the Sultan. It was not possible to exclude them once the original rules of service were relaxed. The Ottoman system failed because, having admirably solved the problems. offered by a particular environment and set of conditions, it was unable to formulate machinery that would enable it with equal efficiency to react to the conditions of a changing world.

SUMMING UP

What lessons in public administration are supported by Ottoman experience? The following five are suggested for consideration:
1.   Administration must adapt itself to changing social and political conditions. Technical efficiency may serve brilliantly the problem of the moment, but only those institutions which have as part of their essence the faculties of adaptation and renewal will be able to evade the persistence of social decay.
2.   An efficient administration can be improved by the special training of its members.
3.   Since it was the aim of the Ottoman system to fit the square pegs into the square holes, steps were taken to ensure that those in the lower class who were subsequently found to have abilities suitable to the higher should be advanced. Ample facilities for such transfers are even more urgently required in any system where the nature of class divisions rests, even in the smallest degree, on social distinctions.
4.   The need for constant simplification and planning of administrative processes —to secure essentials and avoid unnecessarily involved methods of a bureau- cracy—was not provided for in the Ottoman system. The results were serious.
5.   The Ottoman system was in many ways a tour de force which achieved a brilliance that theory would not have dared to prophesy. Ultimately its suc- cess depended upon inspired leadership and hereditary genius: administration requires a more dependable motive power. Democracy has one supreme advantage; its gradual substitution of the ideal of community service for that of personal allegiance.

Blanche D. Blank

Personnel Policy
in New York City

Politics is *won*; administration is simply *done*. The former is a game that attracts the average citizen as an occasional participant and as a reasonably regular specta- tor. The latter seems drudgery worth only distant, infrequent and cynical nods. It is hard then to direct public attention to what I have come to believe is the real

From "The Battle of Bureaucracy," by Blanche D. Blank, *The Nation*, 203, December 12, 1966, 632-636. Reprinted by permission.

adversary in the battle for better urban services and creative, healthful urban living. But the truth of the matter is that today's cities move more upon the backs of their bureaucrats than upon the shoulders of their politicians. And the bureaucrats are found wanting fully as often as the politicians.

Unfortunately, even the professional watchdog associations relaxed their interest in bureaucracy once the public service establishments of our largest cities transcended the "spoils system" about a generation ago. With the adoption of the so-called "merit system" (in which employees are largely immune to political whim), the critics no longer saw a chronic danger. They were wrong. The elected officials, to be sure, should provide the spark for imaginative urban policies; but they must have a bureaucratic base that is prepared to ignite. That base is still sodden in most cities. Reorganization (along the lines already initiated by Mayor Lindsay in New York City) takes care of the shape of the bureaucracy—the number of units and their relative position. It is now necessary to introduce positive practices to insure a supply of first-rate personnel and sufficient incentive to keep them primed.

I recently visited one of Mayor Lindsay's most vigorous new commissioners, who after three months in office was almost overcome by the situation in which he found himself caught. "Do you realize I've got a quarter of a million dollars worth of personnel not doing any productive work for this city? I can't put them *on* a job or *off* the payroll. They're either under criminal indictment or just totally incompetent." In another department (one of the city's largest and most essential) the men in the bureau of transportation average no more than three and a half to four hours of actual work per week while drawing salaries of more than $100. Moreover, the typical malingerer in this operation has no sense of guilt. He sees the situation as "normal operating procedure" and is quick to point out the complicity of middle management.

The good will, ideas, and moral stamina of the much-publicized city leadership must somehow be allowed to percolate throughout the entire bureaucracy. At present the system is clogged by poor public relations, budgetary restraints, statutory anachronisms, procedural rigidities and an inappropriate outlook.

In New York City, close to a quarter million civil servants are charged with carrying out the mayor's programs. They currently operate out of ninety agencies and do virtually every known type of work from fence mending to physics. Two thirds of this group are employed through the City Department of Personnel; not more than 12 percent are direct political appointees. There are, however, some 16,000 noncompetitive posts (mostly manual jobs, but also about 2000 at high levels) for which only general qualifications are required, instead of the usual competitive examination score.

The overwhelming majority of these civil servants are able and honorable people. Indeed, the city often gets better than it deserves. But there are other cases in which the recruitment, development and retention of excellence lag. Some of the failure arises from an "image" of city employment that falls far short of actual conditions. Time and again I found people (including some who were professionally concerned with government service) seriously misinformed about the city's bureaucracy. One high-ranking federal personnel officer, for example, thought incorrectly that stenographers in federal agencies were better paid than those working for the city. Similarly, a banker was surprised to learn that in many areas the city pay scale was competitive with wages in his bank.

Of course, there are also valid reasons why City Hall does not attract Columbia the way Washington does Harvard. New York City's civil service (like that of most other large cities) needs considerable revision. The most frequent complaint inside the service comes from men at or near the top who feel that they have been asked to do big jobs without being given sufficient power. A new, eager, inexperienced, politically appointed commissioner is likely to see his department as a vast immovable herd of automatons in whom imagination and a high sense of urgency have long been deadened. When he has mellowed he may come to find that all is not as black as he first thought, and that he alone does not have a monopoly on intelligence and virtue. But even if he attains this wisdom (instead of drowning in either bitterness or despair), he will accumulate a set of legitimate gripes, all stemming from his desire to run his own show in his own style and to approach the goals of his assignment.

When you talk to such a man, you discover that the leading devils in his purgatory are the Budget Office and "the system" (the latter being a set of labyrinth procedures reluctantly administered by the City Department of Personnel). To imprint his style, a commissioner needs considerable freedom to use both the carrot and the stick. But in New York City, his carrot (merit increases, promotions, training, compensatory time off) is all but nibbled away by budget restrictions, and his stick (reprimand, demotion, dismissal) is all but broken by legal but ossified personnel practices. On top of this, his reservoir of new blood is considerably thinned by impossible exam procedures and unrealistic eligibility qualifications.

When he blasts out against budgetary restrictions, to take the major adversary first, a commissioner is not likely to be conscious of the fact that in large measure he is complaining about the mayor, to whom he owes his job in the first place. Nonetheless, many of the restraints that chafe him are traceable to policies and personalities that come directly under the mayor's control. Sooner or later, most department heads come to sense (however subliminally) that they must operate by "pull." Indeed, a New York City commissioner needs more "blat" than a Soviet commissar. His pull index, moreover, is a composite measure of his political strength, his professional reputation, his personal connections with the mayor, and his persistence. It is apparent to even a casual observer that some commissioners are more equal than others.

An average commissioner cannot do what he wants with his budget primarily because it is a line-by-line affair that must be agonized over with the Budget Office, and this despite the fact that the new charter in New York appears to have liberalized departmental control over budgets. The city now has a "performance" budget in which presumably a department head need justify only overall amounts and within which he can reasonably juggle his own personnel needs. But the charter also permits the mayor to withdraw this privilege, and that is exactly what former Mayor Wagner did, and what Mayor Lindsay continues to do. There is extant an executive order which allows only specifically named departments to enjoy the new flexibility. Few departments have to date received the accolade (and one which did, was made to feel that it had better not abuse its privilege).

All commissioners, moreover, are prisoners of the "accrual system," again a policy patently condoned by the mayor. Under this procedure no department gets its *published* budgetary allotment. Instead, it receives that portion left after the Budget Office has subtracted the expenses likely to evaporate during the year by reason of deaths, retirements or other departures. Any personnel replacements must then be newly justified to Budget and will almost invariably be made at the beginning salary level in the department. This naturally greatly reduces a commissioner's personnel leverage, and means that departments are more likely to "fatten up" their personnel requests than search for savings. From the commissioner's viewpoint, in short, the Budget director has his grasp on too many departmental personnel operations: from what positions should be filled and when, to job classifications, merit increases, and salary rates for certain posts.

In fairness, however, most Budget men have developed their jaundiced outlook from the depressing discovery that all too few *political* personalities are ready to buck the unions, or the internal bureaucratic pressure group, or even to restrain their own instincts for patronage. Furthermore, the Budget director necessarily takes an overall view of the city system. It is he, more than any other official short of the mayor, who must visualize the total implications of any individual move in the civil service establishment. To him, a raise or classification change in a particular department is two things: it is a *permanent* escalation of city costs; and it is a potential trigger to a host of hierarchically related raises and reclassifications.

Moreover, if you ask a budget officer why a department must concoct a phony budget in order to make up for "accruals," he will tell you that the city simply must have uncommitted funds for emergencies. (There is no year without unusual snowfalls, unexpected demonstrations, a blackout, etc.) If you then ask, logically, why the city cannot have a contingency fund written specifically for this purpose, you will be told that such a fund is unthinkable because the unions would see it as an open invitation to come in with wage demands that would reduce the fund to zero in the first week of every fiscal year.

Finally, you may wish to suggest to a Budget man that after all the commissioners are also the mayor's men: why shouldn't *they* be trusted with personnel decisions? You will then be assured that the mayor does not invariably trust or respect his appointees. Some commissioners may be necessary political payoffs, others unfortunate mistakes. In any event, the mayor can hardly be expected to keep a close eye on as many as eighty "top dogs." By working through Budget, he can keep every one of his commissioners constantly dancing to the tune he himself calls.

Complaints against the Personnel Department are less frequent. The average commissioner tends to look on Personnel with more pity than pique—if indeed, he does not overlook them entirely. A few agency heads, however, do feel checked by this staff arm.

One commissioner contended that a Personnel Department classification officer had withheld a critical reclassification of a title in which his agency had had more than 300 vacancies in three years. He had fought a long, hard, time-consuming and ultimately unsuccessful battle for *his* version of what was needed in the job specification. Another commissioner charged that the Personnel Department's failure to honor his request for a short delay in the scheduling of an administrative promotional exam resulted in the exclusion of a group of well-trained, younger recruits who needed the extra weeks demanded in order to comply with the experience qualifications. By Personnel's refusal to postpone this test, an "in-group" of older employees (about whom the commissioner was less than sanguine) had this field for promotion to themselves.

In most instances, however, the Personnel Department tries to be an ally to the agency chiefs and is so accepted by them. They generally see eye to eye and are equally distressed by the overelaborate grievance procedures, the laxity of performance evaluations, the prolix exam system and the budgetary rigidities. The effectiveness of the city Department of Personnel as an aide to the commissioners is, however, heavily curtailed by financial, psychological and legal considerations.

Unlike Budget, the Department of Personnel is not at all close to the mayor. It has never had the administrative status, parallel to Budget, as staff arm to the chief executive, and its position vis-à-vis Budget is exacerbated by the fact that it too must depend on that office for its own lines, classifications, and other benefits. The department includes an unusual cadre of highly intelligent, well-trained and hard-working men, but they have been the "second team" too long. They are so used to being hemmed in by legalistic restrictions through which they must thread clever and devious routes, that they rarely consider fighting a pitched battle.

In addition to being administrative stepchildren, they are also the official custodians of the Civil Service Law and of the merit mentality. These once fashionable goals are today generally obsolete. The mission is not to keep rascals out but to bring excellence in. It is not enough to be fair; one must also be fruitful. But procedural "fairness," as well as a number of other outmoded objectives, are immortalized in everything from the state constitution through state laws, city ordinances, Civil Service Commission regulations (both state and city), the myriad court decisions interpreting all of the foregoing, and the very habits of the Personnel Department itself.

It is the state constitution, for example, that marries the personnel operation to a well-meant but currently inappropriate competitive examination procedure for promotions as well as entrance. Other sections of state law set up arbitrary qualifications. Welfare workers are now required to be college graduates (though not necessarily with anything in their academic records resembling professional social-work training). Yet much of the work they do is investigatory—some of it routine paperwork—and much better suited to junior college people or even bright high school graduates. But aside from other difficulties that here might stand in the way of reform, the standards are perpetuated by a law which requires a department receiving state aid (about half the welfare budget) to use college graduates. Similarly rigid state requirements concerning registered nurses have received unfavorable publicity.

A recent State Supreme Court decision, to take another facet of the legal problem, questioned the lawfulness of a long-used Personnel Department interpretation that its own rules did not require State Civil Service Commission confirmation. Now, even this limited latitude is in doubt, along with a whole series of past actions taken under that reasonable amplification. Years of pussyfooting among such legal booby traps have made the department understandably cautious. "I'll tell you why we can't do that" is the hallmark of its style.

Much of the difficulty that besets the Department of Personnel in its attempt to cope usefully with the civil service establishment stems from preoccupation with an often spurious type of "fairness." This is presumed to flow from all sorts of devices: entrance examinations, promotional exams, veterans' preference rules, labyrinthine grievance procedures, overweening concern for nondiscrimination policies, and from detailed regulations concerning reprimands, demotions and dismissals. These safeguards are frequently inadequate even to their own narrow limits.

The Personnel Department is asked, for example, to administer about 300 different examinations to close to 200,000 people in an average year. Many of these are entrance exams, and *too* many are promotional ones. (There are typically six steps from one rung to the next in a promotional ladder and it takes many years to move through them. In one department, the yield from this system was a median age of 55 among the eighty-five persons earning $10,000 per year or more.)

A typical self-defeating "fairness" requirement in the exam procedure is that every civil service test be published immediately after it is used, so that all may see the questions and the acceptable answers and be able to protest any item believed to be unjust. What is the actual outcome of this expensive procedure? A certain number of relatively minor mistakes are caught, while the more serious problem of running out of decently perceptive questions is insured by the publicity. "Cram schools" inevitably build portfolios of potential questions that must at some point be repeated. Indeed, a year or so ago, almost half of those taking a fireman's exam left after only one hour of what was scheduled to be a three-hour test; they had studied precisely this exam in a cram course. I have just been told, however, that this requirement is about to be lifted.

The following case history is typical of the civil service exam procedure. In January 1964, just before graduating from college, an entirely suitable Hunter senior "filed" for a "planning" exam. The test was held on April 11 (after her application had been scrutinized for "eligibility") at the Abraham Lincoln High School in Brooklyn. A few hundred people from all over the city took the test.

After three months she was finally notified of "passing." Later in July she was asked to appear for an oral interview. In August there was a medical exam, and the following November she was required to report (replete with diploma, marriage license, and other newly acquired credentials) at a "character exam." From that point on she received no further communication from the city except what she herself initiated. She telephoned in September to find out her status. She was then informed that her "list" had expired the previous July. When she tried to discover whether *any* appointments had been made from that exam, she could originally get no firm information. Only after a number of subsequent phone calls (many of which were rudely answered) was she able to ferret out that "a few" people had been appointed to three of the five departments in which vacancies were originally announced. She also discovered at this late date that 153 persons had passed the written test.

A story like this should elicit questions. Why is it necessary to cast such a broad net for so tiny a catch? Having once cast it (perhaps on the ground that nothing is too costly for excellence), why bother with oral interviews, physicals and other such expensive folderol except for the few top people who are *likely* to be ultimately appointed to the handful of vacancies? One might also want to know why (since the exam was an objective one geared for machine marking) it took three months to notify applicants of their fate.

But the really basic questions are: Why should we think that we are likely to get the best of anything when eight months is the average time between filing and appointment for all civil service exams? And why should we cling naively to the hope that objective exams of the sort so often used really elicit the capacities we ultimately need in the service? Would not college grades, the Graduate Record Exam, or some other equally cheap and painless device serve as well? Exams for promotion, it should be noted, offer most of the same disadvantages, plus the fact that they are frequently either confined to an "in group" or designed to favor them.

If getting good people in has its frustrations, getting poor ones out is even worse. Dismissals in the New York City civil service run to less than 1.5 percent a year. The required proceedings are highly formal, almost like a trial—and generally suggestive that it is the supervisor rather than the employee who is being tried. Appeals from a departmental decision can be taken to the city Civil Service Commission or to the courts. (Just recently, a state judicial decision threw doubts on the proposition that these are necessarily alternative procedures; so it may now be that *both* avenues of appeal are open to disgruntled employees.) Although both the commission and the courts are more than likely to uphold departmental disciplinary decisions, a sufficient number of reversals are on record to worry most supervisors. In fact, a very high-ranking personnel officer ventured that if the commission or the courts adopted ordinary business management standards, 50 percent of the grievance procedures now decided in favor of employees would be reversed. Considering, therefore, the risk of the unsettling effects on various segments of personnel, the tremendous consumption of agency time, the heavy cost and the ordinary human reluctance to do unpleasant things, it is remarkable that *any* dismissals are achieved under present conditions. A former powerful and important executive assistant to Mayor Wagner rated dismissal difficulties as the key morale obstacle in the civil service. Good people are irritated by the retention (and occasionally even the promotion; in a number of instances employees were actually promoted while dismissal procedures were under way) of mediocrity, or worse.

Even the probationary period that follows all original appointments to the competitive civil service provides a dismissal flexibility that is more apparent than real. Civil service rules require that an incumbent must serve the *entire* probationary period (either three or six months, depending on the post), before he is vulnerable to summary dismissal. Prior to that time he must be given the full-dress hearing described above, even if his conduct during the period is blatantly irresponsible. Moreover, there is actually only one brief day during which it is legal to dismiss him. Eight hours later, if he is not released, he becomes a "regular." Most probationers become full-fledged civil servants almost automatically.

Merit increases, moreover (which a commissioner might think to use as a "carrot"), have in most instances degenerated into automatic increments because of the difficulties attached to stigmatizing an employee with a "below-standard" rating and the almost equal reluctance of supervisors to designate anyone as "superior." The resulting barrage of "standard" scores makes a farce of the whole merit idea.

Still another type of "fairness" that plagues the city's civil service and is necessarily administered by the Personnel Department is the requirement that the city's own employment practices vigorously reflect the state's generally laudatory attempts to prevent discrimination. The most recent addition to the anti-discrimination coverage is the criterion of "age." On quick reading this may seem as beneficial as the race and religion clauses; nevertheless, it is the bane of many city supervisors. In one department, for instance, an exam that was designed to reap a group of vigorous career-minded youngsters, produced instead a crop of 60-year-old widows. Not only was career development impossible with such a group but one supervisor complained that he could not even get his clerical tasks done properly since many of his files required the use of a 6-foot ladder. Another department chief told me that it had been years since he had seen a "healthy youngster of forty." Even the exams designed for bright young college graduates are apt to turn up 50-year-old college-bred retirees from other careers. While there is every reason to provide meaningful work for older (and disabled) citizens, it is doubtful that the city service alone can carry the burden.

3
Bureaucratic Behavior

Why is bureaucracy a dirty word? Anyone who has applied for a driver's license, gotten married, filed an income tax return, been subjected to a security clearance, or tried to fight city hall will tell you why, in angry frustration. The French call it *paperasserie*, the interminable paper-shuffling that bureaucrats seem to love. The bad behavior of bureaucrats, to put it precisely, is the result of the foibles of many individuals working in a complex system that restricts their freedom to be sympathetic to the aggravated citizen.

Bureaucrats can, of course, perform admirably in some instances. That is, their behavior sometimes accords closely with the Weberian ideals of rationality, efficiency, and impartiality, and this—under favorable circumstances—allows them to complete very complicated tasks quite successfully. Examples are few, to be sure. One of the best is the outstanding achievement of the Hoover Commission for European relief during and after World War I; this bureaucratic task force was largely responsible for saving millions of Europeans from starvation. The selection from the report by Surface and Bland on the Hoover Commission tells this bureaucratic success story. One interesting feature of the report is that it is a document written by bureaucrats, presumably to inspire other bureaucrats. An immensely long and detailed document, it rather dryly heralds the results of the Commission as much in statistics as in human terms. One can conjecture about the reasons for the extraordinary bureaucratic performance of the Commission. In the first place, European relief was an easily understandable goal that won enthusiasm from the American people. The Commission was directed by an able and respected man.

Nobody interfered with his work. The resources and transportation were available. The climate of emergency made quick action a must. Administration, though complex, was clearly thought out. Finally, the program was a short-term project, as these things go, and it had immediate, visible results, satisfying to its sponsors, recipients, and participants alike. Perhaps the only parallel today is the American program which landed men on the moon, but even this enterprise was not blessed with the unusually favorable circumstances of the Hoover Relief Commission.

If all bureaucratic undertakings went as smoothly as did European relief, bureaucratic behavior would not be a problem. But one of the essential characteristics of bureaucracy—namely, its mediating function among various groups within society—provides the arena in which problems of bureaucratic behavior do indeed arise. This is because the mediation of different interests inevitably creates tensions and disagreements, according to the analysis of S. N. Eisenstadt in "Political Struggle in Bureaucratic Societies." Political struggle is Eisenstadt's term for fighting out these disagreements. The most basic political struggle is between the bureaucracy and the head of state, because both have their own claims to legitimate authority. Actual skirmishes in this struggle are fought over such things as specific policy issues, maintenance of bureaucratic discipline, or simply the different styles of administration practiced by conservative bureaucrats on the one hand and impetuous rulers on the other. Political struggles also occur because bureaucrats must mediate interests within the bureaucracy as well as without. Finally, bureaucracy may come into conflict with other social groups, such as a hereditary aristocracy, even though many of the upper bureaucrats may have personal ties to extra-bureaucratic groups. These sources of tension, deriving from the mediating function of bureaucracy, provoke bureaucrats to use all the tricks at their disposal. It is not surprising that, depending on one's point of view, they appear to be dirty tricks.

In the selection from *The Ruling Servants*, E. Strauss discusses specific kinds of bad bureaucratic behavior. He concentrates on the unfortunate effects of the bureaucratic mind, red tape, and departmentalism. Strauss contends, however, that not all bad behavior is willful. For example, the use of standardized forms is necessary for reducing the enormous expense of routine administration, despite the aggravation that forms may cause the outsider. Then too, when a large problem arises, the interests of different parts of the society or the bureaucracy may legitimately conflict, and an acceptable compromise inevitably takes time. The resulting delays appear to be procrastination, but there is really no other way consistent with a fair solution to any serious problem. Excusable defects in bureaucratic behavior, according to Strauss, arise from technical difficulties. On the other hand, wholly inexcusable is "the great social evil of bureaucratic degeneration" born when the power of mediation is sought for its own sake, by bureaucrats intent on creating little empires for themselves.

One of the most repellent forms of bad bureaucratic behavior is corruption, especially the buying of special favors and the unfair exercise of bureaucratic influence. Left unchecked, bureaucratic corruption can reduce the large bureaucracy of a modern industrial nation to a wretched mess. But O. P. Dwivedi, in his article "Bureaucratic Corruption in Developing Countries," provocatively argues that corruption is not completely harmful in emerging societies. He contends, for instance, that bureaucratic corruption may mitigate the effect of overly harsh governmental regulation of private interest groups. He assumes that voluntary associations and interest groups can contribute to the strengthening of the social fabric of a developing country, and he feels that corruption may permit them to play this role more effectively. Dwivedi also maintains that allowing minority groups representation and access to power in the bureaucracy, by special exemption from the merit principle, can prevent minority frustration from exploding in the future. Naturally, Dwivedi's point of view is controversial. To begin with, he does not share with most members of Western-trained intellectual elites in developing countries their hatred of corruption, which they consider the worst enemy of modernization. Furthermore, the "compromise between necessity and morality" proposed by Dwivedi offends many people's sense of right and wrong. Iconoclastic though Dwivedi is, he shows clearly that the question about that dirty word *bureaucracy* ought to be: What do you mean by *dirty*?

Frank M. Surface and Raymond L. Bland

A Bureaucratic Success Story

From the beginning of the World War in August 1914, up to the close of the Russian relief work in 1924, Herbert Hoover created and directed organizations which were responsible for securing and delivering vast quantities of foodstuffs to the peoples of various European countries. The importance and magnitude of this work and the results accomplished can hardly be overestimated. To mention only a few of the possibilities, it may be pointed out that a large portion of the 10,000,000 people in the occupied regions of Belgium and Northern France might have perished. The results of the World War might have been far different, for the final decision depended as much upon food as it did upon armed forces. In the armistice period the peoples of Central and Eastern Europe would have died by millions in the greatest famine the world had seen in three hundred years. Millions of young men and women in Europe today owe their very lives and their present physical fitness to the child-feeding work carried on from 1919 to 1923, and finally, still further millions of the Russian people owe their lives to the relief work in the terrible famine of 1921-1922.

From *American Food in the World War and Reconstruction Period*, by Frank M. Surface and Raymond L. Bland, 1931, Stanford University Press, pp. ix, 3-4, 5-9. Reprinted by permission of the authors.

These outstanding achievements in that decade of service were accomplished in the face of world-wide disorganization and the desire of every nation to concentrate on its own problems of reconstruction.

During the ten years, 1914 to 1924, operations were carried on under Mr. Hoover's direction and by the organizations which he headed involving the expenditure of the enormous sum of almost five and a quarter billions of dollars ($5,234,028,208.56). Part of these funds came from charitable donations, part were funds from the United States Treasury donated for relief or loaned to other governments, part came from other countries or from other organizations.

For this sum there were delivered to the people of Europe more than thirty-three million (33,841,307) tons of commodities, mostly American foodstuffs but including some clothing and medical supplies.

Much of this relief work was carried on under the stress of great emergency and under pressure to make food available at a definite place in a limited space of time in order to save human life. Through it all, detailed records were kept of every ton of supplies from the moment of their purchase until they left the hands of the American organizations. Considering the magnitude of the work and the conditions under which it was carried on, the statistical records are remarkably complete, with no serious gaps . . . .

In August 1914, some 200,000 panic-stricken American tourists were stranded in the meshes of the Great War that had so suddenly enveloped continental Europe. At the first opportunity these Americans piled into England by tens of thousands, most of them without available funds because of the moratorium, and all of them without transportation home. In this emergency, the Honorable Walter Hines Page, the American ambassador to Great Britain, persuaded Herbert Hoover, a mining engineer with an international reputation in his profession, to organize these chaotic groups of tourists and direct their homeward movement. Accustomed to coordinating big engineering projects, he soon reduced these confused groups to something like order. With ten other Americans he guaranteed an American Bank in London against loss and announced that all sorts of American paper, even personal checks, would be exchanged for currency. He arranged transportation with the steamship companies and soon the stream of tourists was homeward bound in an orderly fashion. Five thousand or more Americans a day passed through the hands of this organization during these first six weeks of the war. And although Hoover's Committee accepted checks and other evidences of credit to the extent of $1,500,000, with little opportunity to scrutinize the security, they lost in all only $150.

Hoover himself had engaged passage home for the last week in September 1914. But the gods had another fate in store for him. Before he could sail, the German armies had invaded Belgium and left the people of that little country in a desperate situation. American and Belgian representatives importuned him to undertake the delicate and difficult task of organizing some means of saving the lives of these ten million people within the occupied territories. Hoover knew what this decision meant. He knew it was a long and difficult job and that if he undertook it he must sever his connections with all commercial activities. At that time, by reason of his numerous mining connections, he was in a position to control a large share of the world's supply of base metals, particularly zinc and lead. These were bound to be enormously valuable if the war continued and if he held on to these it was certain to result in a very large fortune. For three days he sat with Mr. Page and the Belgians, discussing details and imagining possibilities. And for three nights he weighed his own perplexities before he finally decided to cast his lot with the relief for the Belgians.

With that decision was born the Commission for Relief in Belgium—a decision of supreme importance for himself and for the world.

The story of the Commission for Relief in Belgium has been told many times: of how this organization, beginning as a purely philanthropic enterprise, soon received the financial support of the Allied and American governments; of how the C.R.B. without incorporation or definite legal status came to have many attributes of a government, flying its own flag, issuing its own passports, operating its own fleet under agreed immunity from all belligerent powers, and operating to feed a civilian population within its enemy lines. In April 1917, the United States entered the war and it was necessary to delegate the distribution in Belgium and France to a neutral Spanish-Dutch committee. Mr. Hoover, now U.S. Food Administrator, continued as chairman of the Commission and arranged for financing the purchase and transport of the food supplies.

In the meantime, President Wilson had asked Mr. Hoover to take charge of the food situation, which was rapidly approaching a crisis, in this country. Mr. Hoover arrived in the United States on May 19, 1917, and immediately initiated the preparatory work which led to the establishment of the United States Food Administration. Under the authority of the Food Control Act, which became a law on August 10, 1917, Mr. Hoover was appointed United States Food Administrator. From that time until after the Armistice, he directed all measures relating to the conservation and distribution of food in this country to insure an adequate supply to support our own needs and those of the Allies in Europe.

In the summer of 1918, Mr. Hoover, anticipating the distress in the liberated and enemy countries on the cessation of hostilities, caused a survey to be made of world food resources and prepared a definite plan for initiating relief measures. Immediately after the Armistice had been signed, President Wilson requested Mr. Hoover to go to Europe and represent the United States in such measures as had to be taken according to the plans already prepared, in order to relieve the impending suffering. He sailed from the United States on November 18, 1918, only seven days after the signing of the Armistice, having arranged before his departure for the dispatch of large quantities of food supplies. From that time until the following September was the most strenuous, the most difficult, but probably the most fruitful period of Mr. Hoover's relief activities. As Director General of Relief for the Allied Governments during these nine months he secured the finance and directed the delivery of more than 4,000,000 tons of food valued at more than one billion dollars.

With the 1919 harvest it was possible to bring this form of relief in Central and Eastern Europe to a close, but in the meantime it had been found that there were millions of children in these countries, many of them orphans, suffering from under-nutrition, many facing death, but all certain of permanent disability unless some means of relief were found. Mr. Hoover immediately set about perfecting an organization which could take care of this need. For three years the American Relief Administration European Children's Fund raised money and fed some 10,000,000 children in these stricken countries.

Before this work was entirely completed, the great famine in Russia again raised the need for "mass feeding" relief on a tremendous scale. The A.R.A. organization, although ready to liquidate, again responded to the call, and under Mr. Hoover's direction, relief to the value of more than $63,000,000 was furnished to these stricken people.

With the close of the Russian relief and the withdrawal of the child-feeding operations in Central Europe, this vast work extending over ten years came to a close.

SCOPE OF REPORT

The present volume attempts to give a statistical summary and a brief outline of relief activities by the organizations with which Mr. Hoover was connected, and also of the activities of other organizations in respect to their cooperation in this work. This is by no means a complete summary of all the relief work in Europe during this period. Many of the relief organizations mentioned in this volume spent millions, even hundreds of millions of dollars, entirely on their own activities, of which no account is taken in this report. To mention a few of these organizations: The American Red Cross spent upwards of $200,000,000 in relief activities in Europe during this period, yet in this report we have included less than $7,300,000 as the amount spent by the Red Cross in activities in cooperation with the American Relief Administration. The Near East Relief, the Jewish Joint Distribution Committee, the American Friends Service Committee, the Knights of Columbus, and many other organizations each spent vast sums which had no relation to the work of the organizations which Mr. Hoover was then directing and, hence, are not included in this report. These facts are pointed out in the discussion of the work of each of these organizations but it is important that the reader bear in mind that the volume of relief attributed to many of these organizations in this report is only that portion carried on in cooperation with the American Relief Administration or its subsidiaries and often is only a small fraction of the total activities of those organizations during this period.

ORGANIZATIONS INVOLVED

. . . The Commission for Relief in Belgium (C.R.B.) was established October 22, 1914, and was the buying and shipping organization for all relief supplies to the occupied regions of Belgium and Northern France for the entire duration of the war. Until the United States entered the war the C.R.B. was responsible to the belligerent governments for the execution of the agreements relative to the distribution of the relief in occupied territories. The Commission remained in active operation until August 31, 1919, by which time both the Belgian and French Governments were in a position to take care of their own people and the Commission had liquidated its stock of commodities.

Operating under the C.R.B. were two committees: one composed of Belgians and known as the "Comité National de Secours et d'Alimentation"; the other the corresponding committee of Frenchmen known as the "Comité d'Alimentation du Nord de la France." These two committees carried out the actual internal distribution of relief supplies within the respective countries. Under these committees there were numerous district and local committees through which the supplies moved to the people.

The United States Food Administration was created by Executive Order of President Wilson on August 14, 1917, to carry out the provisions of the Food Control Act of August 10, 1917. Under the United States Food Administration there were several organizations set up to carry out particular functions. The first of these referred to in this volume is the Food Administration Grain Corporation, which was charged with the responsibility of maintaining the guaranteed price of wheat and which engaged in buying and selling wheat, flour, and other cereals and was the source from which the Allied Governments secured their supplies of these commodities during the remainder of the war. The Food Administration came to a close officially on June 30, 1919, and in order to maintain President Wilson's guaranty of the minimum price of wheat to the producer for the 1919-1920 crop, the President directed a new corporation to be formed, known as the United States Grain Corporation, which was the successor to the preceding corporation.

The second organization under the Food Administration was the Sugar Equalization Board, which was incorporated, and purchased both the Cuban and the United States crops of sugar in 1918 and attended to the distribution of the available supplies; both to the Allied countries and internally in the United States.

The third organization under the Food Administration was the Division of Coordination of Purchases, through which all food purchases by the Allies, except cereals and sugar, were allocated.

Immediately after the signing of the Armistice, Mr. Hoover went to Europe at President Wilson's request and through his efforts there was formed an Interallied Council of Supply and Relief, which later became the Food Section of the Supreme Economic Council. Mr. Hoover was made Director General of Relief for the Allied Governments and was given direct charge of all official relief work during the armistice period.

In order to handle the official relief from the United States, particularly the supplies furnished under the Congressional Appropriation of $100,000,000 for Relief in Europe (Act of February 25, 1919), President Wilson directed Mr. Hoover to form the American Relief Administration (frequently designated A.R.A.), which was an official organization to handle the allocation and distribution of relief furnished by the United States Government. In addition to the relief paid for from the specific Congressional appropriation, the A.R.A. handled relief furnished from United States Treasury loans direct to certain of the newly established governments, supplies furnished from the President's National Security and Defense Fund and certain relief furnished against cash payment.

Under authorization of President Wilson, the Food Administration Grain Corporation cooperated in the buying and shipping of all relief supplies distributed by the American Relief Administration. The Grain Corporation established a London office which took care of all shipping activities in European waters, handled all the accounting work, and made all settlements with the European governments. In the present report all relief deliveries are referred to as handled by the A.R.A., although to be exact the Grain Corporation should receive joint credit.

With the signing of the Treaty of Versailles on June 28, 1919, the armistice period ended and with it all official relief from the United States. From that time on the A.R.A. and the Grain Corporation were engaged solely in liquidating commitments.

In order to render further aid to the millions of destitute children in Europe, Mr. Hoover proposed the organization of an association which could mobilize charitable contributions from the United States. With the approval of President Wilson, it was arranged that any surplus which might have been earned by the Grain Corporation on the relief shipment in the armistice period should be turned over to this new organization for the relief of European children. The name of this new organization was the American Relief Administration European Children's Fund. In the present report this is usually referred to as the European Children's Fund or simply as the E.C.F. This was a purely private charitable organization and should not be confused with the American Relief Administration of the armistice period which was a semi-official organization.

At a somewhat later period, a separate but correlated organization was set up and known as the American Relief Administration Warehouses (sometimes designated by A.R.A.W.), which handled all food draft and bulk sale operations during its existence.

During this period there was also set up the European Relief Council (E.R.C.), which was an association of a number of charitable organizations under the leadership of Mr. Hoover which pooled their appeal for charitable contributions from the American public.

Finally, when it became necessary to expand an organization to take care of the crisis in the great Russian famine, the name American Relief Administration was again adopted. This latter organization was an outgrowth of the American Relief Administration European Children's Fund, but since the Russian relief included both adult and child feeding the latter name was regarded as inappropriate. In this book this new organization is frequently referred to as the "American Relief Administration, Russian Unit," or as "A.R.A., Russian Unit." It should not be confused with the A.R.A. of the armistice period.

The origin and work of each of the above organizations is fully explained in the appropriate section of this volume but perhaps the above brief discussion will make clear some of the interrelations which might otherwise prove to be confusing.

TOTAL RELIEF DELIVERIES

As indicated in the preceding brief summary, this decade of relief work may be divided into four major operations or periods of activities. Although even these were often overlapping and graded one into the other, they stand out as four distinct major developments in the work with which Mr. Hoover was connected. The first of these was the work of the Commission for Relief in Belgium, which took care of the food supply of the occupied territories of Belgium and Northern France during the war. This work was started in November 1914, and continued during the armistice period and up to August 31, 1919, before the respective governments were in a position entirely to take care of their people.

The second major activity was that of the United States Food Administration, which among other things was charged with the responsibility of furnishing the Allied nations with such food supplies as could be spared from the United States. Although the Food Administration was not definitely established until August 1917, yet for many months prior to that, Mr. Hoover, under authority from President Wilson, was directing the work of furnishing food to the Allies. In this report we have included all food supplies furnished to the Allied Governments which were paid for from United States Treasury loans from April 6, 1917, to June 30, 1919, when the Food Administration passed out of existence.

The third major activity was the relief to European countries during the period from the signing of the Armistice on November 11, 1918, to the signing of the Treaty of Versailles on June 28, 1919. This was the period of official relief during which Mr. Hoover was Director General of Relief and had direct charge of all relief activities of the Allied Governments. Deliveries of relief commitments made during this armistice period were completed by the end of August 1919.

The fourth and final period of relief activities considered in this report is that of the reconstruction period, which began with the work of the American Relief Administration European Children's Fund, in August 1919, and included many phases of charitable relief, ending with the work in Russia in 1922 and 1923. The major portion of this relief was in the nature of child feeding, but it also includes many phases of adult relief, such as the food draft and bulk sale operations, intelligentsia relief, and much of the Russian work.

Table 1 summarizes the grand total of all relief work accounted for in this report under these four major operations. . . . This table shows that the total deliveries accounted for in this report reached the enormous amount of 33,841,307.0 metric tons with a net delivered value of $5,234,028,208.56. Some idea of the volume of these activities may be had by considering that this tonnage would have filled more than 500,000 American freight cars and would require more than 6700 vessels of 5000 tons each for its transatlantic transportation.

Table 1

Grand Total Of All Food And Other Relief Delivered During The World War And The Reconstruction Period—By Major Operations, 1914-1924

Major Relief Operation	Duration	Total Metric Tons	Total Value
Commission for Relief in Belgium	November 1914 to August 1919	4,988,059.0	$ 861,340,244.21
U.S. Food Administration	April 1917 to June 1919	23,103,266.2	3,050,496,599.23
Armistice Period (Director General of Relief)	November 1918 to August 1919	4,178,447.7	1,101,486,783.34
Reconstruction Period	August 1919 to July 1923	1,571,534.1	220,704,581.78
Grand total net deliveries	November 1914 to July 1923	33,841,307.0	$5,234,028,208.56

Table 1 shows further that some 60 percent of these deliveries represent food supplies furnished to the Allied Governments during the Food Administration period. . . .The exigencies of the Allied food and shipping situation resulted in throwing almost the entire burden of feeding these countries during the last two years of the war upon the United States. By the extraordinary increase in the total production by the American farmers and by strict conservation measures, the latter under the guidance of the Food Administration, this country was able to export more than three times the amount of foodstuffs which had been sent abroad during the prewar years. To a very considerable extent this was due to measures inaugurated under Mr. Hoover's guidance.

Table 2 shows the division by commodity groups of the total tonnage delivered under each of the four major operations. It will be noted that flour and grain in the total constitute by far the major tonnage. These two groups make up approximately 22,000,000 tons, or roughly 65 percent of the total quantity. Pork products, including all fats, totaled approximately 2,000,000 tons, but in value this was a relatively much more important item than the tonnage figures indicate.

Table 3 gives the grand total deliveries of all food and relief by countries of destination.

Deliveries were made to 23 separate countries exclusive of sundry accounts, which include chiefly local cash sales and deliveries to prisoners of war or refugees from one country but located in another so that it was difficult to allocate the relief.

The largest deliveries were made to the United Kingdom and France, both of which obtained supplies in excess of one and a quarter billions of dollars. Deliveries to Italy were nearly $800 million. These were the three major Allies which received the bulk of food delivered during the war under the United States Food Administration.

Deliveries to Belgium amounted to nearly $700 million, the major portion of

Table 2 Grand Total of All Food And Relief Delivered During The World War And The Reconstruction Period—By Commodities And Major Operations

(Metric Tons)

Commodity	C.R.B.	United States Food Administration	Armistice Period	Reconstruction Period	Total
Flour	411,421.0	4,904,600.4	1,253,568.0	767,191.5	7,336,780.9
Grain	3,310,898.0	10,083,228.8	983,979.6	389,007.1	14,767,113.5
Rice	317,455.0	143,514.0	99,039.1	49,811.0	609,819.1
Beans and peas	171,434.0	108,860.4	104,833.6	45,796.5	430,924.5
Corn grits	. . . .	. . . .	. . . .	103,301.1	103,301.1
Pork products	379,926.0	1,363,799.6	266,979.6	29,594.8	2,040,300.0
Milk	80,921.0	451,346.9	50,653.7	103,612.1	686,533.7
Cocoa	12,870.0	. . . .	511.5	10,762.6	24,144.1
Sugar	51,024.0	1,947,936.8	43,276.7	44,295.7	2,086,533.2
Misc. food	173,272.0	922,736.5	873,062.2	4,076.0	1,973,146.7
Forage	. . . .	3,177,242.8	. . . .	3,134.3	3,180,377.1
Soap	39,129.0	. . . .	1,110.5	2,276.6	42,516.1
Medical Supplies	. . . .	. . . .	4,377.5	8,283.9	12,661.4
Clothing and misc.	39,709.0	. . . .	497,055.7	10,390.9	547,155.6
Grand Total	4,988,059.0	23,103,266.2	4,178,447.7	1,571,534.1	33,841,307.0

which came from the C.R.B. A portion of the Belgian supplies was furnished under the Food Administration on direct loans from the United States Treasury.

Of the countries receiving relief after the Armistice only, the deliveries to Germany of nearly $300 million were the largest. The major portion of these were sold for cash and paid for by German gold during the armistice period. Deliveries to Poland exceeded $200 million. Those to Austria were more than $145 million and to Czechoslovakia they exceeded $115 million. Other countries received smaller amounts, some of the largest of which were those to Russia, Roumania, Jugoslavia, Finland, and Armenia.

Table 3
The Grand Total Of All Food And Relief Delivered During The World War And The Reconstruction Period—By Countries Of Destination 1914 To 1924

Country	Total Metric Tons	Total Value
Armenia	135,764.1	$ 28,795,426.49
Austria	822,200.1	145,481,222.30
Belgium	4,198,856.3	697,140,348.91
Bulgaria	22,862.4	4,856,647.53
Czechoslovakia	545,134.6	115,438,351.98
Danzig Free State	573.2	127,700.69
Denmark	19,912.0	2,147,059.30
Esthonia	67,358.5	21,017,263.56
Finland	188,520.9	30,282,047.90
France	8,425,699.7	1,289,488,622.47
Germany	1,272,934.1	294,373,692.75
Greece	20,374.0	1,211,949.95
Hungary	21,393.5	4,607,139.37
Italy	7,479,780.7	799,608,264.01
Jugoslavia	127,359.0	45,898,651.43
Latvia	26,366.6	7,550,021.69
Lithuania	12,877.7	5,980,781.39
Netherlands	25,027.4	4,219,498.41
Poland	751,135.6	200,864,857.73
Roumania	229,202.8	53,637,311.31
Russia	768,159.9	78,305,318.49
Turkey	20,278.3	4,369,404.30
United Kingdom	8,652,668.6	1,386,102,780.05
Sundry Accounts	56,529.2	23,654,740.07
Grand Total	33,890,969.2	$5,245,159,102.08
Less duplication	49,662.2	11,130,893.52
Grand total net	33,841,307.0	$5,234,028,208.56

S. N. Eisenstadt

Tensions and Conflicts
in Bureaucratic Societies

PROBLEMS OF LEGITIMATION IN BUREAUCRATIC POLITIES

The basic problem here is that there are two necessary levels of legitimation in bureaucratic systems, and two parallel sets of activities on behalf of their maintenance and propagation. These two levels reflect the existence within such systems
of at least two major political elites or ruling groups—namely, the bureaucracy itself, and the "head of state" and the upper political group connected with him
(whether a hereditary king, a dynasty, an oligarchic "collegiate" authority, or
modern elected rulers). For obvious reasons, the ultimate headship of the bureaucratic state, as of any political system, cannot be selected in terms of bureaucratic
criteria; it has to be chosen and maintained with more direct reference to the
ultimate values of a society. This means that within such systems there have to
exist at least two types of legitimation—the more legal-rational one of the bureaucracy, and the more symbolic and cohesive one (whether traditional or secular-
social) of the headship of the polity.

Dual legitimation has some special consequences for the social and political
orientations of a bureaucracy, as compared with those of a head of state. Because
it is difficult to maintain the basic position of the bureaucracy, especially in more
traditional societies, through legal-rational legitimation alone, the bureaucracy usually tends to "usurp" some of the ultimate legitimation of the king, or to propa-
gate a similar one of its own. By way of example, the tendency of bureaucracies to
establish many of their own titles as social titles or designations is clearly discernible in the Byzantine state, in many periods of Chinese history, and in the attempts
toward self-legitimation of the *noblesse de robe* in France and other European
countries. In many cases, it may even claim for itself controlling power over the
political heads, in the name of some of the basic values of the system. In China,
where such self-legitimation was probably carried the furthest, this was done in the
name of Confucian ethics and by claiming the "Mandate of Heaven." In Byzantium, somewhat weaker claims were put forward by the legalists and by the church;
in absolutist Western Europe, the legalistic claims were quite often very pronounced and effective.

From *Political Struggle in Bureaucratic Societies*, by S. N. Eisenstadt. *World Politics*, IX, No.
1, pp. 20-34, 36. (Copyright © 1956 by Princeton University Press). Reprinted by permission
of Princeton University Press.

All these tendencies posed difficult problems of control for the kings, who quite often tried in turn to assume all the effective decision-making powers within the framework of bureaucratic organizations. The constant quarrels between the "inner" and "outer" courts which we find in China, Byzantium, and the Ottoman Empire, and the parallel relations between, for instance, the Wardrobe and the Exchequer in medieval England, as well as the kingly attempts to manipulate titles, etc., are recurrent manifestations of this problem.

But the outcome of these struggles cannot be understood merely in terms of attempts at legitimation by the different groups. These very attempts have important repercussions on the whole structure of political struggle within bureaucratic societies, and it is only within this larger framework that these particular conflicts as well as certain additional structural characteristics and differences among the bureaucracies can be fully understood.

GENERAL CHARACTERISTICS OF POLITICAL STRUGGLE IN BUREAUCRATIC POLITIES

What, then, are the basic characteristics of political struggle within these societies? In general, it can be said that political struggle here is much more diversified than in primitive, nomadic, or feudal political systems. In every bureaucratic polity there are many more elements participating in the struggle, and many more issues involved, than in any of the less-developed political systems. The general framework of this struggle is determined by the basic characteristics of the bureaucratic system itself—that is, by the distinctiveness of political goals and by the necessity for the political elite to mobilize and organize the main types of facilities and support. This means that the political elite (in most of the cases under discussion here, the kings, the emperors, and the bureaucracy) is not entirely identified with any hereditary-ascriptive group or with any other center of power. It therefore strives to control some of the main centers of power in the society, and to minimize the possibility that any of these centers or groups will be able to monopolize influence and power within the society and determine the goals of the polity. The instruments of control that interest the political elite are financial, material, and political. In the field of finance and manpower, and in the area of loyalties and political support, the elite is interested in the continued existence of some "free-floating" resources which are not entirely committed to certain fixed groups, as they are in primitive, feudal, and patrimonial societies.

The most important illustration of this tendency is the various efforts of kings to restrict the power of the aristocracy—especially the landed aristocracy—and, to a smaller degree, to control merchants and other urban economic interests. Other examples are found in the efforts of the Byzantine emperors of the seventh to the tenth century to establish a free peasantry at the expense of large landowners, the struggle of many of the Chinese emperors to support the literati and gentry as against the hereditary aristocracy, and the Ottoman experiment in establishing a ruling institution based on slavery.

The kings also tend to use bureaucratic administration and policies in order to "level out" some of the centers of power, and to organize them within the framework of bureaucratic policies. Of great importance from this point of view are the taxation policies undertaken by kings through their administrative organs, and the parallel attempts to limit the legal autonomy of tax-gathering units or groups. We can find in these societies many other efforts by the kings and the bureaucracy to regulate different aspects of the economic, social, and cultural life of the society. These attempts usually had the objectives of regulating the various centers of potential power in the society in such a way as to hinder any of them from attaining full monopoly of power and influence, and of assuring the continuous flow of the various "free" resources to the polity.

This tendency, inherent in the structure of a bureaucratic polity, determines one of the basic elements of political struggle within it: the contest between the king and the bureaucracy, on the one hand, and the landed aristocracy as well as the merchants and cultural and religious groups, on the other, concerning the scope of bureaucratic activity in the society and the relative immunity of various groups to such activity. The main objective of the aristocracy is to influence in a negative way the general goals of the bureaucracy: to limit its autonomy and distinctiveness and the resources available to it.

STRUGGLES WITHIN THE BUREAUCRACY

This type of struggle, however, is but one aspect of the political process. Side by side with the struggle over the general scope of bureaucratic and central political activity, there occurs a struggle over the relative influence of different groups on the king and on the bureaucratic administrative organs—on their chief policies, on the principles of allocation of facilities, rewards, influence, and the like. This conflict is carried on *within* the framework of the administrative and central political organs, to determine who will monopolize the major bureaucratic positions and formulate major policies in the fields of taxation, foreign relations, etc. In some countries, the centers of this struggle are the king's immediate entourage, his "inner court" or harem, cliques of eunuchs and the holders of the highest administrative positions. In many European countries the various representative bodies and councils, and in Byzantium the Senate and sometimes the popular circus-parties, have also been important participants in this struggle.

Significantly, in most of these cases there is a basic acceptance of the bureaucratic framework; instead of limiting it, the major objectives are to utilize and exploit it. Only in relatively exceptional cases, usually in periods of total disorganization of the bureaucratic polity, is there a complete identity between some of the general anti-bureaucratic tendencies in the first type of struggle and the various conflicts within the bureaucratic framework. Close relations, however, may often be found among the different groups engaged in these struggles. In Byzantium, for instance, there may have existed a close relationship, but not a complete identity, between the great landowners and the civil bureaucratic aristocracy (*Beamtenadel* in Ostrogorsky's nomenclature). Usually, in an internal struggle within the framework of the central political administration, many more social groups, such as merchants, military groups, and church elements, would participate—groups which were identified in one way or another with the basic premises of a centralized and bureaucratic polity, and whose main concern was not to limit its general effectiveness but to influence and utilize it. The constitutional struggles in various absolutist countries in Europe, and especially in England, are perhaps the best illustration of this tendency. It is obvious that these struggles took place not merely between the king and different groups within the society, but also among these different groups and strata, over their relative position and influence vis-à-vis the king and the bureaucracy. In most cases, the basic problem was the relative distribution of riches and privileges within the framework of the goals of the polity and its basic administrative institutions. In these societies we do not find many attempts by these groups to usurp the executive power of the king and the bureaucracy. Attempts to substitute the political control of the general polity for that of the king are found only in Europe in the seventeenth and eighteenth centuries, and constitute an entirely new type of political struggle, involving new principles of selection of the political elite and determination of political goals. Within most of the historical societies studied, the main struggle centers on the question of influence on the king.

Of special interest and importance within this context are the relations between the central political elite and bureaucracy, on the one hand, and the major religious and cultural elites and institutions, on the other. It is significant that in most of these societies these latter elites are also highly organized, very often on a bureaucratic pattern. The Byzantine Church, the "Muslim Institution" of the Ottoman Empire, the whole body of literati (holders of examination degrees) in China, and the church and the parliaments in France and Western Europe are all outstanding examples. One way or another, these groups are always drawn into the political struggle, for two main reasons. First, they are very important in the legitimation of the political system, and are prone to seek various restrictions of and control over the exercise of executive power. Second, they usually constitute important centers of power, in terms both of property and of potential political influence; consequently, they invite the intervention of the king and of the central administration. The exact relations between the latter and these religious and cultural elites—as well as other socially and politically active groups—differ greatly from one society to another. This relationship, as we shall see in detail later on, constitutes one of the important influences on the structure of bureaucracy.

THE BUREAUCRACY IN RELATION TO THE CENTRAL POLITICAL AUTHORITY

In addition to these types of political struggle, there are others in which the bureaucracy, or at least some of its main constituent groups, is more directly involved.

The first of these is closely related to the problem of legitimation analyzed above. In these societies there is a continuous contest between the king and the non-bureaucratic groups around him (such as the royal family, his personal advisors, sometimes various groups of nobles) on the one side, and the bureaucracy on the other, regarding their relative power over each other and over policy and decision making. Such a struggle may become especially acute when the king is wholly corrupt and capricious, interested only in his private pleasures, and bent on utilizing the state machinery for his own nonpolitical ends and for the benefit of members of his immediate entourage. Good examples of this can be found in various periods in China, in the later stages of the Ottoman Empire and, to a smaller degree, in Byzantium. An important aspect of these struggles is the king's attempt to "pack" the bureaucracy with his own protégés without regard to their qualifications or to the usual procedure of appointment, and to dismiss any displeasing officials arbitrarily—even if, or especially if, they are honest and scrupulous.

However, this kind of struggle occurs not only in extreme situations but also in normal and relatively stable times. The bureaucracy tends very often to emphasize its own basic political philosophy and experience as against those of the emperor or king, and tries to limit his innovations. The struggle between the legalists and the Confucianists at the beginning of the Han Dynasty is a very good example, as are the relations between the *noblesse de robe* and the parliaments in France, and the whole complex of relations between the sultan and the vizir, and the Ruling Institution, in the Ottoman Empire.

In most of these countries, the bureaucracy develops a "professional morale" and ideology that emphasize its own autonomy and direct ethical (and sometimes even legal) responsibility, as contrasted with the caprice of policy and the vicissitudes of politics. It is only in some of the relatively "underdeveloped" countries, in borderline cases of semi-feudal, semi-patrimonial societies—for example, Ancient Egypt—that such an ideology seems to be lacking. Its clearest exposition can be found in China, where the bureaucracy fostered many aspects of the Confucian code, emphasizing its own responsibility and ethical functions. Similar tendencies, couched to a greater degree in legal terms, can be found in Byzantium and in European countries.

While the concrete points of difference may vary from one society to another, in general it seems that the bureaucracy manifests more traditional and legalistic attitudes than the emperor, is much more bent on the maintenance of any given status quo (subject to limitations to be discussed later), and is much less prone to take the initiative in the executive field, although from time to time it may produce great reformers and innovators. But it is not easy to discern continuous patterns of difference in principle as between bureaucratic and executive powers. Elements of personal competition, of general attempts to maintain influence, and different basic orientations always have some place in these controversies between the more "political" and the more "legal-rational." The more "conservative" and "legal-rational" attitude of the bureaucracy can be clearly seen in its relationship to legal problems and reforms. The bureaucracy usually seems to have a greater respect for legal tradition than do the kings, as well as a greater propensity for systematization and codification and a lesser predisposition to employ *ad hoc* measures. It may be closely related to the legal profession, and even try to incorporate parts of it.

The arena in which this struggle is waged encompasses the various administrative organs and mechanisms that are designed to maintain the king's control over the bureaucracy and to carry out the major policy decisions. Some of the sources of conflict have been mentioned earlier in the discussion of legitimacy, but we shall deal with them somewhat more systematically now. First is the constant effort of the kings to maintain a body of personal officials and advisors who are independent of the bureaucratic machinery and cliques, in the face of the equally constant effort of the bureaucracy to penetrate these circles and to influence them. The wide use made of eunuchs in many of these monarchies, and the ambivalent position of these eunuchs in the political struggle, are one feature of this kind of conflict. Another is the attempt of the kings to develop a core of officials of the "inner court," directly under the throne's control. The fact that many of these officials tended, in time, to achieve relative independence and to lose touch with the king explains the very frequent changes of the officials' positions and the continuous creation of new positions and titles.

A second source of conflict is created when a chief official and a general council are at the head of the bureaucracy, acting as the king's major policy- and decision-making body. In many cases, the king tried to dispense with such a corporate body, or to play it off against the bureaucracy. It is significant that the greater extent of what may be called "conciliar" centralization is found in Byzantium in the periods of the relative predominance of the aristocracy, and that during them the Senate had a relatively greater importance. In China, on the other hand, a council and particularly a prime minister were usually most influential during the periods of the predominance of the bureaucracy.

Closely connected with this is the problem of the maintenance of discipline in the bureaucracy. Here we find a tendency on the part of the king either to concentrate most of these matters in his own hand or, alternatively, to delegate them to as many heads of department as possible, in contrast to the tendency of the bureaucracy to establish its own regulations and organs, through which it might be able to influence the king's policy and attitude. Of special interest from this point of view are the "controlling officers" established from time to time by the kings and sent out to supervise the local officials. The most noteworthy examples are the Chinese inspectors, the French intendants, and the Spanish "visitors." Most of these officers stood outside the administrative hierarchy; quite often the first appointments were special confidants of the kings. But with their passing, and with the gradual institutionalization of the offices, many efforts were made by the bureaucracy to assimilate them. There was generally a struggle of some sort over who was to control these controlling officers.

The Chinese censorate is perhaps the most important illustration of the tendency of bureaucracies to maintain their own regulations and supervisory systems. Others are found in the dealings of French parliaments with the regulation of the sale of offices and other disciplinary matters, and in some of the activities of the Byzantine legalists. Certain special posts within the bureaucracy have also been utilized to control the executive and ensure its compliance. The astronomer in China provides the best example, perhaps, but many others could be offered. In the European countries we find many attempts by the bureaucracy to gain control of some of the main representative institutions, especially the parliaments—attempts which were sometimes very successful at the height of absolutism, and which tended to influence the composition of the kings' councils.

The policy area dealing with titles is one of the most interesting fields in which this struggle occurred, especially in Byzantium, China and, to a lesser extent, in the Ottoman Empire. In most of these cases, a distinction was made between the official designation of a function and an honorific title which denoted the general status of the official in the hierarchy. While there was some correspondence between the two, they were never identical; and the distinction was often used by kings to control the bureaucracy and to hinder it from monopolizing both status positions and administrative positions. Sometimes the honorific titles were used to compensate for loss of power, or as a means to create new "nobles" more directly dependent on the king. On the bureaucratic side, there was a continuous effort to make the titles more or less hereditary and to develop a strong sense of group cohesion among the title-holders. Some of the developments in Europe in the age of absolutism are parallel to this. The most important among these is the creation of the *noblesse de robe* by the king as a counterweight to the *noblesse d'épee*, and the strong efforts of the former to become an autonomous and self-perpetuating status group, mainly through the development of various devices for the sale of offices.

Another interesting field in which this aspect of political struggle has been waged is the whole system of sales of offices, which was prevalent in most of the countries in question. This system was usually inaugurated by the kings in order to solve their financial problems and to let new, non-aristocratic elements into their service, thus diminishing their dependence on the aristocracy. But in time, in most of the societies, the bureaucracy came to look upon its offices as units of property, and to transmit them within families or sell them in the market. Thus, despite their own efforts, the kings tended to lose control over these offices.

THE BUREAUCRACY AND MAJOR POLITICAL AND SOCIAL GROUPS

This brings us to the last and perhaps most important aspect of political struggle in bureaucratic polities: the relationship between the bureaucracy and other social strata, especially those which are politically active and from which many of the upper bureaucracy are recruited. Does the bureaucracy tend to have a policy or orientation of its own, or does it only represent the interests of the major social strata? Are the different policies of a bureaucracy a reflection of the different social groups and cliques who vie with one another within its framework, or can more autonomous tendencies be discerned? Is the bureaucracy only a representative of the gentry and the literati in China, of the different landed and urban groups in Byzantium, of the rising bourgeoisie in Western Europe? In other words, does the bureaucracy constitute an autonomous force in the political struggle vis-à-vis other groups in the society?

In some extreme cases, the answer is clearly yes. These are mostly instances in which the bureaucracy is very closely identified with the king or central political authorities against all other groups in the society. The best examples are the Ottoman Empire in its first flourishing stages, some of the periods in the development of Muscovite bureaucracy between the reigns of Peter the Great and Catherine II, Prussia in the eighteenth century and, in modern times, some of the bureaucracies of the Balkan countries in the period between the two world wars. In all of these cases, the major social strata were politically and economically weak, while there was a very strong "punishment orientation" and alienation on the part of the bureaucracy and, usually in cooperation with the king, a very strong legalistic and "leveling" policy. In all of them we also find that the bureaucracy—at least in its upper echelons—tended to become a very cohesive status group, arrogating to itself many of the basic positions of prestige and power. But, to repeat, these are extreme cases, arising from rather specific conditions.

These tendencies in the bureaucracy usually accompanied its strong subjugation to the king and, even in these cases, the bureaucracy was rent by internal struggles. It can perhaps be postulated that at certain stages in its development, a bureaucracy is almost completely identified with the upper political elite. In the early development of a body of officials by a king who may still be fettered by patrimonial or feudal restraints, such "private" officials (as distinct from the more honorific aristocratic officials) usually tend to identify themselves totally with the king.

It can be claimed, of course, that these tendencies are inherent in any bureaucracy, even if they cannot be fully worked out in all circumstances. But can any of these tendencies actually be discerned in other, more stable, bureaucratic polities?

It is difficult to argue that at any given time the whole bureaucracy of a country has a unified and homogeneous policy and orientation, entirely distinct from those of different groups or classes. Writing of China's experience, Wang Yü-ch'üan has put this in a rather extreme way: "In spite of the basic interests of its members, the bureaucracy did not constitute a homogeneous body. It was made up of a number of factions, all struggling for supremacy, which were formed on the basis of personal ambition for power and position or on the basis of the interests of the social group which a particular faction represented. The bureaucracy was maintained by the equilibrium of the forces between the various factions or by the domination of one of them."* For example, in different stages of Chinese history the administration was more or less dominated, in terms of policy, by certain upper gentry and even merchant groups, the Byzantine administration by certain landowning or military interests, and the French by certain groups of the rising upper bourgeoisie.

*I am indebted to Professor W. Eberhard for this suggestion.

These groups did not have absolute control over personnel or decision making; rather, they had to deal with other groups and cliques contending for power. Most of these struggles were carried on within the basic framework, rules, and orientations of the bureaucracy. These groups may have quarreled over details of taxation or economic policy, but they tacitly recognized the necessity for some kind of policy, or the need to uphold certain basic legal frameworks that would not admit all the privileges demanded by certain groups, some of which would deny the legal rights of lower strata of the population. Thus a degree of universalism in orientations and regulations was upheld by most of the bureaucracy, even if it ran against the interests of the social strata closest to them. The bureaucracy tended to maintain these basic orientations to, and identifications with, legal and universalistic principles because its own position was largely dependent on its doing so, and because some of its basic duties, such as maintenance of peace, minimal provision of food, and river administration, could be discharged only within such a framework.

Sometimes there exists a tendency on the part of the bureaucracy to organize itself into a status group differing even from those strata with which it is most closely related or identified. Thus in France many of the *noblesse de robe* gradually dissociated themselves from the bourgeois families from which they originated. In Byzantium, as has been mentioned earlier, even in the period of decline from the eleventh century onward, there was not a complete identity between the urban civil nobility and the great landholders and military magnates. In Russia and Prussia, the emperors succeeded in disciplining the nobility into a bureaucracy which was more an instrument of the emperor's will than a reflection of the nobility's own interests. Even in China, where the relation between the gentry and the bureaucracy was the closest, complete identity did not exist. The bureaucracy tended to differentiate itself from both the gentry and the literati, and to maintain a framework and policy of its own. This is perhaps most evident at the first stages of the establishment of the examination system, but it persisted thereafter.

Moreover, in many of these bureaucratic systems, reformers arise from within the bureaucracy; this happens particularly where the system is dominated and, from the point of view of its own premises, corrupted by the monopoly of one group. The most interesting and best known examples of such reformers are Wang An-shih in Sung China, Sari Mehmed Pasha in the Ottoman Empire, and the great European ministers in the age of absolutism. True, they do not always succeed in their efforts at reform, and the bureaucratic apparatus may continue to be corrupted. This can easily bring about the end of the system—whether the dynastic changes in China, the gradual shrinking and disintegration of the Byzantine and Ottoman Empires, or the political revolutions in Europe. It is significant from the point of view of our analysis that many of these downfalls are related to the abandonment of a unified and equitable policy of taxation, which is the basic financial and political mainstay of a bureaucratic polity.

It is also important to note that in the periods following these disorganizations, one of the first steps is the reinstallation of a relatively autonomous bureaucratic organization and policy. This is especially well known and well documented for China, and it seems to be true also for several periods of Byzantine history.

A close analysis of various attempts at bureaucratic reform and of patterns of change in bureaucracies reveals another very important aspect of the relationship between bureaucracies and other social groups. The main functions of a bureaucracy in these societies seem to include mediation between the major political and economic interests and groups, and the maintenance of some of the rules of the game in political struggle. The fact that the political institutions in these societies have their own goal orientations, and that they must consolidate support from various groups and strata in the population, necessarily means that in turn they have to provide these groups with various facilities and rewards, such as prestige, influence, or power. The bureaucracies usually administer the technical aspects of these facilities, and in addition they allocate rewards according to certain general rules and expectations. The concrete details of such rules differ greatly from one society to another, and may be biased in favor of certain social groups, but maintenance of such rules is necessary to the maintenance of the bureaucratic polity. It is this fact that gives the bureaucracy its main power in relation to the king, who may not be as sensitive to the various problems of balancing out different interests; this is more likely to be the case in countries that are without any type of representative institution.

This need to maintain a set of rules, however, sets limits to the degree to which a given bureaucracy can be dominated by any one group without causing the whole system to disintegrate. This, of course, is closely connected with the whole range of problems of the legitimation of the polity in general and of the bureaucracy in particular. It also explains an important and nearly universal feature of bureaucratic systems: their development of relatively systematized and unified legal codes, and their strong tendency to uphold these codes and to inculcate the basic norms and orientations inherent in them. The codes and their norms may often be enforced against the special privileges and interests of various social groups, a process that involves a strong element of mediation.

The performance of mediating functions by the bureaucracy and its at least partial autonomy do not mean, of course, that it acts outside the basic framework of a given society or that it performs really important and integrative functions for it. Nor do they mean that in these societies the principles of polity and organization are not biased in favor of one or more groups. First of all, it is quite obvious that the interests of politically and socially passive groups, especially the peasantry, were minimally represented in most of the bureaucracies—Byzantium being the exception. Secondly, the bureaucracy itself, and the kings who directed it, did not usually stray very far beyond the basic principles of stratification that existed within a given society; they tried to adjust their policies to these principles, to modify the principles to some extent, or even to isolate some of their more difficult aspects, but they did not seek to abolish them entirely.

But all this does not negate the basic fact that the bureaucracy, sometimes with the king and sometimes in opposition to him, tries to maintain some basic mediating functions that are not entirely identical with the interests of any single group or stratum. Even in its relations with the lower groups and strata, the bureaucracy tends to maintain a measure of continuity; and, unless it is totally corrupted or punishment-oriented, it generally entertains a minimal defense of the interests of these strata. . . .

In this article we have attempted to analyze some of the basic social and political characteristics of bureaucratic polities. We have tried to show that in order to understand the structure and complexities of various bureaucratic polities, as well as the major differences among them, it is necessary to consider not only the formal aspects of bureaucratic organizations, but also, and perhaps mainly, the basic sociological characteristics of bureaucratic polities. It is these characteristics that provide the social and political framework within which various bureaucratic organizations develop. In this article several aspects of this wider framework—especially the main elements of political struggle within bureaucratic polities—have been singled out for discussion. We have tried to show the basic political and social issues that exist in such polities, and the relation of the major political elements— the king, the aristocracy, and other social groups and strata—as well as of the bureaucracy itself to such issues. We have also demonstrated how some characteristics of the bureaucracy—chiefly the extent of its autonomy—are related to these aspects of the political struggle. The analysis presented here has necessarily been preliminary; its main purpose has been to clear the way, as it were, for more systematic comparative analyses of bureaucratic polities and structures.

E. Strauss

Varieties of
Bureaucratic Conduct

THE BUREAUCRATIC MIND

The bureaucratic defects of large organizations may arise either from the effects of administrative duties on the behavior of the individual official or from the

From *The Ruling Servants, Bureaucracy in Russia, France—And England?* by E. Strauss, 1961, pp. 43-61. Reprinted by permission of George Allen & Unwin Ltd.

structure and processes of the administrative system. They are naturally most prominent in the government service; the public official, civil servant, *fonctionnaire* or *Beamter*, for this reason looms overwhelmingly large in the popular picture of the bureaucrat, but many of his characteristic traits can also be discovered amongst the professional administrators of other large bodies.

A useful summary of the everyday criticisms of the bureaucratic official was given towards the end of the second World War by a British parliamentary committee on the training of civil servants, and it undoubtedly forms an impressive catalog: "The faults most frequently enumerated are over-devotion to precedent; remoteness from the rest of the community, inaccessibility and faulty handling of the general public; lack of initiative and imagination; ineffective organization and waste of manpower; procrastination and unwillingness to take responsibility or to give decisions."

With the exception of ineffective organization and waste of manpower, which are defects of the administrative system, all the faults mentioned relate to the individual official and his behavior. They are not all due to the same circumstances, nor are they equally important in all types of organization or in all countries. "Remoteness from the rest of the community" is more characteristic of the public official than of the employee of a trade union or corporation, and perhaps more typical of the English civil servant and the German *Beamter* than of their American counterpart. Nevertheless it is comparatively easy to see the extent to which these faults reflect the position of administrative officials and are, therefore, to some extent inherent in their work, but the logical sequence is somewhat different from the order in which the public, and the parliamentary committee of inquiry, tends to look at them.

The typical administrative official is a professional who devotes most of his time and energy to his employment, and public administration in particular is normally a lifetime "career." The difference between success in a profession and in a career is the existence of a definite organizational framework for the latter. In the professions, success may at least to some extent be measured by technical achievement. Professional eminence may be associated with outward rank, but this is not invariably the case, and the two are by no means necessarily identical. It is, to say the least, possible to be a great lawyer without being a Lord Chancellor, or a great divine without being an Archbishop, and vice versa. Even in the armed forces, acknowledged greatness is not necessarily identical with highest rank—the greatest genius produced by the British navy died as a Vice Admiral. In an administrative career, on the other hand, success is identical with promotion: there is no "great" junior clerk. It is a career in the sense of an obstacle race, where success is measured entirely by the official position attained within the hierarchy, with promotion the key to higher rank, greater power and bigger income. The chances and effects of promotion are, therefore, of overriding importance for the individual official and influence his outlook to an extent which can hardly be exaggerated.

The individual official may only be a small cog, but he forms part of a very large wheel, and his modest share in the power wielded by the organization as a whole tends to color his attitude towards all outsiders who have no part in his great mystery. If he is in the service of the government, the consciousness of belonging to the paramount organization of the country naturally intensifies this attitude, but every large organization has its full-time staff, with its scale of ranks, its promotion system and its material rewards. This setting is the primary and decisive fact which conditions the daily life and outlook of the individual official. He is, therefore, inevitably somewhat removed from the rough-and-tumble of the outside world and primarily concerned with the official world to which he belongs, with its rules of procedure and conduct, its chances of promotion and its gossip, which is of absorbing interest to the initiate, however fatuous it may appear to the outsider.

Although inherent in the position of the administrative official, and therefore to some extent inevitable, this aloofness is a definite drawback to the proper functioning of the organization. There are many routine jobs within a large organization whose holders have little or no contact with the outside world, but the body as a whole is not a self-contained and self-regulating mechanism but an instrument for the furtherance of specific social interests, and therefore intimately concerned with the world at large and its problems. Its officials, therefore, have to maintain contact with the outside world, and the ability to respond quickly and correctly to changes in the social environment is vital for the success, or even for the survival, of the whole organization.

The administrative official thus belongs to two worlds, and has to perform the difficult task of balancing their requirements in his daily work. One of the symptoms of failure consists in "faulty handling of the general public." This defect is most acute at the base of the administrative pyramid, where routine officials are in daily contact with the public. In the higher ranks of the administration different problems arise, and the "remoteness from the rest of the community" with which many higher officials are charged is largely due to the insulating effect of a number of administrative layers between themselves and the outside world. Although the senior official usually has his own outside contacts and deals directly with important problems or personalities, the bulk of his duties normally consists of official matters reaching him at the second or third remove through the administrative chain.

"Overdevotion to precedent," combined with "lack of initiative and imagination . . . procrastination and unwillingness to take responsibility or to give decisions" are closely related bureaucratic defects, due in the last resort to the hierarchic structure of large-scale administration. The ordinary official is far below the policy-making level, where the primary purposes of the organization are transformed into a scheme of administrative action. For him, policy consists of definite, though not unalterable, instructions governing his behavior in typical circumstances and supplemented by rulings on special cases which he obtains in case of need from his superiors.

While he is dealing only with matters adequately covered by his instructions, the routine work will run smoothly, but social life is essentially a changeable and unruly element, and sooner or later the official will be confronted by an unexpected combination of circumstances, because the policy of the organization and the instructions given from the top are based on past experience and have not caught up with the march of time. When this happens, the subordinate official may have to choose between different courses: either to apply his rules to a case which they do not properly fit, or to deviate from his orders and make an independent decision, or to do nothing and ask for new instructions.

The attempt to force changing facts to fit the established policy of the organization, though always made by routine officials, cannot be indefinitely kept up, because sooner or later it is bound to end in failure. The disregarding of official rules by junior officials is for very good reasons discouraged in every large organization, for it is incompatible with orderly administration. More important from the point of view of the individual, it may have serious repercussions for the culprit, and "disobeying orders" is, therefore, one of the gravest steps a subordinate official can take.* Barring acute emergencies, a display of independence is neither expected from a junior official, nor would it be countenanced by authority.

The decision of administrative cases by precedent is, therefore, deeply rooted in the structure of the whole system, and where precedent is lacking, or where its application is resisted by powerful outside interests, the official will not feel entitled to give a decision on the spot and thereby accept a responsibility which the rules of the administration withhold from him. He will instead refer the matter to his superior, and if the case is unusually difficult it may slowly travel along the "return line of responsibility," until a decision is made at top level, whence it will return to the starting point in the form of an instruction, after an exasperating time lag.

RED TAPE

The peculiar habits or failings of the official mind have their counterpart in the cumbersome procedure of the administrative machine which goes by the name of Red Tape. In a racy American definition, this includes "delay, buck-passing, pigeon-holing, indecision and other phenomena which contribute to, and end in, inaction."

1. Procrastination or delay is the most obvious form of administrative inefficiency, and widely regarded as the archetype of bureaucratic incompetence. However simple the service required of an organization, if it has to be rendered on a sufficiently large scale, it cannot be performed at all without a regular procedure. What is criticized as "red tape" or "procrastination" may, therefore, simply be the legitimate time needed by the organization for doing its work. As in many instances the services undertaken by such organizations are far from simple, and may require

*A characteristically illogical recognition of the inherent dilemma was to be found in the Order of Maria Theresa in the Imperial Austrian army (c. 1757), which could be obtained by successful action by an officer in disregard of orders—with the court martial as penalty for failure.

reference to a number of different departments for their proper performance, delay need not be identical with culpable procrastination. But popular insistence on this point is too strong to be dismissed as a common prejudice, and there are good reasons for it.

By and large, the operations of every organization may be divided into "routine matters" and problems raising "policy issues." The working procedure laid down for the latter must be flexible, that for the former must be detailed, specific, and fairly rigid. Without a certain measure of rigidity it might, indeed, be impossible to cope with the flood of routine operations which form a large part of the day-to-day work of most large organizations, but a price has to be paid for this convenience in the form of a certain lack of consideration for individual circumstances. In addition, even if the working procedure governing the routine operations is intrinsically sound at the time it is laid down, it may be rendered wholly or partly obsolete by changing conditions. This applies particularly to large government departments whose rules must be determined in advance in considerable detail, thereby frequently being too rigid in practice, particularly in times of quick social changes.

Sometimes the only remedy is a change in the law; thus an Income Tax Code which may be perfectly adequate for dealing with a small number of well-to-do taxpayers may become hopelessly inadequate when applied to the mass of the wage-earning population. Similarly, an inflationary rise in income levels may compel the revenue authorities to tax large numbers of small wage earners for trivial sums at an excessive collection cost, but only an alteration of the law can provide relief.

On other occasions, the excessive rigidity of the administration may well be the cause of the trouble. Thus it has been argued that the "disease of making no errors at all costs" involved the American government during the last war in disproportionate expenses through the detailed checking of comparatively trivial traveling expenses of huge numbers of officials, with the result that "the total money disallowed is much less than the salaries of the auditors. Not only that, the amount of money disallowed is for the most part less than the cost of keeping it." This may not be an adequate standard for passing final judgment on the issue, but it is a good illustration of the different outlook of the official and the outsider.

Financially much more important was the state of the American government system for purchasing goods from the commercial world: "A maze of laws and regulations surrounds the whole process with unnecessary red tape. The emphasis of the laws is not on promoting efficiency and economy but on preventing fraud. Over-regulation encourages routine buying and prevents economy and the exercise of initiative. Purchasing is consumed in red tape. It is estimated that, on over half of the three million purchase orders issued by civilian administrations, the cost of paper work exceeded the cost of the items purchased." There is no reason to believe that these defects are confined to the United States, although it is unusual to see them pilloried with such admirable clarity.

Where administration is completely governed by public law, there is little room for administrative ingenuity, but this is rarely the case, and in general working routines may be rigid or elastic, out-of-date and hidebound, or alive and forward-looking over a fairly wide field. A typical cause of unjustified delay is the processing of simple routine matters through an excessively complex procedure, and this is particularly characteristic of money claims against large organizations, licence applications, etc.

Broadly speaking, an administrator confronted with a sharp rise in the volume of work in his department will demand more staff to carry out the prescribed routine operations on every case or document; the correct reaction might well be a new survey of the whole problem leading to changes in routine, with different methods for cases of different importance. However, the need to keep administrative procedure under constant review in the light of changing circumstances must be balanced against the need for administrative stability. The technical efficiency of the whole system, and of its individual servants, depends to a great extent on the smooth application of an established drill by trained staff. In this tug-of-war between the ideal and reality, the result is more often than not excessive adherence to tried and trusted methods.

Only when the disadvantages of a routine become patent and cause considerable public dissatisfaction, will it be supplanted by another system less out of step with the demands of the time—but destined to grow obsolete in turn with the next substantial change in conditions. Administrative reform, therefore, proceeds comparatively rarely by small and more or less automatic adjustments to gradual changes in conditions but by large and jerky steps intended to bring the whole machine into line with changed circumstances.

Delay in the settlement of "policy issues" is due in many instances to the limited authority of the individual official who must refer certain matters to his superiors; however much this may be criticized by justly impatient outside interests, it is inevitable that such issues should occur from time to time. The limitation of the junior official to the handling of a definite working routine may however narrow his field of vision so much that he fears and resents the need to use his own judgment even where this forms part of his duties. Delay may, therefore, arise because the official prefers to deal with the simple cases first and intentionally defers tackling more complicated jobs, thus combining procrastination with indecision. This is a well-known tendency, and an efficient administrative system will provide adequate safeguards against its harmful effects, if it wants to avoid the charge of bureaucracy.

2. Forms.   Another popular bugbear is the use of forms. As a device for simplifying and speeding up the work of an organization, forms are an essential part of a regular administrative routine, but their abuse may easily defeat their ends.

Standardized forms for accounting, reporting and record purposes are indispensable within the administrative system, but their use in the relations between an organization and the outside public may become contentious. Outsiders frequently resent them as little short of an affront, because they compel them to express their individual requirements, wishes, and complaints in the way in which the administrators want them presented for their own convenience, and not according to the individual's judgment of their relevance and order of priorities.

Wherever administrative operations of a simple type have to be carried out very frequently, e.g., in the issue of driving licences or passports, forms are undoubtedly necessary. In their absence, each letter from each individual applicant would have to be scrutinized in detail for the essential information, ignoring superfluous verbiage and frequently following up for missing data. In other words, information obtained in this way would have to be used for the construction of "forms." To employ ready-made forms for work of this kind is not simply a saving of time, but the necessary condition of the efficient handling of routine matters on the required scale; to this extent the sacrifice of the free expression of individual personality involved in their use is inevitable. "The abolition of forms would make most administrative processes excessively expensive and in some cases too cumbersome to be practicable."

There are, however, two types of abuse to which the employment of forms may lead in the relations between the government and the public. They undeniably express the growing ascendancy of officialdom and its success in adapting the facts of the outside world to the needs of the administrative process. This may ultimately induce the official designers of forms to elicit information from the public which has nothing to do with the ostensible purpose of the form. The more harmless type of this abuse would tend to exploit forms for intrinsically useful purposes like the collection of statistical information, while its more virulent type would transform them into a sort of trap for extracting particulars designed to increase official control over the individual by back-door methods.

Such practices are open to serious abuse and their social dangers far outweigh their administrative advantages. At least in democratic countries, they are less frequent than the incomprehensible form, which is a bureaucratic defect of a less dangerous kind. As a rule, forms are designed by officials for the convenience of officials who usually have a fairly clear idea of the purpose for which they need the information provided by the form, but who are much less familiar with the outlook of the private individual who has to complete it. Forms which make insufficient allowance for the lack of expertise on the part of the general public cause unnecessary queries and errors; if the point of view of the user is completely subordinated to administrative comfort, the result may be unintelligible forms, and mistakes in their completion will increase to such an extent that they will become a source of friction and delay instead of a means of eliminating waste and speeding-up routine.

3. Buck-passing.   The study of a recent American President is said to have been decorated with the categorical inscription: "The Buck Stops Here." As the President occupies the apex of the administrative pyramid of the American government, this statement was both lapidary and true.

Where failure to give final decisions is due to the inefficiency of the officials concerned, cases are bound to travel upwards from one administrative level to the next, until the top of the machine is reached. Such lack of moral courage is, however, much more frequent amongst juniors than amongst senior officials who are, indeed, more often accused of an inordinate lust for power, except in instances where decisions are "charged with political dynamite." The normal course of "buck-passing" is, therefore, not vertical but horizontal; its usual cause is not the refusal of the competent official to make a decision but lack of functional competence, although both factors may occur in combination.

As a rule, the irritating migration of cases and files from one official to another reflects not so much the hierarchical structure of the administration as its functional division into a number of separate departments. Usually the process is set in motion through the approach of an outsider without detailed knowledge of the organization with which he is dealing—typically a department of the national government. If he contacts its nearest local representative, he may be referred to a different department which, in the opinion of the local official, may be better able to deal with his problem; if he addresses himself to headquarters, his request may not be properly formulated or it may be misunderstood, and in either case it is likely to take some time and effort until the proper pigeon-hole is discovered. Being hazy about the technicalities of his case the claimant will express himself clumsily and it may only be after protracted correspondence that an official comes to the conclusion that the case is, after all, not within his competence. However infuriating for the victim, such difficulties may occasionally arise without malice or even without palpable inefficiency on the part of the administrator as an unfortunate by-product of the complicated process of large-scale administration.

The subdivision of authority between different departments and between different officials of the same department often leads to unwelcome complications even in the hands of experts. In the *cause célèbre* of British bureaucracy, the Crichel Down case, a critical stage in the confused proceedings was reached, when the objecting party obtained the assistance of the local member of parliament who personally intervened with the Parliamentary Secretary of the Ministry of Agriculture. The result was a request for an authoritative report for the personal attention of the ministerial chiefs of the government department concerned.

Although it might be expected that particular care would be taken in such a case, this did not prevent it from being passed on from one official to another: "So Mr. Nugent (Parliamentary Secretary, Ministry of Agriculture) wanted a report. He asked Mr. Payne (Assistant Secretary, Ministry of Agriculture), who asked Mr. Smith (Secretary of the Land Commission), who asked Mr. Hole (Provincial Land Commissioner at Bristol), who asked Mr. Lofthouse (District Land Commissioner at Taunton). At that point, it might be supposed, there would have been action. So indeed, there would have been but for the unfortunate fact that Mr. Lofthouse, when he received the request on July 17, was about to go on holiday. Mr. Lofthouse deputed the work to Mr. Brown, his assistant working at Taunton . . ."

The movement of the file in this case was comparatively simple, for it consisted of one vertical step followed by one horizontal and three vertical steps. It commenced near the very top of the pyramid and was backed by the authority and expertise of some of the highest civil servants in their own department. Nevertheless, the transfer of the file from hand to hand so strongly distorted the purpose and meaning of the original request that the final report was seriously inaccurate and misleading, although "no blame whatever" for its defects attached to the official who finally dealt with it, because he had received faulty instructions for carrying out his work.

The criticism of the results of "buck-passing" may, therefore, be justified even where the organization of the administrative machine leaves the official without any choice in the matter. In practice, officials sometimes indulge in this far from harmless pastime, because the lines of responsibility are not clearly drawn or because they want to economize their own efforts at the expense of some other department, and of the efficiency of the organization which they are supposed to serve. The dividing line between administrative necessity and bureaucratic defect may thus be perilously narrow.

4. Duplication.   Specialization of functions and the resulting multiplicity of departments is the cause of a host of other bureaucratic defects which reduce the working efficiency of an administrative system and lead to a good deal of friction with outside interests. A typical case in point is duplication of efforts by different departments.

Although servants of the same organization, the officials of different departments look at the same events from varying angles, and consequently find it difficult to agree with each other on the proper weight attributable to the facts with which they are dealing. In most large organizations, certain basic records enter into the work of a number of departments and must be accessible to various officials for their different purposes. Almost invariably, the same arrangement does not suit all of them equally well, and the difficulty is solved, wherever possible, by the duplication in a number of departments of near-identical records with slight variations, irrespective of the fact that the bulk of this information is already available elsewhere.

The Hoover Commission found that in 1947 "about ten thousand five hundred employees in some fifty different civilian agencies of the (US) Government were engaged in statistical work at a cost of about $43 million." As a result of this proliferation of small service units, there was hardly a crime against the principles of sound statistics which was not committed by the departmental statisticians. Apart from defective training, the Commission criticized "incomplete coordination, overlapping of functions, jurisdictional conflicts, lack of comparability, lack of standard concepts, definitions and classifications. There are conflicts between reports, faulty coverage in various areas and gaps in the statistics assembled." This is one of the most commonplace examples of duplication of effort. A rarer illustration from a very different field is provided by the statement that "more than half of the departments and administrations of the Federal Government conduct medical or health activities. These administrations compete for doctors and other technical personnel, and for funds. There is no central supervision of their activities; and they operate under diverse policies with respect to quality of treatment, types of beneficiaries served, types of research, and areas of authority."

Duplication becomes a scandal and a public nuisance, when it leaves the privacy of official buildings and occurs in the relations between the administration and its public. It is bad enough for different departments of the same organization to approach the public with identical demands, requests or even advice, but the mischief rarely ends there: as no two experts ever agree on the same question, their disagreement becomes even more blatant, when the experts come from different departments with different tasks. To the layman a problem may appear single and indivisible, but to the specialist it reveals subtle differences which prevent him from working with the existing information of another department and compel him to issue yet another questionnaire, return or set of instructions.

Examples of this tendency abound in the public administration of most modern countries. In Great Britain, a wartime parliamentary committee established that as many as nine different official investigations in one and the same household could occur, resulting "from the numerous forms in which inquiries are made before social assistance, dependent on a means test, or relief from taxation is granted." In the United States, "forty-seven employees attached to seven districts and separate field services of the Department of Agriculture in one cotton-producing county in Georgia were working with fifteen hundred farmers; a fruit and grazing county in the state of Washington has 184 employees of separate field services working with some six thousand seven hundred farmers. . . . Farmers are confused and irritated, as climaxed in one Missouri county, where a farmer recently received from five different administrations varying advice on the application of fertilizer to his farm."

This failure of a service intended exclusively for the benefit of a section of the community is less serious than corresponding failures of the machinery of the State in its regulative functions. Thus in wartime Britain, the official arrangements for the supply and welfare of workers involved "the inspection of each firm by officers of at least two departments, and where, as is often the case, the firm is working for three departments, it may be visited for the same purpose by four inspectors. . . . The Labor Division of the Ministry of Supply and the Directorate of Labor of the Ministry of Aircraft Production duplicate to a considerable extent the work on labor supply and welfare of the Ministry of Labor. There is in consequence both waste of effort and failure to cover properly the *whole* field."

DEPARTMENTALISM

Departmentalism is the most serious bureaucratic defect and invariably indicates a serious deterioration in the efficiency of the administrative system as a whole. The symptom of this disease is a decay of the consciousness of an overriding common purpose between different departments and a corresponding decline in the authority of the central leadership. Its result is the replacement of cooperation between different departments in the service of common aims by chronic friction which may flare up into acute interdepartmental warfare.

A common and comparatively harmless form of this disease follows the sudden expansion of existing organizations. Where new purposes have to be carried out with insufficient preparation, the administrative center of gravity moves away from its traditional place, and new men may dispute the authority of the established leaders. The sudden growth of the administrative machine may affect its balance and overtax the technical abilities of the administrators, and a few important departments may attempt to supplant the aims of the whole organization by their own interests.

In great emergencies the dividing line between legitimate ruthlessness and departmental megalomania is difficult to lay down and still more difficult to observe; admirers of the methods used by Lord Beaverbrook as British Minister of Aircraft Production during the second World War will probably never be able to agree with his critics on this point. However, healthy organizations may survive even gross excesses without permanent damage, provided the emergency does not last so long as to destroy the existing balance between the primary purpose of the organization and its institutions.

In *politics*, the classical modern illustration of rampant departmentalism in a comparatively healthy environment is, curiously enough, the United States government of the New Deal and the second World War with its aftermath. The number of new federal organs, departments and agencies, among them the notorious "alphabetical" agencies, created between 1933 and 1943 reached the fantastic total of 195, including not only the special New Deal departments but also the massive block of wartime emergency organizations. Thus it is not surprising and hardly even shocking that the great inquest carried out by the Hoover Commission on the structure of American government after fifteen years of almost uninterrupted expansion brought in a general verdict of departmental anarchy: "Instead of being unified organizations, many departments and agencies are but loose federations of bureaus and subdivisions, each jealously defending its own jurisdiction."

In this "chaos of bureaus and subdivisions," the National Security Organization held, perhaps, pride of place, because its growth had been particularly precipitate, and the Commission found "continuous disharmony and lack of unified planning, extravagance in military budgets and waste in military expenditure." The Veterans' Administration was taken to task for the excessive number of its staff officers and the complexity of its structure, with its 88 different manuals, 665 varieties of technical bulletins and over 400 circulars of various kinds, adding up to a wealth of "instructions on internal methods and procedures which defy intelligent execution."

The coexistence of the manifold departments of the American government, whether old or new, was and is by no means always peaceful. The outstanding example of interdepartmental rivalry in the civilian field is an administrative heirloom going back well before the origin of the New Deal. It concerns the soil conservation services of the Departments of the Interior and of Agriculture, and particularly the Forestry Service. Their vendetta warfare went well beyond official levels, and at times the Forestry Service was lobbying against a bill put before Congress by the Department of the Interior, while the latter submitted programs to Congress without even informing the Secretary of Agriculture. More recently, such breaches of decorum have been completely eclipsed by the notorious wrangling between different branches of the armed forces which show a remarkable latitude in their interpretation of military discipline and the constitutional proprieties.

Not even the severest critics of the American system of government would describe it as a full-fledged bureaucracy, however alarming some of these recent manifestations. The growth of departmentalism, though spectacular like all things American, has so far not gone unchecked, but if it is allowed to proceed without the self-assertion of the top leadership which is the guardian of the conscience of the organization as a whole, such processes may reach the point of no return.

Soviet Russia provides unsurpassed illustrations of these tendencies, particularly in the *economic* field. The economic bureaucracies of capitalist countries function in the discreet seclusion of private enterprise, but in the Soviet Union glimpses at the way in which things are done, or remain undone, may be obtained as a by-product of official "self-criticism" on the occasion of changes in policy. Thus it was at least one of the purposes of the great Massacre of the Ministries carried out in the summer of 1957 under Khrushchev's leadership to break the stranglehold of central departments on the operation of industry.

In his speech in May 1957, Khrushchev complained: "It is very difficult indeed to carry through specialization and cooperation in production where there are so many ministries and departments, because the departmental interests of the numerous ministries and central boards raise obstacles in the way." The meaning of this general statement was made clear with the help of everyday illustrations, of which there was obviously no shortage: "Often enterprises that are closely linked with one another and situated side by side operate as independent units, because they are managed by different central boards of one and the same ministry. . . . The directors of those enterprises copy the methods of the central boards in seeking to shut themselves off from each other as best they can. Comrade Maximov, who heads the Zhdanov coke and by-products plant, being intent on upholding his "sovereignty," had a slag stone wall 915 meters (3000 feet) long and 2½ meters (over 8 feet) high built to shut off the Azovstal works, spending about 200,000 roubles on this useless idea."

The next example is less naïve and much more serious, because it emphasizes the threat of departmentalism to administrative efficiency. It concerns a cement works and an asbestos and slate plant occupying the same premises and processing the cement produced by the former: "The two enterprises are virtually one. But see how the bureaucratic practices prevailing in some departments deform industry. The Ministry of the Building Materials Industry has artificially divided that single production unit into two independent ones under two different central boards—the Glavzapadsement and the Glavasboshifer respectively. The result is two directors, two chief engineers, two independent accounts departments and other departments that are duplicating each other's work . . . and in Moscow there are two central departments in charge of the twin enterprises, and hence if there are any differences between the two departments, the matter can only be settled by the top level executives of the ministry."

With an acute sense for the intrinsic logic of this process, Khrushchev finally quotes the following result of the division of responsibility for the Moscow electrical works between three ministries: "What used to be factory shops have been turned into three different plants with three independent managements and the corresponding staffs."

Large departmentalized organizations tend to reproduce bureaucratic defects on a much bigger scale; whole departments behave like individual officials, and departmental inertia, refusal to make decisions and other forms of procrastination are added to, and intensify, parallel tendencies amongst individuals. The acknowledged impotence of the private person faced by the lack of sympathy of a bureaucratic machine may then be matched by the helplessness of one department in obtaining the necessary cooperation of other departments.

This state of affairs is, perhaps, more characteristic of old-established administrations whose efficiency has been allowed to run down than of new mushroom organizations like the "alphabetical" agencies of the New Deal in America. There is more than a suspicion that something of this kind occurred in the British government service during the 1930's. This was at least the experience of a somewhat unorthodox British diplomat of the period, Sir Walford Selby, who attributed a good deal of the responsibility for the unsatisfactory diplomatic policy of the British Government "to the seeming inability of the Foreign Office to obtain decisions of any kind from other departments of Government." This agrees well enough with the impressions of an experienced politician like Dr. Dalton who reflected on the vagaries of the "Whitehall obstacle race—of trying to push or pull some piece of policy over, or through a long series of obstacles. This included in this case [an amendment to the Statute of Arbitration of the International Court of Justice] first, some of our own officials in the Foreign Office; second, some other Departments, particularly the Service Departments; third, some members of the Cabinet; fourth, some of the Dominion Governments."

Unchecked departmentalism does not exhaust itself in protestations of one's own good intentions and protests against unsympathetic and, therefore, ignorant critics. Every department easily convinces itself that it cannot carry out its functions (which are invariably interpreted in the most liberal manner and may include a growing amount of duplication) without bigger and better staff, and is thus firmly set on the way towards carving out its own empire. In this virulent stage of the disease of departmentalism, self-aggrandizement becomes the main principle of every department, either on its own or in temporary coalition with others. At this point the original purposes of the organization are in imminent danger of losing their creative and guiding function, although they may still be evoked as formulae. It will depend on the vitality of the primary organization whether such dangerous tendencies can be curbed by a reform regime, or whether the whole administrative system degenerates into a jungle of jarring and warring departmental factions.

This is the watershed between bureaucratic defects, which arise in the common soil of technical difficulties, and the great social evil of bureaucratic degeneration.

O. P. Dwivedi

The Case for
Bureaucratic Corruption

No visitor to a developing country can escape hearing about bureaucratic corruption. Such accusations are voiced most widely by the modernizing elite—in particular the educational elite—who tend to be cynical about the existing state of affairs and who charge that the process of modernization is stagnant because of administrative inefficiency and corruption. But we may pause to ask whether bureaucratic corruption is really obstructing economic and political development in developing countries? Or does it act as a catalyst in harnessing the process of modernization? If so, does it have some constructive character? In this article we shall examine these questions with particular reference to the Indian situation.

Corruption carries different meanings. Many writers have avoided defining it mainly because the meaning of unethical behavior—and corruption comes under it—differs from one culture to another. An unethical act in one culture may be socially acceptable in another. We shall examine this problem later, but the word corruption in this article will include nepotism, favoritism, bribery, graft, patronage, and other unfair means adopted by government employees and the public alike to extract some socially and legally prohibited favors.

Some writers have found that "corruption is the end-product of a process of administration and is preceded by maladministration. For eradicating the former the latter should be checked." Others think that the cause of widespread corruption are the conditions of extreme inequality as well as considerable absolute poverty. A person who resorts to bribery to gain government employment expects enormous benefits compared to penalties because of his low standard of living. Or, "the pay scales involved may be so low that some form of supplementary graft or corruption is necessary if a civil servant is to achieve even a modest living

From "Bureaucratic Corruption in Developing Countries," by O. P. Dwivedi, *Asian Survey*, 7, No. 4, April 1967, 245-253. Reprinted by permission.

standard." Embezzlement of government funds may be encouraged by the fact that the punishment is modest relative to the financial gain. It would appear that corruption is inseparable from great inequality of wealth. In developing countries, corruption seems to increase with inequality of distribution; where great riches and acute poverty exist side by side, the corruption rate is high. But is economic disparity the only cause?

BUREAUCRATIC CORRUPTION: A COLONIAL LEGACY?

Some observers have argued that bureaucratic corruption in developing countries is merely a logical evolution of the acceptance of Western behavioral patterns. Colonial people discovered that Western norms were not applied universally by their rulers. To their bewilderment, these people found that two sets of norms were used by their colonial masters: one for Europeans and another for natives. Corruption was abhorred if Europeans were involved but was accepted as the natives' way of life. The British Indian Civil Service officers, for instance, had separate clubs and a general tendency to exclusiveness from the people whom they were ruling. Exclusiveness was essential in order to maintain impartiality and the ability to disengage. But Victorian norms to these officers were of a high order in relation to "Arabs, Indians, and—in Kipling's words—the 'lesser breeds without the law' [who] revealed very different and, superficially again, much less honorable standards of conduct." To most colonial administrators, nepotism, bribery, the institution of polygamy, and the publicly condoned acts of cruelty, all suggested inferiority of race and norms. And it was perhaps because of this that they became apathetic and cynical toward corrupt practices prevalent in colonial society, and did little to control such unethical behavior among natives although at the same time they were not permitted among themselves. The result was that some forms of corruption became institutionalized, and were carried over even after independence.

It also became apparent to colonial people that merit and achievement criteria were disregarded by their masters when the question of religious affiliation was considered. Neo-converts into Christianity were given preferences over qualified non-Christians in civil service appointments and promotions. In Africa, according to James S. Coleman, "indiscriminate recruitment into the Christian fold (entrance into which meant opportunity for Western education and eventually high status in the emergent territorial society) brought about a status reversal in many societies. Africans drawn from the lowest stratum of traditional society have been elevated, through the activities of missionaries, to the highest strata of the social structure of the larger territorial societies." Favoritism, on the basis of religion, was thus accepted by some colonial people as normal social behavior. In India, Anglo-Indians were recruited in several government departments largely on an ascriptive basis. Today, when the widespread ascriptive considerations in the appointment of government employees in India are criticized, some Indians refer back to the British Indian recruitment system to rationalize the present situation.

ASCRIPTION AND CORRUPTION

The reasons for corruption in developing countries, however, go much deeper than the factors suggested above. In these countries primary associations are still dominant; family, kinship, caste, neighborhood, village, ethnic origin, and religious affiliations are the associational forms that have the first and the greatest call on individual loyalties. There are modernizing elites in each developing country but they too are swayed by such ties. Most civil servants, though possibly recruited on the basis of merit and competition, maintain their traditional ties. As Fred W. Riggs points out, "given a choice between loyalty and competence, a sala official (a civil servant in a prismatic society) will choose traditional loyalty." An administrative system influenced by such traditional loyalties will tend toward an ascriptive rather than achievement-oriented pattern of recruitment. And that is why a person who asks favors from officers belonging to his caste does not consider his act unethical. Similarly, when a government official "fixes" applications and licenses in utter disregard to merit but in accordance with family and caste loyalties "he is obeying a law of social conduct more ancient than that of the upstart state." Moreover, in any traditional society the family forms the common interest group *par excellence*. The extended family system is based on a comprehensive system of mutual obligations. A member may call upon his uncles or cousins for assistance when he is unemployed. When he attains any place of importance, be it a civil service employment or a public office, his relatives have first claim on his support. Nepotism, therefore, assumes a form of strict family obligation.

Some civil servants whose families may have spent considerable sums on their education are obligated under the traditional pattern of social life to support the family once he is employed. Since family in this usage includes uncles, cousins, nephews, grandparents, and other near and distant relatives, a great deal of pressure to "fix" jobs for them or to find some other source of income to support them is not uncommon. To resist bribery and not to resort to nepotism may very well constitute avoidance of the responsibilities of customary citizenship. Moreover, these relatives are themselves aware of the problem posed by the eventual retirement of their "man" in government service; and so they would like to take advantage of his position in securing jobs, procuring permits, etc., while he is still influential. They do not consider the exploitation of a relative's official status as something bad or unethical. Such ascriptive considerations help the perpetuation of bureaucratic corruption.

ASCRIPTIVE CORRUPTION AND IDENTITY CRISIS

W. H. Morris-Jones points out that in a traditional society a bureaucrat faces two sets of values. Trained in Western norms, he publicly adheres to the norms of objective and achievement-oriented standards of recruitment and selection. But privately, he subscribes to more subjective and ascription-oriented standards—a rigid hierarchy of caste and particularistic norms. Thus it should not surprise a Westerner visiting a developing country to find civil servants publicly condemning "bribery and corruption, but secretly encouraging them. He can be found, at one moment, insisting on a strict and literal enforcement of regulations, but the next moment supporting the open violation." Is the existence of such a double-standard due to the identity crisis faced by civil servants?

An administrator in a developing country may be inclined to regard that position in both Western and traditional terms. Even if he himself does not profess a belief in traditional values, he will be, nonetheless, subjected to constant pressures framed in these terms; and it will be very difficult not to give in. The same person found attacking publicly the prevalence of corruption in administration will resort to unethical activities privately because he is torn between two different sets of ethics. This dilemma—living in two different worlds of norms—creates an identity crisis for a civil servant. This identity crisis will continue until the extended family system and caste and tribal loyalties have been abolished, for "much of the alleged corruption . . . is nothing but the prevalence of these nonrational norms on the basis of which these administrations operate."

PUBLIC ATTITUDE TOWARD BUREAUCRATIC CORRUPTION

Joseph LaPalombara found in Italy that the public attitude toward bureaucrats is a combination of disdain, hostility, frustration, and helpless resignation. To a great extent the Indian public holds a similar view toward their government officials. Most of the public, and especially villagers, do not expect fair treatment from civil servants. A widespread notion prevails that the administration is corrupt, and that an efficient and responsive hearing is rendered in direct relationship to the number of currency notes given. In 1964, the Indian Institute of Public Opinion asked a sample of 1999 respondents the following question:

> If you had some problems that you had to talk about with a Government official, such as a question about taxes, agricultural regulations, shortage of water, and so on, how do you think you would be treated?

The first of the two tables prepared for the analysis of answers received illustrates the different expectations the public may have from government officials in an attempt to gain hearing.

Several interesting results are shown in this table. One is the difference in the rural-urban response on the "politely with interest" category—eight percent of the respondents in small villages and triple that number in cities. On the other hand, the same percentage of rural and urban respondents (ten percent) expected an interested hearing from officials who were offered bribes. It would also seem probable that the "it depends" respondents were thinking in terms of influencing officials through pressure exerted by caste, tribe, religious or regionals groups, including political leaders. Nearly one third of the respondents who gave answers (i.e., excluding the 26 percent of the total who did not answer) thus indicated a belief that bribery and its related ascriptive forms could be used to influence officials.

Table 1
Expectations About Treatment From Civil Servants
(Respondents distributed by locality)

Expectations	Small Village N = 638	Large Village N = 713	City N = 648	Total N = 1999
Politely with interest	8%	27%	24%	20%
Politely with no interest	12%	9%	16%	13%
No interest	8%	9%	8%	8%
Rudely—hostile	11%	7%	9%	9%
It depends	9%	15%	15%	13%
Yes—if given money	10%	15%	10%	11%
Don't know/no answer	42%	19%	19%	26%
Total	100%	100%	100%	100%

Table 2
Expectations About Treatment From Civil Servants
(Respondents distributed by level of education)

Expectations	No formal education N = 465	Some primary N = 540	Some secondary N = 668	College university, technical N = 321	Total N = 1994
Politely with interest	11%	15%	27%	25%	20%
Politely with no interest	4%	15%	14%	16%	12%
No interest	8%	10%	9%	7%	8%
Rude—hostile	10%	10%	7%	9%	9%
It depends	3%	10%	16%	26%	13%
Yes—if given money	6%	11%	16%	11%	12%
Don't know/no answer	58%	29%	11%	6%	26%
Total	100%	100%	100%	100%	100%

The type of expectations was also dependent upon the education level of the respondent. As demonstrated in Table 2, one striking aspect is that nearly 60 percent of the uneducated respondents were uncertain whether they could get any response at all from civil servants even through bribery. This percentage declines with the rise in formal education; only six percent of the respondents with college or university education expressed doubts on this question. Also, attitudes toward the efficacy of bribery vary from one educational level to another, as the uneducated still believe that bribery does not pay a great premium whereas more educated people think civil servants are susceptible. Could it be that this cynical attitude on the part of educated people in India means that bribery is a process through which politically less-sophisticated citizens may ease the impersonality of a great inherited bureaucratic system?

ROLE OF BUREAUCRATIC CORRUPTION

It has been suggested that a certain "level of corruption, *if* practiced and detected during the formative stage of the political system, can have beneficial effects, by discouraging excessive deference to civil servants and by encouraging the public to be forever watchful of its servants in offices high and low." But another authority argues that "there is no historical evidence to support the belief that bureaucratic corruption is merely a stage in a nation's political development and that it will disappear with political modernization or maturity." He brushes aside all arguments which suggest that bureaucratic corruption may help to some extent the process of modernization, and instead proposes ten measures to cure this "social disease." Instead of prescribing remedies I would suggest that the following be given consideration.

Bureaucratic corruption contributes to the survival of voluntary associations and interest groups: In India, a series of restrictive laws have been passed by the Parliament and provincial legislatures which attempt to regulate individual monopolies and limit their profits, make public the financial structure of the press, and regulate the activities of syndical organizations. These laws have been carried too far because of the discretionary and controlling powers provided to the administrative machinery. It has been noticed that bureaucrats have a built-in suspicion against the business community and these laws and regulations have been enforced more literally than perhaps desired by the legislature. Instead of promoting the growth of voluntary associations and interest groups, these laws have been used to restrict the very freedom of association that is essential for the democratization of the political process in India. As lobbying is generally ineffective, businessmen have difficulty influencing the legislative process; rather, they have to establish highly particularistic relationships with individual civil servants who are appealed to on the basis of kinship, personal friendship, or financial rewards. These bribes have "generally been recognized as the oil that makes the administrative machinery operate quickly." Many Indian businessmen do not consider such payments immoral unless some are denied the "right" to bribe when others are obtaining similar services.

Centralized administration checks individual initiative within the bureaucracy which can be fused only by some outside incentive: Bureaucracy in developing countries operates mostly on extreme centralization of the decision-making process and on the basis of rigid rules and regulations. Permanent heads of operating departments and other administrative units or agencies would rather delay a decision than face the displeasure of their political bosses who are ever doubtful of the administrative jungle. Administrative decisions occasionally are kept pending awaiting the counter-signatures of senior officers. Civil servants at the lower level of hierarchy are deferred from taking initiative lest their actions become subject to departmental inquiry, which is a time-consuming process. Some civil servants prefer to avoid such trouble and adhere closely to rules and regulations, unless offered a financial inducement.

The system of recruitment in government service should be changed to merit-cum-ascriptive criteria: As pointed out earlier, ascriptive appeals are often made to influence administrative decisions, but the same criteria is not applied in civil service recruitment and selection. In India there are many ethnic groups which are far less advanced educationally than other castes and groups. If they are to be integrated into the administrative process, strict adherence to the merit system would have to be modified for some time to come. Otherwise the acculturation of these groups into the political process may be delayed.

> This is not to argue that India should give up her merit system for recruitment into the administrative services or colleges and universities but only to suggest that patronage—and even corruption when widely applied and involving many individuals from many communities—may facilitate an adjustment to democratic institutions.

Of course, there will be difficulties in applying such an approach in a developing country, but Pakistan would seem to have solved this problem to some extent by using an ascriptive-cum-achievement system of civil service recruitment under which 80 percent of the vacancies in the administration are divided equally among East and West Pakistan and the remaining 20 percent are filled on merit basis. This problem of regional or communal representation in the public services exists in almost all developing countries—the case of Nigeria is one of several examples. Unless the present recruitment and selection system is overhauled, the fears entertained by backward and minority groups and regions will continue. Changes in the existing system can be effected in such a way that each community and region is guaranteed adequate representation in the administration by means of a recruitment program that is based equally on merit and ascriptive considerations.

Ascriptive corruption should be replaced by universalistic bribery: In a traditional society a move from a particularistic to a universalistic oriented social and political system has been regarded as an integral part of the process of modernization. But where administrative decisions can be and are influenced by ascriptive appeals, persons belonging to other castes, tribes, regional and religious groups will become increasingly frustrated. To avoid this, they should be provided with equal opportunity to influence administrative decisions. As long as businessmen and villagers can obtain what they want from local administrators through the payment of money, there is less likelihood of the revolution of rising frustrations than if those who can and wish to offer money discover that ascriptive considerations are more decisive.

Bureaucratic corruption cannot be studied separately from political corruption. Any prescription for its cure should take into account the social, economic, political, and cultural environments. I would like to conclude by summarizing the main point in this article. Charges of corruption generally originate from the modernizing elites—the group to whom the responsibility for political, economic, and social development has been entrusted. Trained mostly in Western norms but brought up in a traditional environment, these people abhor the increase in corruption. In the recent Fourth General Election in India, charges of corruption and administrative inefficiency levelled from all sides have punctured the hitherto omnipotent Congress Party. But it is not realistic to assume that the situation will improve by bringing another political party into office. Rather, there is a need for a compromise between necessity and morality. The modernizing elites should be induced to accept an altered perception of the nature of bureaucratic corruption. The transitional stage of these developing countries would seem to require that, as Herbert Spiro has argued: ". . . instead of the impersonal, machine-like honesty and efficiency of the ideal type of Western civil servant, they may prefer public officials who are more 'human,' approachable, amenable to influence, and leisurely than European civil servants under the conditions of highly industrialized, densely populated, and intensively bureaucratized societies."

4
Control of Bureaucracy

An ideal bureaucracy ought to do its job efficiently and reliably. But no bureaucracy is ideal. Left to its own devices, a large bureaucratic organization is as likely to work against the goals of the society as for them, as we have seen in the section on Bureaucratic Behavior. Therefore, it is essential that some form of control over bureaucracy be exercised.

Control of bureaucracy is usually imposed from above—from the ruling elite, from the Party, from duly constituted political authority. (The only significant exception is the system of ombudsmen, a recourse for the ordinary citizen, which operates with fair success in several modern European countries.) Establishing the appropriate degree of control from above is a delicate process. If control is too lax, it does not achieve its purpose. If it is too harsh, it will be counter-productive, because it will encourage the inherent tendencies of the average bureaucrat to follow the letter of the law blindly, and thus will stifle imaginative administration. Very few bureaucracies have achieved an optimum balance.

The first stage of control, naturally, is control over the entrance of bureaucrats into the system, discussed in Section Two. But bureaucracies as whole systems are more than the sum of the individual bureaucrats, so they also must be controlled as institutions. A wide range of problems may arise. For example, one particular part of a bureaucracy may be operating unsatisfactorily. If that department cannot be abolished outright, it may be possible to circumvent it by establishing another department to do the job more reliably or to provide a multiplicity of operational standards and channels of communication to balance flexibility of operation and centralized control. If, on the other hand, it is felt that the entire bureaucracy does not respond precisely enough to the wishes of the ruling group, elaborate cross-checking procedures and heavy penalties can be instituted to change the character of bureaucratic behavior. Or, if the rulers think that even stricter, day-by-day control of operations and ideology is necessary, they may establish special control organizations to permeate the regular bureaucracy, watching its every move. Milder long-term reform of bureaucracy, which not only controls but changes the role of bureaucracy to make it more controllable, is also a possibility. The selections in this section illustrate the operation of such methods of control in Imperial Spain, Prussia, the Soviet Union, and the United States.

J. L. Phelan, in the selection from his article "Authority and Flexibility in the Spanish Imperial Bureaucracy," provides an example of how a central administration can secure the performance of its "real" desires by allowing flexibility of action among bureaucratic personnel. Instead of enforcing strict controls over the administrators responsible for the colonies, central policy makers encouraged seemingly undirected action. Because of the size of the empire and the difficulties of communication, the Spanish king and his council made it possible for the colonial officials to take local conditions into account in carrying out central administration policies. To facilitate this, although there were strong orders issued constantly, the orders were conflicting and channeled through conflicting hierarchies. The goal was performance, not merely compliance. The result was a system that survived far longer than a rigidly controlled bureaucracy with consistent instructions could possibly have done in that age of inadequate communication and less-than-expert personnel.

Control through elaborate checks and a policy of strict subordination of the bureaucracy were the hallmarks of the Prussian civil service system, as Hans Rosenberg explains in *Bureaucracy, Aristocracy and Autocracy*. The overall objective, in pursuit of which checks and penalties were complementary means, was control of bureaucrats by making their internal motivations consistent with the purposes of the state. The Prussian kings called this policy the moral purification of the administration. Checks on bureaucratic freedom were everywhere. Frederick William I and Frederick II (the Great) insisted on the committee system to guard against private initiative; they laid down standards in a plethora of detailed regulations; and they happily encouraged mutual spying and informing within the ranks of their bureaucracy. Their policy of strict subordination was modeled on military discipline. This was a jarring fact of life for every bureaucrat, because punishment for misdeeds extended even to death. Although the Prussian rulers ". . . sought to promote a peculiar attitude of career service, pervading the whole of one's activities and resulting in hard and faithful work and superior performance," they actually succeeded in producing what Rosenberg calls a class of nodding automatons. It was not accidental that Prussian methods of bureaucratic control, in conjunction with Prussian militarism, had a profound effect on the state as a whole.

Soviet attempts to control their bureaucracy resemble Prussian methods in many ways—mutual suspicion, heavy penalties, and high pressure are characteristics of both regimes. The Soviet leadership has added to this arsenal a comprehensive system of control organizations that permeates all levels of the bureaucracy. As Merle Fainsod shows in the selection from *How Russia Is Ruled*, the Russian rulership ". . . depends heavily on the separately organized Party and police hierarchies to control administration, and it supplements this type of surveillance and pressure by planning, financial, personnel, legal, and investigatory controls which are built into the system." The controls are supposed to guarantee that the wishes of the leadership will somehow trickle down through the bureaucratic pyramid to the bottom, where the work is really done. The omnipresence of controls means that pressure can be pinpointed, and turned on and off, with a degree of accuracy that leaves the ordinary bureaucrat helpless. Those who learn to operate within the Soviet system behave, and misbehave, in ways far more subtle than the unimaginative Prussian bureaucrats. Ironically, the same clever psychological techniques used to control the Soviet bureaucracy are used by the Russian bureaucrats every day on their superiors.

Reform of the American civil service has been characterized by a long-term effort at control, in which historical events and the mood of the nation have played an important part. As such, it contrasts with both Prussian methods, which were essentially manipulative efforts to change the system permanently and quickly, and Russian methods, which, though long-term, are under the strict direction of an elite. According to Paul Van Riper, writing in *The History of the United States Civil Service*, the grave exigencies of the First World War and the Great Depression did as much to change the nature of the American bureaucracy as did the reform and control measures of the Populists and Progressives in the late nineteenth and early twentieth centuries. The great growth in twentieth-century civil service rolls forced the people of the United States to pay attention to bureaucracy in a more sustained way than had their forebears. The faith of the Cleveland era in the efficacy of good men was no longer enough; nor were the simple-minded appeals for economy in the Taft years. America in the 1940's and 1950's saw increasing popular concern over the "mess in Washington." The strengthening of the Civil Service Commission, the departmental reorganization, and the new personnel policies of the Truman and early Eisenhower years were, at least in part, responses to the public mood. As it turned out, these measures damaged bureaucratic morale, since they implicitly cast doubt on the growing self-respect of the civil service. The history of American reform efforts shows that public control of bureaucracy is extraordinarily difficult, because coordinating popular attention to the problem at hand with effective action is such a haphazard process. Even in the 1960's, the vital necessity of controlling a large bureaucracy like the Defense Department comes as a great surprise to many Americans.

J. L. Phelan

Authority and Flexibility
in the Spanish Imperial Bureaucracy

Societal and political stability was a predominant feature of Spain's vast overseas empire. In an age of slow communications Spain was able to preserve her widely scattered colonial dominions in both America and Asia against frequent foreign threats and occasional internal revolts without heavy reliance on military coercion.

Two institutions were primarily responsible for the maintenance of a social status quo that endured for three centuries. They were the Spanish Catholic Church—and it was more Spanish than Roman—and the imperial bureaucracy. The effectiveness of these two institutions became apparent in the period following the wars of independence. Political emancipation swept away the imperial bureaucracy, and the Church emerged from the struggle with its traditional sources of power considerably undermined. Political instability resulted. The new republican ideology inspired by the American and the French revolutions did not fill the vacuum created by the abolition of the colonial bureaucracy and the weakening of the Church. Actually the military organization seized control after independence, and the various ideologies were scarcely more than a façade for masking this control.

In view of the predominate role of the colonial bureaucracy in creating conditions of durable social stability, the dynamics of this system merit some scrutiny. The aim of this essay is to examine the Spanish bureaucracy in terms of a thought-provoking hypothesis recently advanced by Andrew Gunder Frank. Although Frank's hypothesis was inspired by his study of the operation of the industrial system in the Soviet Union, his model illuminates the functioning of other bureaucratic systems as well.

THE HYPOTHESIS

Mr. Frank outlined his model as follows:
More than one hierarchal channel of communication is maintained. Multiple and, at least, in part conflicting standards are set by superiors for subordinates. Conflict may arise among standards set within each hierarchy as well as among those set by different hierarchies. Subordinates are free to decide which of the conflicting standards to meet, if any. However, subordinates are responsible to superiors for their performance with respect to all standards; and subordinates may be held

From "Authority and Flexibility in the Spanish Imperial Bureaucracy," by John Leddy Phelan, *Administrative Science Quarterly*, 5, No. 1, June 1960, 47-64. Reprinted by permission of the publisher and the author.

responsible for failure to meet any standard. The relative importance of standards is neither well, nor completely defined, nor is it entirely undefined. The priority among standards is ambiguous. Subordinates make their assessment of priority to guide their decision making and task performance. Each subordinate appeals to those standards which are most in accord with his incentives and the circumstances of the moment and to those which are most likely to be invoked by superiors in evaluating his performance. Superiors in turn make their assessment of priority to guide their necessarily selective evaluation of subordinates' performance and enforcement of standards. The entire process is continuous: superiors modify the set of standards to comply with their changing objectives; subordinates adapt their decisions to changing standards and to changing circumstances; superiors enforce standards in accordance with the changing priority.*

In this model two outstanding features are flexibility and authority. Flexibility encompasses (1) the response of subordinates to changing objectives of their superiors, (2) the adaptability of subordinates to adjust to changing circumstances, and (3) the initiative of subordinates in sponsoring innovations. In this context of the term, authority means sensitivity of subordinates to their superiors' objectives rather than mere adherence to their rules. The Weberian distinction between formal rationality and substantive rationality is pertinent. Formal rationality refers to rational calculation and predictability based on adherence to specified procedures, which result in task performance; substantive rationality refers to the achievement of task performance itself regardless of the means employed. The bureaucratic systems under discussion exhibit substantive rather than formal rationality.

The multiplicity of standards permit superiors to make their ever-changing wishes felt by adding new standards or shifting the emphasis among existing ones. By their very incompatibility, multiple standards allow a wide latitude of discretion to subordinates, resulting in the decentralizing of decision making. Selective evaluation of performance and selective enforcement of standards makes the incompatibility among the standards operationally feasible.

This system also generates authority. Superiors can invoke, if they wish, one of the many standards that has not been met. Selective enforcement permits superiors to convert potential authority into real authority at any given time. Hence subordinates remain sensitive to the wishes, both formal and "real" of their superiors. The existence of multiple hierarchies and alternative channels of communications prevent subordinates from obstructing the upward movement of information about their own malperformance. By providing superiors with a wide fund of knowledge about conditions below, subordinates are made more responsible to their superiors.

In applying this hypothesis to the Spanish imperial bureaucracy, the structural features of the colonial administration must first be outlined. . . .

*Andrew Gunder Frank, "Goal Ambiguity and Conflicting Standards: An Approach to the Study of Organization," *Human Organization*, published by the Society for Applied Anthropology, 17 (1958-1959), p. 11.

THE STRUCTURE
OF THE COLONIAL ADMINISTRATION

At the summit of the Spanish colonial bureaucracy was the king. Directly under the monarch was the Council of the Indies, exercising by royal delegation supreme jurisdiction over all phases of the colonial administration: legislative, financial, judicial, military, ecclesiastical, and commercial. Only at the top was the imperial bureaucracy highly centralized in the persons of the king and his Council. The Crown's agents in America and in the Philippines were the viceroys, the governors, and the Audiencia. The viceroys and the governors ostensibly held supreme sway in both civil and military matters; in their territories they were the immediate representatives of the king. Command of the military establishment and the secular aspects of church government were under their jurisdiction. They nominated most of the lesser colonial officials subject to the eventual confirmation of the Council in Spain.

The centralization of authority in the viceroys and the governors was, however, more apparent than real. In various spheres the jurisdiction of those magistrates was rigidly limited. Many of the viceroy's subordinates as well as the judges of the Audiencia and the exchequer officials, who were his quasi peers, were appointees of the Crown. They corresponded directly with the Council. Under these circumstances the control of the viceroy over some of his subordinates and his quasi peers was frequently nominal. Although the viceroys had virtually unchallenged freedom in matters of routine administration, even in this their powers were limited; for every aspect of colonial life down to the most minute and insignificant details was regulated by a voluminous body of paternalistically inspired legislation issued by the Council. Viceroys and governors were under standing orders to enforce these mandates. These regulations were codified by 1681 in the celebrated *Recopilación de leyes de las reynos de los Indias*. In matters of policy the viceroys were supposed to refer all decisions to Spain.

The viceroy shared many of his powers with the Audiencia, the second hierarchy in the system. Those bodies were the highest court of appeal in their respective districts. The Audiencia also served as an advisory council to the viceroy or governor and exercised certain legislative functions. In any clash between the two, ultimate authority usually rested with the viceroy. Yet a vacillating presiding officer or a refractory Audiencia could easily upset this rather delicate balance of jurisdictions.

In addition to the viceroys and the Audiencia the two other administrative hierarchies were the ecclesiastical and fiscal. Under the system of the *real patronato de las Indias* the king, as patron of the Church of the Indies, acted as the Pope's vicar in ecclesiastical administration. Royal agents administered ecclesiastical taxation, and they nominated all church dignitaries from archbishop to parish priest. Discipline and doctrinal matters were the only significant spheres beyond the immediate control of the Crown. Although the viceroy acted as vice-patron of the

Church in his district, the ecclesiastical hierarchy enjoyed a wide degree of quasi-independent action. The prelates could appeal directly to the Council in Spain. They often played the viceroy off against the Council and vice versa. . . .

The officers of the royal exchequer, while of lower rank than the viceroys and the governors, were of coordinate authority in their sphere of administering royal revenue.

The viceroy, in reality, was the coordinator of the various administrative hierarchies. He served as the presiding officer of the Audiencia in its role as a Council of State, as vice-patron of the Church, and as president of the *junta superior de la real hacienda* (the exchequer office). Furthermore, the functions of each hierarchy were sometimes exercised by members of another. In the event of the sudden death of the viceroy, the Audiencia assumed supreme command of the government until a successor arrived from Spain. Archbishops sometimes served as viceroys. In spite of these occasional mergers of offices and the nominal centralization of power in the viceroy, the three other hierarchies retained a substantial amount of autonomous power, and each one was responsible directly to the Council of the Indies in Spain.

The Crown deliberately maintained several channels of communication with its colonial agents. The purpose was to ensure that superiors in Spain would have multiple sources of information as to actual conditions. As Clarence Haring has put it:

> The only real centralization was in the king and his Council in Spain. Spanish imperial government was one of checks and balances; not secured as in many constitutional states by a division of powers, legislative, judicial, executive, but by a division of authority among different individuals or tribunals exercising the same powers. There never was a clear-cut line of demarcation between the functions of various governmental agencies dealing with colonial problems. On the contrary, a great deal of overlapping was deliberately fostered to prevent officials from unduly building up personal prestige or engaging in corrupt or fraudulent practices.

Motivated by an abiding distrust of its agents overseas, the Crown gradually fashioned during the course of the sixteenth century a complex bureaucratic pyramid with multiple, partly independent and partly interdependent hierarchies. Under this system the conflicts between the various bureaucracies were continuous and acrimonious, since their jurisdictions often overlapped. Internal conflicts within the bureaucracies themselves were perhaps somewhat less frequent, but did occur. In the ecclesiastical bureaucracy the tensions were particularly severe. The bishops and the secular clergy were pitted against the regular clergy, and conflict between the various orders of the regular clergy was not uncommon. The bishops and the Crown often clashed over jurisdictions.

THE NATURE OF THE STANDARDS
IN THE SPANISH ADMINISTRATION

Standards refer to that multiplicity of pressures to which all colonial administrators had to adjust in order to survive in office. The most apparent standards were those interminable directives issued by the Council of the Indies. These mandates were often mutually contradictory. The incompatibility of the Council's directives in regard to the Indians stemmed in part from the Crown's desire to reconcile the needs of the natives and those of the colonists. The Spanish monarchs partially justified their sovereignty over the Indies from the missionary obligation to convert the Indians to Christianity. Both as infidels and even more so as "new Christians," their property rights and personal liberty merited some protection. Furthermore the Church threw its considerable weight toward the protection of native rights. The spirit and intent of the Indian legislation of the Crown reflected the conviction that the Indians constituted an inferior group in society whose rights and obligations, however, deserved paternalistic protection. The conditions under which the Indians might render labor services to the colonists were minutely regulated in a voluminous body of legislation eventually codified in the *Recopilación*, but these edicts were more frequently honored in their breach than in their observance.

This wide gap between the law and its enforcement resulted partially from another source of pressure. Colonizing had to be made profitable for the Spanish colonists, and that meant some form of exploitation of native labor. The Crown usually sought to reconcile the welfare of the Indians and the general well-being of the colonial economy. Harmonized they sometimes were, but there were striking cases when the two objectives stood in naked conflict with each other. The economic crisis created by the diminution of the Indian population in Mexico after 1576 is one notable case in point; another one was the crisis in the Philippines (1609-1648) precipitated by the Hispano-Dutch war in the Orient. There were also countless other cases in which magistrates in the Indies had to cope with mutually incompatible directives handed down by the Council in Spain.

The prevalence of mutually conflicting standards was further compounded by the ignorance of the central authorities as to actual conditions in the colonies. These local conditions could make the directives of the Council either impracticable or even impossible to enforce. In many cases the Council deliberately defied local conditions. The tendency of the central authorities was to eliminate regional differences, as the Council's aim was to standardize practices throughout the empire. Hence circular cedulas [instructions] were often dispatched to all the Audiencias of the empire. Such a practice reflected the supreme indifference, if not the active hostility of the central authorities, to local conditions. The Philippines, for example, would be treated on occasion as if they were another Mexico.

In view of the Spanish procedure of assigning the same functions of government to different agencies, bureaucrats had to cultivate a sensitivity to the aims and the procedures of their peers in the other administrative hierarchies. In the sphere of Indian legislation, for example, the viceroys had to take into account the views of the clergy. The bishops in their ex-officio role as protectors of the Indians could intervene in those cases where the economic demands of the state or the colonists encroached upon the religious welfare of the neophytes. Given their countless missions among the natives, the regular clergy also had a vested interest in all matters pertaining to the welfare of the Indians. The officers of the exchequer were concerned with the fiscal aspects of Indian administration. A special responsibility of the Audiencia was the legal defense of the natives. In the administration of Indian affairs a viceroy or governor would be ill-advised not to take into account the viewpoints of his judicial, ecclesiastical, and fiscal peers. Decisions were often the result of tension and conflict, the consequence of the fact that the jurisdictions of these partly independent and partly interdependent hierarchies overlapped. Nor could the governors or viceroys ignore their subordinates. The middle-echelon officials, by virtue of their long tenures in office covering many administrations, were not without the means to influence the conduct of their superiors, the viceroys.

Although there was no organized and articulate press to serve as a vehicle of protest against bureaucratic incompetence, colonial subjects did not lack means for voicing their grievances. The wealthy and the educated often corresponded directly with the Council of the Indies. The Archivo General de Indias in Seville contains countless petitions and protests of corporate groups like town councils or class groups like encomenderos as well as memoranda from private citizens.

A system of incentives and penalties further encouraged colonial magistrates to adjust to the multiplicity of pressures. The offices in the colonial bureaucracy were in effect monopolized by peninsular Spaniards. They formed a class of career bureaucrats. They were likely to be sent to any region of the empire. Promotion and spoil were their incentives, as was assignment to a favored geographical location. Posts in an isolated and economically underdeveloped colony like the Philippines were considered far less desirable than stations in Mexico or in Peru, where a more agreeable climate and more lucrative emoluments of office attracted ambitious royal servants. Notwithstanding severe and widespread clashes of interests and values among the members of the system, colonial bureaucrats appeared to share an underlying esprit de corps that they belonged to a common body whose existence ought to be perpetuated. Most of the members seem to have been motivated to some significant degree by a feeling of personal involvement in the system's ultimate welfare. In addition to the incentives of advancement there was also a whole series of penalties. They ranged from reprimands, demotions, loss of office, fines, and criminal prosecution for those who miscalculated the pressures of a given situation.

All of these pressures—orders from Spain, local conditions, the peers and subordinates of bureaucrats, public opinion, incentives, and penalties—served to create a whole complex of standards, which guided and conditioned the conduct of colonial officialdom.

The very multiplicity and the often mutually contradictory character of the standards contributed both to maintaining authority and to providing flexibility. The issuing of new directives by superiors made those objectives known to their subordinates and hence contributed to the maintenance of authority, whose two components are knowledge by subordinates of the wishes of their superiors and compliance by subordinates. Multiplicity of standards also increased flexibility. Superiors had the opportunity to change directives and standards as the occasion demanded. In view of their contradictory nature, subordinates necessarily had a certain latitude in their choice of what standards to enforce.

FLEXIBILITY

There were a variety of ways in which colonial administrators responded to those manifold pressures created by mutually incompatible standards.

A well-documented example occurred in Mexico. New Spain's century of depression originated in the great epidemic of 1576-1579, in which the Indian population was massively diminished by the spread of contagious diseases against which they had no acquired immunity. The crisis was hastened by the accompanying rapid decline in available native labor, the increase of the non-Indian population (Spaniards and mestizos), and the extensive use of native labor by the regular and the secular clergy for their many architectural enterprises. Another factor complicating the plight of the Indians was a change in land use, in which a large portion of the land of central Mexico was removed from the production of maize and given over to the raising of livestock. The landscape of Mexico was radically altered by the advance of herds of cattle, sheep, and goats. The non-Indian population was determined to maintain its customary standard of living, with the result that the pressure on the rapidly diminishing Indians for increased grain production became almost intolerable. Stopgap measures such as the establishment of public granaries and a crude system of price fixing did not succeed in guaranteeing an adequate flow of foodstuffs to the cities.

The *repartimiento* (a system of compulsory draft labor) and the rise of a latifundia system based on Indian debt peonage by the middle of the seventeenth century arrested the contracting economy. Earlier, during the first administration of Velasco the Younger (1590-1595), the *repartimiento* was failing to draft enough labor from the steadily diminishing Indian population to meet even those demands which crown officials recognized as having a prior demand on what labor was available.

As the labor market was tightening, new orders arrived from Spain. The reform projects contained in the cedulas of November 24, 1601, and May 26, 1609, envisaged a drastic lightening of the labor burdens of the Indians. Motivating the Crown's policy were a variety of considerations, ideological as well as humanitarian and economic. The Indians as recent converts to Christianity merited the Crown's special protection. Compassion for the plight of the Indians who were being decimated by famine, disease, and overwork was another factor. Thirdly, enlightened self-interest advocated measures of relief. The Indians must be preserved, for they were the colony's principal labor force. The viceroys, the Audiencia, and even the clergy did not discount the pertinence of these arguments. Yet the same officials realized that the implementation of the cedulas of 1601 and 1609 would only aggravate an already desperate crisis. Famine in the cities of New Spain instead of the threat of famine might ensue. In the face of conflicting standards, the responsible authorities in New Spain gave priority to the overall economic crisis rather than the specific plight of the Indians. Invoking a traditional formula of Spanish administrative procedure, the viceroys and the Audiencia obeyed but did not execute the orders of the Council.

The actual operation of this formula merits closer examination. Geographical isolation of the colonies, wide divergence in regional conditions, and only partial awareness of these conditions on the part of the central authorities made some such institutional device desirable. The formula's origins go back to the Roman law concept that the prince can will no injustice. The "I obey" clause signifies the recognition by subordinates of the legitimacy of the sovereign power who, if properly informed of all circumstances, would will no wrong. The "I do not execute" clause is the subordinate's assumption of the responsibility of postponing the execution of an order until the sovereign is informed of those conditions of which he may be ignorant and without a knowledge of which an injustice may be committed.

Presiding magistrates in the Indies were permitted by law to postpone the execution of royal orders whose implementation might create an injustice or undesirable social conflicts. Colonial administrators were required to justify immediately their conduct to the Council. The central authorities in return might reissue the orders in their original form, or they might modify them in accordance with the suggestions of the local authorities. The latter in turn might invoke the formula again in the hopes that by procrastination the unwanted proposals might be buried by bureaucratic inertia.

Colonial administrators had to apply with discretion the "I obey but do not execute" formula. A reckless use of this power might arouse the ire of the Council. Offenders might incur any number of penalties, ranging from reprimands to demotions, to loss of office or imprisonment. The colonial bureaucrat constantly needed to strike a delicate balance between the orders of his superiors in Spain and the dictates of local pressures. Many a bureaucratic career ended in disgrace that could be traced back to a miscalculation of the relative importance of the pressures in a given situation. The Spanish colonial bureaucrat like his modern Russian counterpart had to orient himself to his superiors' "real" objectives, which were often not reflected in the actual instructions emanating from Spain.

Thus, the "I obey but do not execute" formula appears as an institutional device for decentralizing decision making. Its frequent use enabled colonial officials to postpone indefinitely the execution of royal wishes. Furthermore, its operation reveals the more positive role of subordinates as policy makers. By postponing the execution of royal mandates and presenting fresh proposals, viceroys, Audiencia, and archbishops could influence the reformulation of their superiors' directives. New instructions from Spain often reflected to some extent, at least, the viewpoint of officials in the Indies.

The dialectic of the Spanish administrative system may be clarified by

Hegelian formula. The thesis is the wishes of the Council embodied in its directives dispatched to the colonies. The antithesis is that complex of pressures or standards to which colonial administrators had to adapt, pressures often in conflict with the Council's instructions. The synthesis is what actually emerged. That was not only a satisfactory but usually a workable compromise between what the central authorities intended and what local pressures would permit.

The Spanish colonial administration was, in effect, a dynamic balance between the principles of authority and flexibility, in which the highly centralized decision making vested in the king and the Council was counterbalanced by some substantial measure of decentralized decision making exercised by bureaucratic subordinates in the colonies.

INSTRUMENTS OF CONTROL

If the "I obey but do not execute" formula gave colonial magistrates some measure of freedom in which to maneuver, other institutional devices made officers in the colonies sensitive to the wishes of their superiors in Spain. There were two institutional procedures by which superiors in Spain enforced standards and reviewed the performance of subordinates in the Indies. They were the *residencia* and the *visita*.

The *residencia* was a judicial review of the conduct of a magistrate at the end of his term in office. All appointees of the Crown with the notable exception of the clergy were required by law to submit to a *residencia* at the termination of their tenure. A specially designated *juez de residencia* conducted a public court of inquiry in which he heard all charges of malfeasance against the former incumbent. After receiving the latter's defense, the judge passed sentence and remitted his findings to the Council of the Indies for final review. Heavy fines, confiscation of property, imprisonment, or all three, were customary sentences in cases of grave misconduct in office. The fact that sentences in the Indies were often reversed or altered in Spain does suggest that decisions sometimes reflected the personal bias of the judges or that the official under investigation was able to bring to bear commanding influence at Court. . . .

The *visita* differed from the *residencia* in respect to procedure. Both devices, however, shared a common purpose, that is, to serve as agencies of royal control over subordinates in the colonies. The *residencia* was public and statutory. It took place at the end of a magistrate's term of office. The *visita*, on the other hand, was a secret inquiry which could be made at any time during a magistrate's incumbency. Generally applied as a crisis measure, it usually reflected the discontent of the central authorities with a specific situation in the colonies. The aim of the *visita* was to prod apathetic subordinates into taking more vigorous action, whereas the *residencia's* objective was to expose and to punish illegal practices. There were restricted *visitas* applying to a single official or to a single province, and there were general *visitas* in which an entire vice-royalty or an Audiencia district came under investigation. The visitor general could examine all aspects of administration. He might interrogate any magistrate from the viceroy or the archbishop downward.

It is indeed a moot question as to whose authority was supreme during the term of the visitation—that of the viceroy or that of the visitor.

The opinion of the Marquis of Montesclaros, viceroy of Peru (1607-1615) has often been quoted. He likened the *residencia* and the *visita* to gusts of wind which one frequently encounters in the streets and in the public squares and which accomplish nothing but to raise the dust and refuse and cause everyone to cover his head. This bon mot may be an apt contemporary evaluation of the institution from the viewpoint of subordinates subject to investigation. Yet the perspective of the investigators, the Council of the Indies, was a different one. These twin procedures enabled superiors in Spain to enforce standards in the colonies and to review periodically the performance of subordinates. The *visita* functioned as a means of enforcing old standards, establishing new ones, or enunciating a new priority among existing standards. The *residencia* became an instrument for reviewing the past performance of subordinates. Both procedures were highly selective. Some standards were violated in order to enforce others, as the wide gap between the law and its observance in the colonies amply attests. Magistrates in the Indies, however, never for a moment forgot the existence of this highly institutionalized system of enforcement and review, however selective its application may have been in practice. Its operation certainly encouraged them to keep in harmony with their superiors' "real" wishes.

The key to this hypothesis about social organization lies in selective evaluation and selective enforcement. Selectivity makes a system with conflicts among the standards operationally feasible.

CONCLUSIONS

In summary, the operation of the Spanish colonial system apparently has some features common to the Soviet industrial system.

1. The members of both organizations were motivated to some significant degree by personal involvement in the system and its welfare.
2. Looking at the Spanish administration as a whole, one can see no single guiding goal or objective save that tendency common to all bureaucracies— the tendency toward self-perpetuation. Nor are there several goals commensurate with each other. Hence the goals are difficult to rank. The standards to which individual agents were subject often clashed with one another, and no clear-cut priority among these standards was available for the agents. A notable exception to the overall goal ambiguity of the Spanish system is the case of the Church. The spiritual welfare of the natives and the colonists was a clear-cut goal from which the Church could scarcely deviate, although various branches of the clergy clashed over the means of reaching that goal.
3   The Spanish system like the Russian was task-performance oriented.
4. Both systems are hierarchal and bureaucratic organizations.
5. In short, both administrations constitute multiple, partly interdependent and partly independent, hierarchies with mutually incompatible standards, selective enforcement of standards, and selective review of performance. . . .

Historians have assumed that the Spanish bureaucracy like other bureaucratic organizations had only one goal or a set of commensurate goals and that standards of conduct for members were not mutually conflicting. If this assumption is cast aside in favor of goal ambiguity and conflicting standards, new light is thrown on the chasm between the law and its observance in the Spanish empire. The wide gap between the two was not a flaw, as has been traditionally assumed. On the contrary, the distance between observance and nonobservance was a necessary component of the system. Given the ambiguity of the goals and the conflict among the standards, all the laws could not be enforced simultaneously. The very conflict among the standards, which prevented a subordinate from meeting all the standards at once, gave subordinates a voice in decision making without jeopardizing the control of their superiors over the whole system.

Hans Rosenberg

Control of the
Prussian Bureaucracy

The rise of centralized domination under the leadership of autocrats, whether kings, princes, prime ministers, or political cardinals, wrought profound changes in the functions of the central government; in the methods of political and administrative management; in the recruitment and behavior of men in authority; and in the conception of the rights and duties of officeholding.

Absolutism also altered the nature of political power. The new state rulers were not content to add to their "patrimony" the traditional jurisdictions of the estates and to absorb most of their functions. They also built a new bureaucratic empire. They raised sizable permanent armies, imposed ever larger taxes, multiplied fiscal exactions. They extended and intensified the regulative and administrative intervention of the dynastic government into the sphere of private rights and local home rule. And they made a place for the Crown as a strong commercial competitor and monopolist in production and distribution.

Thus, the makers of the absolute monarchy did not merely learn to handle old institutions in a new way. They also invented novel and more effective

Reprinted by permission of the author and the publishers from Hans Rosenberg, *Bureaucracy, Aristocracy and Autocracy*, pp. 12-13, 88-100. Cambridge, Mass.: Harvard University Press, Copyright 1958, by the President and Fellows of Harvard College.

instruments of compulsion. By constructing a large-scale apparatus of finance, administration, and military might operated by a class of appointed career executives accountable to them, they became the founders of a thoroughly bureaucratized state with many strikingly "modern" features. The great political entrepreneurs had the wit to realize that "a bureaucratized autocracy is a perfected autocracy."

An aggressive, methodical, and often oppressive machine of hierarchical state management by dictation and subordination came to prevail over the less elaborate, more slovenly, and infinitely more personal medieval contrivances. Dynastic absolutism itself was only a passing historic phenomenon. But it gave birth to an administrative system which survived to enter the common heritage of contemporary civilization. . . .

It was a stupendous undertaking to whip into shape the mixed crowd of career bureaucrats who represented greatly divergent qualities, habits, aspirations, interests, loyalties, values, and traditions. However contemptible some of the means used to make the "royal servants" function as servile instruments of dynastic policy, the fact that the effort was partly successful was an impressive historic achievement. The new bureaucrats learned to act as an organized group and as reasonably efficient team workers. The collective pursuit of a common professional task and political function was made compatible with the disruptive influences stemming from individual differences and jealousies and from intragroup antagonisms.

The Prussian kings based their personnel management on a flexible combination of calculated external pressures and inducements and internal incentives. They put a premium on dictation and terrorization, mitigated by occasional bribes and paternal deeds, and on the manipulatory efficacy of human selfishness. Both pessimism and optimism—distrust in self-imposed restraints on the one hand and a qualified belief in progress and human perfectibility on the other—sustained the pragmatic personnel administration of Frederick William I [reigned 1713-1740] and of Frederick II [reigned 1740-1786].

In their direct personal contacts mostly limited to flatterers and opportunists, their idea of the best way to manage men rested on a few hasty and primitive generalizations. It sprang from the assumption that, save for a few—a very few—no one was to be trusted, that, "human nature being what it is," government officials were likely to be evil rather than good, corrupt rather than honest, lazy rather than diligent, irresponsible rather than dutiful. In order to make the personal will of the ruler supreme, his agents, therefore, were to be regimented with an iron hand, driven to their work, compelled to acquire a new frame of mind and attitude of service, watched all the time and spurred to greater exertions by the hope of material reward and social honors and the fear of stern punishment.

Carefully planned, neatly defined, and minutely detailed official codes of professional behavior, of disciplinary rules, and of moral proprieties were worked out for the major service branches in the age of Frederick William I. These sets of standardized regulations and the efforts to enforce them had more than local and episodical significance. These were not merely the visionary schemes of a temperamental, eccentric, and frantic crusader, intoxicated with militaristic logic and outraged by lax standards of conduct, who was bent on turning his hired assistants into spineless marionettes. By his threats and blandishments, it is true, Frederick William thought that he might bring the dynastic enforcement squads into line: "They shall dance to my music or the devil take me. Like the Czar I will hang and roast and treat them as rebels."

But this experiment in fabricating a novel kind of nodding conformist had broad human and social significance. It provided a substantial clue to the understanding of the knotty problem of when, where, how, and why there was born, outside the acquisitive business community, the ceaselessly efficient, rationally tempered modern "vocational man" (*Berufsmensch*), who did not work in order to live but who lived in order to work. Collectivist Prussia made a remarkable contribution to the creation of this new species of thoroughly disciplined man, activated by quasi-moral compulsions and chained to a large-scale apparatus and thus to the collective pursuit of objectified, utilitarian tasks. In line with the conception of the bureaucratic state as a machine, man himself was destined to become an automaton.

In Prussia the bureaucrats were supposed to function as figures on the royal chessboard. In this martial state the campaign against individual self-will, slovenliness, waste, corruption, and falsehood in dynastic employment received its distinctive texture from the deification of military values. These furnished the central theme for the legal regulations and the moral canons which the Hohenzollerns imposed upon their civilian servants in the attempt to mold their behavior.

In the poor and backward Prussian state the impatient and over-ambitious royal leaders, apt to overtax the strength of their subjects, did not rest content with the mere improvement of discipline and efficiency. They aimed at superdiscipline, superconformity, and superefficiency. Compliance with garrison standards (*"Kommiss!"*) was the ideal discipline in civil employment. In consequence, they regarded self-resilient initiative, let alone criticism of their orders, as an act of insubordination bordering on mutiny. Loyalty, therefore, they confounded with unquestioning submission to the service code and unconditional subservence to the machine of compulsion, directed by the autocratic commander-in-chief.

The norms of vocational conduct, as laid down from above, were largely concerned with the regulation of the technical terms of employment and of functional duties. The *règlements*, in spelling out uniform rules for particular categories of officials and bureaus, provided a meticulous specification of the division of labor within the service and a minutely defined allocation of individual and collective tasks and responsibilities. The service codes also regulated the hours of labor, many small particulars of the working methods, and the ways of using administrative time.

Frederick William I, with his passion for concrete detail, did not overlook anything. When, for instance, he imposed a mandatory eight-and-a-half-hour day for the summer period and a seven-and-a-half-hour day for the winter season upon his servants, he did not forget to map out the whole day even for the ministers of the General Directory. As for the latter, he gave his stringent requirements a human touch by guaranteeing a complimentary luncheon, consisting of "four substantial courses with the necessary wine and beer."

The standards of efficiency and sober practicality laid down by Frederick II were more ascetic and demanding but also more impersonal and egalitarian. Having gained through his spies and his tours of inspection a comprehensive picture as to how things worked out in daily life, he made Prussian government service even more humorless by dispensing with state-financed sumptuous living during the luncheon period. Thus he terminated the friendly alliance between the royal household as a generous supplier of culinary pleasures to the elite of the *Ministerialbürokratie* and the state as an austere and pedantic extractor of expeditious labor from all dynastic employees. For with regard to upper officialdom as a whole he had arrived at the considered judgment that "if everybody does his duty and works diligently, all current business can be disposed of in three hours during the morning. However, the whole day will not be long enough to get through with the work in hand, if the members of the board tell each other stories, read the newspapers, go for a walk or keep themselves busy with other matters which have nothing to do with the functions of the board."

Infinitely more consequential were the moral obligations which all Prussian bureaucrats were ordered to meet. The building up of an apparatus of vastly extended, legally irresponsible royal power was accompanied by changing conceptions and standards of public morality subordinate to dynastic interests and political utility. In the old days of the supremacy of traditional law and of the private proprietary state it was perfectly respectable, cavalier-like and, in fact, the thing to do for an administrator of the princely domain to alienate its yield. Conduct of this kind, in terms of the new, dynastically decreed public law, was a crime. To clear up the legal and moral confusion that had arisen; to provide a specific guide to human behavior in the new complex organization; to redefine rights and duties, permissible and nonpermissible ways of thinking and of acting—this was the function of the Hohenzollerns' dexterous attempt at effecting a "moral purification of the administration."

The official code of vocational proprieties and professional ethics lumped together, in rather abstract fashion, "loyalty, diligence, restraint, discretion, conscientiousness, adroitness" as particularly desirable qualities. It sought to promote a peculiar attitude of career service, pervading the whole of one's activities and resulting in hard and faithful work and superior performance. Although, time and again, the state bureaucrats were scornfully treated like valets, naughty school boys, and prospective criminals, they were constantly reminded of their special status as a distinctive and superior occupational group. Membership in the powerful organization to which they belonged carried with it singular responsibilities. Their appointment to the select body entailed the duty to be scrupulous and vigilant in the execution of their assignments and to band harmoniously together in the cooperative pursuit of a common end. Theirs was the obligation to practice in their calling unswerving submission, thrift, sobriety, repression of the passions, and stern self-discipline.

The royal drillmasters knew that man does not live by bread alone. They were not unaware of the utility of nonmaterial incentives for both individual and group discipline, loyalty, and efficiency. In fact, to get things done they did not rely exclusively on external coercive controls and sanctions, on the lure of strictly material stimuli, on the exploitation of human vanity, and on the use of ethical norms as technical expedients. In order to reduce expenses, to tap additional sources of energy, and to forge politically indispensable bonds of allegiance, they also attempted to arouse sentimental attachments to the royal service, a spirit of affectionate, selfless dedication, of cooperation freely and eagerly rendered.

In his desperate search for workable means of making his civilian employees and his army officers serve "with great advantage" to himself and his ends, Frederick William I almost drifted into the camp of the "idealists," although he was incapable of conceiving of the state in other than personal terms. The idea that the "vocational man" might come to practice self-denial in the service of an idea and to devote himself to impersonal tasks for their own sake was beyond his grasp. Yet, in his own peculiar way he tried to breed individual idealism. He urged the royal servant not only to give his technical skill, but to merge his personal desires and opinions, his very individuality and whole personality with his professional work. He called upon the bureaucrat to take pride in his vocational activity and to find through it an ideal content of life by functioning as "an intelligent, assiduous, and alert person who after God values nothing higher than his king's pleasure and serves him out of love and for the sake of honor rather than money and who in his conduct solely seeks and constantly bears in mind his king's service and interest, who, moreover, abhors all intrigues and emotional deterrents."

Despite the enormous gulf between fiction and fact and the conflict between intended and unintended results, it was not merely a matter of wishful thinking to expect the administrative executives at all times to give their undivided allegiance to the concerns of the ruler and to stake upon their profession "everything but their salvation." Plans for the "moral purification of the administration" and for the unconditional inner surrender of the administrators advanced faster on paper than in the minds and deeds of the officials. Still, Prussian state service, slowly and inexorably, evolved not merely into a specialized full-time vocation for life but into a rigorously circumscribed professional career. The new bureaucrats were indeed more than common job holders, as their supreme commanders were more than ordinary large-scale employers.

Here were the early historic roots of some of the peculiarities which distinguished the Prussian service estates of the nineteenth century from the government bureaucracies of the West. The authoritarian political outlook, the professional superiority complex and the social group vanity, as developed by the Royal Prussian Bureaucracy and the Royal Prussian Army, were supported by conceptions and illusions which went back to the reign of Frederick William I. For it became a matter-of-course part of the bureaucracy's creed and ideology to advance the argument that the permanent civil official or military officer was a distinctive and particularly valuable type of man, since he sacrificed his whole life to a collective lofty cause instead of selling his labor to a particular employer. Like the monarch himself, he was the bearer of state authority. He deserved therefore special security, special rights, and a special position of dignity and honor. Hence the inclination to segregate the bureaucracy from the general public, to regard the former as the embodiment of the state and to equate its privileges and power with the public interest.

The elaborate machinery for the enforcement of the disciplinary code was formidable enough to assure a substantial measure of superficial conformity. Nevertheless, the striving for discipline and subordination interfered with the goal of consolidating monocratic leadership, of perfecting efficiency and promoting personal integrity. Excessive royal demands were simply self-defeating. They had a harmful influence upon group morale and an evil effect upon human character training.

Bombarded with edicts, ordinances, rules, regulations and, if something went wrong, at once humiliated in snarling language, the oppressed royal servants needed a thick skin to put up with the outbursts of their masters. Flattery and servility belonged in the defense mechanism of upper officialdom. But in protecting their right to self-preservation these well paid and high ranking yet withal pitiable creatures learned to camouflage their real lives, to resort to subterfuges and double-dealing, and to practice calculated deceit. Thus moral obtuseness and degradation became an essential feature of employer-employee relations in the most austere of all the European states of the Old Regime, its respectable façade notwithstanding. The cunning and bad temper of the mighty leaders found an insurmountable obstacle in the crafty and obstinate responses of the subordinates. Those who had enough backbone to refuse to be turned into puppets found manifold ways to revenge themselves for being treated, occasionally, like the scum of the earth.

Even in technical and organizational matters the Hohenzollerns overshot their mark. Their harsh methods failed to eliminate many cumbersome and wasteful forms of management. In fact, the superfluity of regulations, checks, and controls kept alive or produced unnecessary jobs and overlapping functions as well as administrative confusion and jurisdictional disputes which dissipated energy. Nevertheless, incessant drill, underpinned by the dissemination of hope and fear, of promises and threats, produced certain enduring results. Many of the "permanent probationers," for reasons of their own, found it to their advantage to exert themselves fully. The vigorous assault of the autocracy upon the bureaucracy, combined with the forces boring from within, gave rise to infinitely more routinized and more efficient working habits than had evolved in the age of the *Ständestaat*. Regular, standardized individual and team work tended to become a matter of habit. And in the long run, the sense of duty which developed with the changing style of work

made for the glorification of duty as such, often devoid however of critical thinking about ultimate purposes.

In the young and artificial Prussian state, more so than in the modernized
old monarchies of western Europe, it was the salient political function of the
bureaucracy to hold the scattered dominions together by cultivating the arts of
government regimentation and by teaching the subjects unquestioning obedience
to the central power. But since the bureaucrats themselves had first to be taught
subservience and the working rules of large-scale authoritarian collectivism, even
the outward forms of the administrative institutions reflected their function as
strict disciplinary agencies.

The administrative colleges, though adopted in imitation of the old collegial
courts of law and of foreign models, were contrived to produce both pliability and
efficiency. The collegial principle [of shared responsibility] in central and provincial administration played an important role in Prussia, and also in the leading monarchies of central, northern, and eastern Europe, in Austria, Sweden, and Russia.
This unwieldy instrument of absolutist statecraft was not designed to provide "the
public" with legal protection against government by dictation. It was the monarch
who was to be protected against idlers, saboteurs, liars, crooks, and rebels on the
royal payroll.

The stress on the collaborative efforts and the responsibility of administrative
boards was a constructive means of ensuring steadiness, greater uniformity, cooperation, and accountability in the discharge of common professional duties. Group
action under central supervision reduced the dangers of graft, favoritism, and personal arbitrariness. The service code tied the individual official to his department
colleagues. All matters falling within the jurisdiction of a particular board and calling for corporate action upon the completion of the preparatory work by an individual or small subcommittee were, if regulations were followed, freely discussed
in a meeting of the whole department and resolved by simple majority vote. This
democratic intraservice procedure, though sometimes farcical in actual operation,
did much to make administrative management more scientific by basing decisions
on facts and the critical examination of information rather than on loose personal
opinions, preconceived notions, and individual fancy.

The board pattern of transacting executive business facilitated the education
of bureaucrats for discipline in a mutual undertaking and for routinized servicing of
the administrative machine. Group pressure hampered the few strong and imaginative individuals, but when brought to bear upon timorous and slothful workers, it
tended to stir these to greater efforts, and to thereby raise the level of trained
mediocrity.

Collegial organization also proved a valuable instrument for strengthening the
bonds of group solidarity. At the same time, however, it had a disruptive and de-
moralizing effect upon intragroup life in consequence of the disciplinary functions
which the colleges were requested to perform. In accordance with its policy of
divide and rule, the crown used the boards as a double barrier against insubordination by methodically organizing mutual vigilance and distrust through the medium
of both corporate and individual checks.

In the first place, each department was made the responsible sponsor of efficient and honest standards of work. It was the self-governing vehicle for enforcing discipline upon all its members, and for maintaining and refining professional honor under the service code. Highly diversified modes of behavior emerged from this collective guardianship of duty, decorum, and probity which have endured to the present day and, in varied forms, have spread to all modern bureaucracies. Sustained by interservice contacts, by the transfer of individual functionaries from one agency to another, and by the manner with which the administrators dealt with the subjects, the bureaucratic ways of living profoundly influenced the making of a tradition of service. They deeply affected the characteristics typical of the Prussian bureaucracy as a whole.

In the second place, the collegial principle in public administration fostered *esprit de parti* rather than "that complex pattern of emotion and thought which is *esprit de corps*." Both Frederick William I and Frederick II overshot their target when they incited their bureaucratic assistants to engage in little wars of all against all. The royal tactics turned the administrative hierarchy into a hothouse of disharmony, suspicion, animosity, and underhand plotting. The kings inadvertently encouraged the very paralyzing intraservice strife against which they often thundered. In fact, in their attempt to turn human weaknesses into dynastic assets, they converted the bureaucracy into an informer and spy-ridden association.

It was one thing to invest the ministers and privy councilors of the General Directory, the presidents, directors, and councilors of the various Boards of War and Domains and the members of special committees with the responsibility of acting individually as guardians of professional discipline by restraining defective fellow workers and offenders of the service codes. It was quite another matter to call upon them to watch closely and unceasingly their rank equals, subordinates, and superiors and to turn informer upon their brethren by reporting, secretly though not anonymously, weaknesses, irregularities, and misdemeanors, let alone felonies. And it was still another matter to make this sort of "alertness" and "faithfulness" not only part of their normal professional duty, but to offer as an inducement to "qualified informers" the prospect of higher salaries, accelerated promotions, or other special favors.

Other devices were likewise designed to produce formal obedience and internal constraints. The inventive Hohenzollerns made organized spying a major instrument of disciplinary pressure in the new bureaucratic state. To ensure central control over the councilors in the realm of provincial administration, the members of the General Directory were duty-bound to develop a maze of mutual suspicion by working in intimate cooperation with a whole host of secret field agents and petty local informers, such as "substantial tenant farmers, burghers and subaltern royal domain officials, peasants and village officers. . . . By means of such clandestine intelligence they often will get better information as to what is going on in the provinces than from the reports of the Commissariats and Boards."

In addition, throughout the upper service particular career men, mostly of high official rank and of nonnoble origin, were given secret assignments to act as royal watchdogs and informers upon promise of protecting them against all possible adversaries. For these henchmen this task of shadowing their associates was but a by-employment. Part of their assignments they met by doing, so to speak, overtime without expectation of any immediate extra compensation.

Viebahn, for example, when made a minister of state, in 1729, at the same time was appointed special secret agent in the General Directory. As undercover agent of His Serene Highness it was his job to submit confidential memoranda on all fellow ministers who tended to deviate from the instructions, were slack in their work, or engaged in "intrigues" and "malicious gossip." Significantly enough, Viebahn did not express any distaste for the onerous burden imposed on him. On the contrary, he recalled the "happy experience" of his predecessor, the minister-spy Katsch, who, by living up to royal expectations, had managed "to overcome all jealousy and persecutions, to enjoy a pleasant life and to die in a state of unbroken bliss and honors."

Neither Frederick William I nor Frederick II were content with the services of such informers. Discipline through intimidation and fear of reprisals received an additional impetus from the *Fiskale*. These rather ominous men, aside from being ordinary state attorneys, functioned as professional in-service spies in every branch of the central and provincial administration. They formed a special little bureaucratic hierarchy of their own, acting at once as a secret administrative police and as a body of public prosecutors under the direction of the *Generalfiskal*.

This impressive array of controls carried in its train the threat of humiliation, degradation, and more severe punishment. Penalties, as distinct from simple reprimands and mere indignities, varied widely. They ranged from the denial, temporary or permanent, of further professional advancement or the transfer to undesirable positions to money fines, salary cuts, suspension, outright dismissal, jail sentences with or without discharge, mostly without even the semblance of a hearing or trial, and, finally, to death on the gallows.

These penalties were not a dead letter. Frederick William I and Frederick II dealt summarily with some of the more obnoxious offenders of the disciplinary rules. The brutal Frederick William I dared even to hang a noble councilor guilty of petty embezzlement and for a few weeks displayed the corpse in front of the building of the Board of War and Domains in Königsberg as a little memento to his, temporarily, frightened colleagues. Yet, one should not take too seriously Frederick William's promise "to hang and roast" like the czar, "to singe and burn," to inflict "exemplary punishment and in good Russian fashion." Utterances of this kind were but the impotent threats of a frightened individual who from time to time sublimated his rage by getting tipsy on words and expurgatory fantasies.

A consistently serious and strict enforcement of the stark unwritten penal code, which was held like a club over the heads of the Prussian bureaucrats, would have meant the disbanding of the administrative service altogether and the killing of many of its members. The autocratic monarchs of Prussia could oust, banish, jail, or even put to death individual bureaucrats, but they were utterly helpless without the bureaucracy. In real life, therefore, leniency and sluggishness dominated. Rewards proved far more instrumental than penalties in producing the fact as well as the fiction of competent work and of compliance with royal orders. Hope as an incentive to effort, allied, in certain cases, with creative instincts, prevailed over fear. Paradoxically enough, the much talked about "superior efficiency" of the Prussian bureaucracy in the age of dynastic absolutism was at least as much due to the evasion of the disciplinary codes as to their actual enforcement.

Merle Fainsod

The Pervasiveness
of Soviet Controls

One of the salient outgrowths of modern totalitarianism is the bureaucratization of its power structure. The leader who bestrides the peak of the totalitarian edifice is the victim of his own limitations. He cannot decide everything, and even when he exercises his power to decide, he must depend on bureaucratic instruments to project his will. Authority becomes institutionalized, and its fragments are distributed among the manifold sub-bureaucracies which collectively contribute to the illusion of totalitarian omniscience.

The ways of bureaucracy elude totalitarian and nontotalitarian labels. Bureaucracies everywhere generate their own special interests and aspirations. They guard the expert knowledge which is the source of their power and resist the encroachment of interlopers who seek to invade their jurisdiction. They display what Soviet critics have termed "a narrowly departmental approach" and build their loyalties and hopes around the complex of concerns that have been entrusted to their care. They develop their own routines and working habits and are not easily persuaded to abandon them once they have become established. The Soviet bureaucracy manifests many of the traits characteristic of bureaucratic behavior generally.

At the same time, Soviet totalitarianism also imposes its own peculiar requirements on the bureaucracy. Soviet public administration exhibits attributes which sharply differentiate it from the administrative systems prevailing in Western constitutional democracies. Its scope is all-embracing. It seeks to organize the total experience of man in Soviet society. Every branch of the economy and every form

Reprinted by permission of the author and the publishers from Merle Fainsod, *How Russia Is Ruled*, rev. ed., pp. 386-389, 417-420. Cambridge, Mass.: Harvard University Press, Copyright 1953, 1963, by the President and Fellows of Harvard College.

of social expression, from art, music, and letters to sports and the circus, are subject to administrative regulation and direction. The totalitarian imperative drives to transform the nation into a hierarchy of public servants operating within a framework of disciplined subordination to state purposes.

Soviet public administration is one-party administration. The conception of the politically neutral civil servant who serves his successive political masters "with equal fidelity and with equal contempt" is utterly foreign to the Soviet scene. Soviet public administration is suffused with political content. Every field of administration, however technical, is regarded as a channel for the propagation of the Party line and the directives of the top leadership. As Stalin put it, "not a single important political or organizational question is decided by our Soviet and other mass organizations without guiding directions from the Party." The Party itself is a creature of its high command. Functioning in this capacity, it permeates Soviet society, occupies the strategic positions of power in state administration, issues policy instructions which guide administrative activity, checks on their execution, and attempts to serve as an organ of continuous discipline and control.

In practice, this picture of monolithic unity is only imperfectly realized; the struggle of the elite formations of Soviet society for power and influence continues to find expression. The Party apparatus, the police, the army, and the administrative bureaucracy vie with one another for preferment, and the local and departmental interests of different sections of the bureaucracy exercise their counter-influence on the Party. The public affirmations of unanimity on which all totalitarian regimes insist serve to obscure the diversity of interests which they can neither eliminate nor openly acknowledge. Although Soviet totalitarian controls drive some of the most vital interests in the society into a subterranean zone of illegality, other equally important concerns find partial and distorted articulation through the frequently camouflaged processes of bureaucratic representation and manipulation. The play of these pressures continues to operate within the limits imposed by the ruling priorities of the Party leadership. The monolithic control of the Party high command largely takes the form of enforcing its priorities and resolving the conflict which their execution generates. The pressure from above is ruthless and unremitting, and evasion from below is resourceful and not unavailing.

Soviet public administration gives relatively little weight to the rights of the individual as such. Although the arbitrary authority exercised by the security police during the Stalinist era has been curbed and the powers of the courts and the procuracy have been strengthened, public policy remains oriented toward a conception of Party and state interests which every branch of government is dedicated to promote. Safeguards to protect the individual against the abuse of administrative power, which play such an important role in Anglo-American and Continental jurisprudence, are weakly developed. When Soviet jurists speak of administrative responsibility, they have in mind a concept of state service and controls designed to ensure efficient performance of official functions, rather than a set of constitutional or legal restraints on administration aimed to protect individual liberties against state interference. Soviet administrative law in the final analysis is built around the interests of the collectivity as interpreted by the Party leadership.

The Soviet bureaucracy is also characterized by a formidable proliferation of control agencies without parallel in the West. The typical Soviet administrator functions in an environment in which every major decision is subject to the possibility of check, recheck, and countercheck. The long-range plan under which he operates must be approved by the State Planning Commission (Gosplan) and the short-range plan by the All-Union Council of the National Economy. His staff arrangements and financial transactions are subject to the scrutiny of the Minister of Finance. The Party-State Control Committee maintains a watch on his efficiency, seeks to prevent fraud and deception, and checks to make certain that he is fulfilling all government orders and decrees. The Procurator General watches the legality of his actions. The KGB (State Security Committee) enforces security regulations and keeps him under observation to ensure his political reliability. The whole range of his activity, as well as that of the control organs, is always under careful surveillance by representatives of the Party. It is not too far-fetched to describe this complex network of controls as a system of power founded on the institutionalization of mutual suspicion.

The insecurity developed by these arrangements engenders its own antidotes. In order to escape the heavy burden of distrust which the system imposes on those who are involved in it, both controlled and controllers not infrequently cover up for each other's sins and omissions in discharging the tasks for which they are held jointly responsible. The urge to find a peaceful sanctuary is deep-seated among Soviet administrators, and it comes into sharp conflict with the Hobbesian war of all against all upon which the ruling group relies in order to maintain its own control and security. The literature of Soviet administration is filled with criticisms of administrators who enter into so-called family relations with each other and with the control organs that surround them. Despite the virulence of the denunciations, the phenomenon is recurrent, and it apparently registers a strongly felt need to erect barricades against the intrusive checks used by the regime to maintain the pressure of its power. The interstices of every totalitarian regime contain concealed pockets of effective bureaucratic resistance. The Soviet rulers engage in a ceaseless effort to stamp out this resistance and forge the bureaucracy into a pliable instrument of their will.

The history of Soviet public administration is the record of a search for a formula to guarantee both the loyalty and the efficiency of the administrative apparatus. After the seizure of power, the Soviet regime was plagued by an absence of trained administrators in whom the leadership could have confidence. The prerevolutionary bureaucracy was a repository of established governmental routines and procedures, but its skills were not readily adaptable to the new order, and, in any event, many of its members regarded their new overlords with enmity. The Party itself attracted few members trained in the arts of civil administration. The problem of transforming a revolutionary party into a governing party presented real problems. The

qualities which made for success in agitation and propaganda were not easily trans-
ferable to industrial management or other administrative responsibilities. Five years
after the revolution, Lenin commented,

> We now have a vast army of governmental employees, but we lack suffi-
> ciently educated forces to exercise real control over them. Actually, it often
> happens that at the top, where we exercise political power, the machine func-
> tions somehow; but down below, where these state officials are in control,
> they often function in such a way as to counteract our measures. At the top,
> we have I don't know how many, but in any event, I think several thousand,
> at the outside several tens of thousands, of our own people. Down below,
> however, there are hundreds of thousands of old officials who came over to
> us from the Tsar and from bourgeois society and who, sometimes consciously
> and sometimes unconsciously, work against us. Nothing can be done here in
> a short space of time, that is clear. Many years of hard work will be required
> to improve the machine, to reform it, and to enlist new forces.

The Party leadership resorted to a variety of expedients in order to cope with
the problem of its inadequate administrative resources. Since it could not dispense
with the old-regime specialists and bureaucrats, it enlisted them in its service and
surrounded them with Party and police controls in order to ensure their loyalty.
Party members who displayed a talent for administration were sent to special
"industrial academies" for intensive training and assigned to responsible administrative posts. The major long-term effort was concentrated on educating the on-
coming generation for technical and administrative responsibilities. . . .

The Soviet bureaucratic structure is commonly visualized as a tightly centralized
administrative hierarchy in which all initiative and decision-making power are concentrated in the top leadership and in which the lower officials serve as mere
automatons to execute the will of the ruling group. While this stereotype performs
the useful function of emphasizing the high degree of centralization which charac-
terizes the Soviet system, it also distorts reality by ignoring the fluid play of bureaucratic politics that underlies the monolithic totalitarian facade.

The Soviet bureaucracy operates under the strain of constant pressure from
above to accelerate the program of rapid industrialization to which the regime is
committed. This program accords top priority to military needs and the expansion
of heavy industry. Scarce resources are allocated in accordance with these domi-
nating priorities. The "key sectors" which have been chosen for intensive development enjoy a preferential position in the Soviet economy, but no part of the bureaucracy is immune from the insistent and implacable demands of the leadership
for maximum output and effort.

The success of the bureaucracy is judged by its ability to meet the demands
made on it. Since the demands are great and the resources available to meet them

are ordinarily limited, each sector of the bureaucracy is driven to fight for a plan which it can carry out and for an allocation of resources which will enable it to discharge its obligations. This struggle is in essence political. Although it is broadly contained within the framework of the ruling priorities of the leadership, there is still considerable room for maneuver. The planning experts, whose precise calculus is supposed to define the tasks of the bureaucracy, are not divorced from the play of bureaucratic politics. Indeed, the planning bodies are a focal point around which the battle for special treatment rages. The battle is waged by negotiation, by personal influence, and by invoking the assistance of the powerful. Each bureaucratic group is constantly engaged in an effort to mobilize as much political support as it can muster, right up to the member of the Party Presidium responsible for its performance.

Bureaucratic representation in the Soviet context expresses itself in a struggle for preferential advantage. Because each part of the bureaucracy operates with an eye to the feasibility of the demands which are made on it, it becomes an unwitting spokesman for the claims of that sector of Soviet life for which it is responsible. The dictates of survival compel it to mediate between two types of pressure, the drive from above to extract the last reserves of energy from the population and the resistance from below which seeks to tailor commitments to capabilities. In the process, Soviet administrators develop a certain agility in counteracting the squeeze in which they are caught, and the more powerful or influential manage, in some degree at least, to shift the viselike grip to other sections of the bureaucracy or the economy.

This crossfire of pressures occurs at every level of the bureaucratic hierarchy. Once a plan has been determined, the same ministry or regional economic council which has fought for a "reasonable" plan and "favorable" allocations for itself must resist the efforts of its own subordinate enterprises to carve out protected positions for themselves which will shift the squeeze to other enterprises in the same domain. The enterprises, like the ministries and regional economic councils, struggle with every means at their disposal to obtain plan quotas that will be easy to meet and to accumulate large reserves of supplies and other resources to facilitate plan fulfillment. The responsibility of the enterprise is limited to its own performance, while the record of the ministry or sovnarkhoz is the record of all the agencies subordinate to it. The enterprise is in the same difficult position with respect to its component parts.

The tensions generated by the industrialization drive set the stage for a steady tug of war between the central leadership and the bureaucracy. The leadership faces the constant problem of ensuring that the pressure which it exerts will be transmitted to the base of the bureaucratic pyramid and not be diffused and frustrated by bureaucratic manipulation and resistance. The ruling group has developed a variety of ingenious devices to make its control operative throughout the bureaucratic structure. It appeals to the self-interest of the bureaucratic elite by an incentive system which offers attractive bonuses and other large rewards for production in excess of plan. It combines positive incentives with negative controls which impose harsh penalties for failure. It pits one bureaucracy against another and relies on the rivalry between them to enforce its demands on both. It depends heavily on the separately organized Party and police hierarchies to control administration, and it supplements this type of surveillance and pressure by planning, financial, personnel, legal, and investigatory controls which are built into the administrative structure. It endeavors to prevent the growth of "family relations" between the controlled and the controllers by frequent shifts of personnel and by periodic campaigns against officials who cover up for each other's sins. It takes advantage of the activist's desire to move ahead in the Soviet system by stimulating pledges of "over-plan" production and by encouraging denunciations of officials who evade the demands made on them. It seeks to protect the activists and careerists from retaliation by punishing "suppressors of criticism" who attempt to escape the controls which surround them by eliminating the critics in their own domain.

The essence of bureaucratic politics in the Soviet system consists in a search for a viable equilibrium between the pressures from above for maximal output and the inescapable limitations which factors of scarcity and human frailty impose. The successful Soviet administrator must be more than loyal and efficient. He must learn to manipulate the environment around him to meet the demands which are made on him. He cannot afford to be overscrupulous in obeying legal regulations if the price of conformity means failure to meet his set goals. He operates under an overriding compulsion to drive through to plan fulfillment, and every expedient is justified which advances this transcendent purpose. In the Soviet Book of Acts, much is forgiven success, but nothing is forgiven failure.

Despite the remarkable skill with which some administrators manipulate the system for their own ends, the Soviet bureaucracy as a whole responds to the regime's inexorable demand for rapidly expanding industrial production. The pressure from above may be distributed unevenly as it is transmitted through the bureaucratic hierarchy, but it is distributed nonetheless. The administrators who fail to meet the expectations of the leadership disappear from the scene. The drivers and the manipulators survive.

The high-pressure system of Soviet administration imposes its costs. The administrators who drive are also driven, and the toll on their nervous energy and reserves of strength is great. The strain under which they operate is communicated to those below. The ultimate victims are not the administrative and managerial class, but the mass of collective farmers and unskilled and semiskilled workers who bear the major burden of the industrialization effort. The price of forced-draft industrialization is the tensions and dissatisfactions which it inevitably generates.

The Party leadership attempts to protect itself against these consequences by both negative and positive measures. Its powerful instruments of surveillance discourage any overt expression of disloyalty. It acts positively to build a labor aristocracy by reserving special rewards for its Stakhanovites and more productive skilled workers. It places great emphasis on attaching the loyalties of the new Soviet intelligentsia to the regime. It accords a privileged position to its bureaucratic elite and holds out the promise of rapid promotion for the most loyal and talented representatives of the younger generation. This conscious effort on the part of the regime to consolidate a subservient, but nonetheless privileged, layer of bureaucracy between itself and the Soviet populace represents an important aspect of its search for stability. The road which the regime has chosen to tread is that of primary reliance on a system of bureaucratic and Party controls to engage the energies of the masses and to hold popular discontent in check. It builds its power on its elite formations and places its wager on their capacity to command that degree of popular support which even a totalitarian dictatorship needs if it is to function effectively.

Paul Van Riper

American Civil Service Reform

Civil service reform and public personnel management normally lack glamor. We find it difficult to associate heroism with the merit system. Yet this is a topic which has moved men to considerable heights of oratory. It was civil service reform which Senator Roscoe Conkling was aiming at when he hurled his oft-quoted rejoinder to George William Curtis during the New York State Republican Convention of 1877: "When Dr. Johnson defined patriotism as the last refuge of a scoundrel, he was unconscious of the then undeveloped capabilities and uses of the word 'Reform.' "*

Our government is allegedly a government of laws and not of men, but the many and acrimonious quarrels over public office during the course of American history only underline the fact that he who administers the law is often more important than the law itself.

Today it is difficult to conceive of the tremendous changes which have taken place in the American national public service since its reorganization under the Constitution of 1789. Through nearly seventeen decades the federal service has grown from an institution of a few hundred employees to one which, by January 1958, was able to command in peacetime the efforts of some 2,350,000 individuals through its civil branches alone.

Institutional analysis.   The analysis of the development of any modern social institution is, like the whole of which it is but a part, necessarily a complex thing.

*Alfred R. Conkling, *The Life and Letters of Roscoe Conkling* (New York: Charles L. Webster and Co., 1889), p. 541.

Often the interpretative path of least resistance lies in a simple recognition of the metamorphosis of the seeming unities of previous ages into the bewildering multiplicities of a technological civilization. This path has here been foresworn in favor of a more analytical approach. To put the matter another way: the development of the American public service has not been merely the product of a "wonder-working Providence" but rather the result of a developing American social purpose and structure both of which can be systematically outlined. . . .

In broadest outline the evolution of our civil establishment, like that of most other elements in our social system, has involved a peculiar amalgam of largely European theory and practice, catalyzed by and compounded with the events and pressures associated with the dramatic conquering of a continental wilderness. The device of the nonpolitical civil service, which has provided one of the main subjects of study here, and which became embedded in our political system through the Pendleton Act of 1883, was fundamentally a European invention. But from the very beginning the American version of this administrative contrivance assumed a character all its own. We do have today a nonpolitical national service, but it is by no means the precise equivalent of that of England, France, Germany, or any other nation. Many forces have intervened to change the pattern. Unique political habits and institutions, differing views as to the ends to which social institutions ought to be directed, and an enviable and isolated economic position have reacted together to produce a public service which can only be labelled "American."

The first century and the first "reform."   In the early days of the Republic the civil service was designed to serve the needs of a conservative and somewhat aristocratically inclined voting public. While General Washington and his successors in office were interested in competence and efficiency, they were careful to choose as public officials those persons who thought as they did and who represented the interests of what then might legitimately, and in an European sense, have been called the American upper classes. Despite a mild movement toward a broadened base of political action under the Jeffersonian Republicans, the federal civil service remained for forty years primarily the instrument of these classes.

However, as the effects of a rapidly expanding frontier, fostering in turn a more dynamic and free-wheeling economic system, commenced to permeate American society on a significant scale, the government and the politics it represented were reoriented to conform to the individualistic, equalitarian, and decentralizing tendencies of early nineteenth century democracy. A political system designed to assist the commercial and business interests of the Federalists evolved by 1829 into the more inclusive democracy of the agrarian Jacksonians; and the public service, then widely considered to be unrepresentative, was rudely adjusted accordingly. Thus the first reorientation of the American federal service, through the spoils system of Senator Marcy, was the product of an essentially grass roots movement aimed at controlling the government for the benefit of those who, under the stimulus of the Protestant Ethic, would freely exploit the undeveloped resources of a continent.

Andrew Jackson's theories of public office came both to symbolize and to support the individualistic and equalitarian spirit of his times as well as the social mobility characteristic of American society. His concept of the spoils system as "reform" also served to dignify and fortify the organizational system of the new democracy. Democratic politics is considerably more expensive initially than aristocratic politics. In the absence of corporate contributions, the offices furnished that margin of financial and personal incentive which permitted the political machinery of a Martin Van Buren to flourish. The equally important necessity to bridge the gaps within a governmental system based upon both a horizontal and a vertical division of political power, placed a further premium upon any and all devices available for the coordination of public policy now that the unifying forces of the Federalist period were largely gone. But beyond this, the growing size of the executive establishment forced, of necessity, an increasing subletting and delegating of administrative authority, including the appointing power. Thus, the spoils system—and it deserves to be called a system—furnished both a political and an administrative solution to many of the pressing problems of a developing nation.

Nor was the result always as inefficient as frequently charged. In one sense the spoils system as it evolved before the Civil War represented the kind of phenomenon which we now associate with the French cabinet. Every four years or so the "deck was shuffled" again From 1830 to 1860 many of the same familiar figures glided in and out of public office, depending upon the fortunes of politics in that uncertain period of rapidly alternating political control. So, while there was often great turnover in office, there was, as Carl Russell Fish noted a half century ago, never a complete severance from the past. Even the most ardent advocates of rotation in office sometimes wondered if their doctrine was actually as effective as it had been intended to be. And, if efficiency is a function of the accomplishment of social purpose, the spoils system was unquestionably an effective instrument for the implementation of fundamental policy, however repugnant it may seem to fastidious critics.

But, if the spoils system was a radical institution in 1829, it had become a political bulwark of the established order by 1865. Soon, however, this order and all it represented came under attack. The Civil War had greatly accelerated industrialization, the effects of which were quickly felt, if not fully understood, by large portions of the voting public. A society of individualists and equalitarians was gradually conditioned through the sensational and traumatic events of the Gilded Age to an understanding that, in a civilization rapidly being technologically transformed, the Protestant Ethic could lead to some peculiar results not at all in accord with the theories of Jacksonianism. A bewildering rash of stubborn protests against the status quo quickly signified the depth of popular feeling and unrest within many segments of American society.

By the eighteen seventies the problem was not that the voting public failed to understand the nature and value of cooperative effort as a solution to social problems. An earlier age had taught the necessity of collective action through voluntary association in time of need, and corporate enterprise itself was a tribute to the thoroughness with which we had learned that lesson. The difficulty lay in the fact that our individualistic though cooperative society had seldom organized its collective efforts through the compulsory agency of government. In fact, agrarian democracy had fostered a compelling antipathy to the restrictive tendencies of government. Protestantism, here as elsewhere, had reinforced this belief, and there was nothing in a political system based on a separation of powers and federalism to encourage any augmentation of governmental authority.

Nevertheless, large sections of the voting public began to believe for various reasons that they were receiving less than their due of what there was to get. The grass roots pressures for reform steadily built up in strength. Competing for popular favor, there were on the one hand groups like the Populists, who would make fundamental changes in the political and economic structure, and on the other hand, the little eddy of civil service reformers, who desired to attack only the obvious surface symptoms of the underlying difficulties.

The Pendleton Act of 1883 and the second reform.   The proposals of Curtis, Eaton, and Schurz, translated almost verbatim from prior British experience, rejected the approach to civil service reform advocated by Clay, Calhoun, and Webster and typified by the Tenure of Office Act of 1867. The new civil service reformers, aiming at the redirection and refinement of the appointing rather than the removal power, sought to control the distribution of public offices before rather than after the fact. More specifically, the reformers wished to encourage the development in the United States of what we know as the *merit system:* that is, a system of civil service recruitment and tenure based upon (1) competitive entrance examinations, (2) relative security from partisan removal, and (3) political neutrality and nonpartisanship in public office. Had they had their way, the reformers would have gone one step further and, by limiting recruitment to the bottom levels of the service and by emphasizing promotion from within, set the stage for the development of the same closed type of bureaucratic system that was solidifying then in Great Britain.

As has often been the case in this country, the British concept of a neat and orderly devolution of political authority under the parliamentary system appealed to the equally orderly and intellectual minds of American civil service reformers. Congress was, however, much less impressed and, in a series of amendments, modified the original proposals for American consumption. The end product, the historic Pendleton Act of 1883, recognized a growing demand for expertise in the management of public affairs, the need for continuing stability in many portions of the executive establishment, and the popular clamor for a reorientation of the underlying ethics of officeholding. But, it also presaged the evolutionary development of a public service just about as well suited as the spoils system had been to the relatively classless, highly mobile, equalitarian, and individualistic society of the post-Civil War period, and well attuned to the political problems inherent in a constitutional federalism and separation of powers. While we copied the English example in a general way, the civil service law of 1883 clearly indicated that we would take our time about it, that we would develop some characteristics in the organization of our public service which might rightly be considered as all our own, and that we would have extreme difficulty under our fundamental law in developing a service as nonpolitical as that of the British.

Even the reformers themselves, though enamored of British experience, could not tear themselves entirely away from their American environment. First of all, with little or no dissent, they accepted the legislative decision as a proper decision and immediately took an active part in its administrative implementation. But, more important, the ends they sought by means of the reform of the American public service through the merit system were by no means synonymous with those of Northcote and Trevelyan in England. For the British, the renovation of their civil establishment had meant the type of class reorientation of politics which more nearly resembled the American experience in 1829. For the United States, the statute of 1883 was the vehicle for reform and purification of a political system long since democratically oriented. It was in this different guise that the merit system became politically effective in this country.

The American civil service reformers had no quarrel with the basic premises of American society—economic, political, or moral. They had themselves prospered within its framework and saw no reason to question its essential validity. But in the scandals of the era of General Grant, for example, they saw the perversion of the individualistic and equalitarian principles they had always supported. Most of these men had taken an active part in the events leading up to the Civil War, and for them the transference of allegiance from a defunct antislavery movement to civil service reform was simple. To men like Carl Schurz, political bondage to the partisans of the spoils system—whom he and his friends now castigated as the *new aristocracy* of "plunder and patronage"—seemed little more than another form of slavery, with equally vicious implications for the body politic. Curtis, Eaton, Schurz, and the rest merely proposed a sort of purified political man to rescue the economic man from bankruptcy. Through a new and more democratic procedure known as the merit system, they felt many such political men would enter the public service and turn it in new directions. For the second time, the civil bureaucracy was being attacked as unrepresentative of the ideals and aspirations of the nation at large. This time the free competition of the merit system would replace free-wheeling politics as the touchstone to a new democracy and new morality in public life, which, to the civil service reformers, seemed necessary if the nation was to survive.

In simplest terms, all the movement called for was a change in the type of personnel at the helm of the government. Such a program, cloaked in a garb of Victorian morality, was the limit to which the majority of the voting public would permit the legislative branch of the federal government to proceed by 1883. Civil service reform was the reform least objectionable to the immediate interests of the greatest number of voters in the post-Civil War era. It was passed in preference to the more substantive economic measures advocated by Henry George, the Populists, and others like them in their direct approach to reform.

Considered in broader outline, the approval of the Pendleton Act of 1883 represented a temporary resolution of the crucial ethical dilemma then confronting the average citizen, who felt a need for some sort of collective action against the problems then facing him, but who still was deeply and emotionally committed against taking that action through the instrument of coercive public authority. Somehow, if, God willing, *good men*, good more in a moral than efficiency sense, were brought in and left to manage the affairs of the nation, all would be well once again. From one point of view the logic was unassailable, for goodness is, by definition, desirable. What goodness was to consist of in terms of political action was, however, obscure. As Herbert Croly observed, while arguing for another round of reform in 1914:

> . . . The early reformers were not sufficiently thorough. They failed to carry their analysis of the prevailing evils far or deep enough, and in their choice of remedies they never got beyond the illusions that moral exhortation, legal prohibitions and independent voting constituted a sufficient cure for American political abuses.*

Of course, no millennium even approached in the years immediately following the passage of the Pendleton Act. Grover Cleveland, the archetype of the "good political man," was little more successful in solving the problems of the day than his predecessors. As the distinguished reformer, Oswald Villard, later sadly concluded in his autobiography, he and the rest of the country had probably tended to "stress too much getting a 'good man' into high office rather than changing fundamental conditions . . . one always hopes for a short cut."**

In a sense, however, the reformers—and the voting public as well—were right in insisting on civil service reform as the "first" postwar reform. Simple honesty in public affairs and technical competence in administration were necessary before any more fundamental reforms could hope to succeed. The merit system struck a responsive chord in terms of the needs of the modern state, and the new reform, almost the only fundamental governmental reform to be undertaken between 1870 and 1900, was destined to survive and gradually to prosper.

Nevertheless, it began to be quite obvious by the end of the Cleveland era that the placing of good men in office was not sufficient to cure the ills of the body politic. To put it another way: Morality was not enough. Therefore, for the second time since the Civil War, a movement grew urging extensive reforms via the political mechanism.

Progressivism and the civil service.   The Progressives, carrying on under new auspices much of the unfinished business of the Populists, advocated extensive political and economic changes as well as further administrative and structural reforms.

Progressive Democracy (New York: The Macmillan Co., 1914), p. 9.

**Fighting Years* (New York: Harcourt Brace Jovanovich, Inc., 1939), p. 183.

But, for a second time and for similar reasons, the voting public refused to move very far in accepting any stringent control over the distribution of goods and services. Instead, the nation implicitly concluded that, if good men were unable to bring about the changes desired, the trouble lay with the political and administrative *machinery* at their disposal.

Thus, through the late nineties and the early nineteen hundreds, such procedural and organizational reforms as the direct election of senators, the general staff, the Australian ballot, the initiative, referendum, and recall, and the reorganization of state and local government were legislatively implemented in rapid succession. Public administration became respectable as a field of political science; bureaus for administrative research mushroomed; scientific management influenced the industrial as well as the governmental world; and under President Taft the first comprehensive inquiry into the nature of the federal administrative and organizational mechanism was made under the new watchword of "economy and efficiency."

The ethical imperatives of the nineteenth century were still too strong and the reality to which they were related not sufficiently unattractive for most Americans to react to the requirements of social change through much more than another variation of the old morality. Again, the voting public took what seemed to be the easiest way out. Administrative reform immediately threatened the income or position of relatively few individuals and was, in addition, most attractive to a business world which was beginning to feel the press of increasing taxation. Economy and efficiency—in a dollars-and-cents, short-term, business sense rather than in any long-term social sense—was extremely appealing to the large segment of the population which felt that, since it had prospered through such methods, government also could not help but benefit.

Under Theodore Roosevelt the public service began to be subjected to the influence of the drive for administrative and organizational reform. Itself a kind of mechanical procedure, the merit system easily floated along in the main stream of the larger movement, profiting this time from a secondary rather than primary role. Under energetic presidential auspices, the competitive segment of the civil service quickly expanded to a point beyond which it was not to proceed far for nearly thirty years. The rules governing the competitive service were recodified in a form to last just as long. The concept of a career service was formulated and actively promoted; and the boundary lines between the permanent service and the patronage were clarified. Civil service reform thus commenced a metamorphosis into public personnel management. On the outside, the National Civil Service Reform League began to discard the moral diatribes of its youth for calmer paragraphs on the dollars-and-cents value of the merit system; and superannuation, position-classification, and salary adjustments developed into secondary political issues. The prestige of the service was not yet very high and it possessed little sense of corporate unity, but under the stimulating guidance of Theodore Roosevelt, morale was clearly rising. It would not be long before the civil bureaucracy, nourished by the positive state, would be close to the center of political power.

However, great doses of economy and efficiency were unable to forestall the political debacle of William Howard Taft in 1912. The economic problems which had pressed for solution in the eighteen eighties and nineties still cried out for action. Grover Cleveland and Theodore Roosevelt had merely prepared the way for the great ground swell of public opinion which rose to a crest in the election of Woodrow Wilson to the Presidency and which demanded modification of the economic system through governmental intervention. By this date a large proportion of the voting population had implicitly or explicitly concluded that a good man with good organizational machinery could not cope with the times. Morality had not been enough. Nor was a simple renovation of the apparatus of American democracy sufficient, either.

The civil service and the positive state: the first phase.   But bringing the New Freedom to legislative fruition was not accomplished without a struggle in which the heretofore steady growth of the merit system came to a grinding halt. Once again, as the exigencies of economic politics taxed the power of the chief executive to turn his election mandates into reality, the manipulation of the public offices provided a major means for more exalted ends. Despite his previous connections with the National Civil Service Reform League, Woodrow Wilson quickly learned, under the astute guidance of his Postmaster General, that in full-scale political warfare all weapons must be used.

The merit system was not completely eclipsed, but the great progress of the first decade of the twentieth century was rudely interrupted, first by the Democratic demands for patronage after decades of frustration, and later by the requirements of the First World War. Amid the more basic quarrels over fundamental national and international policies, the problems of the federal service tended to drop further and further from the political consciousness of both Congress and the general public. Simultaneously, the wartime inflation underscored the failure of the federal government to keep the pay and perquisites of the civil service abreast of those of private industry. In 1916 the wage curves of government and business finally crossed, with that for the federal service dropping below that of private industry for the first time in American history. Employee turnover skyrocketed to heights hardly contemplated even under the spoils system, and within two years the first service-wide union of public employees was organized and in action. All this only highlighted the chaotic state of federal public administration by the end of World War I and the failure of Congress to pay much attention to the needs of the service as outlined in 1913 by the Commission on Economy and Efficiency of President Taft.

That the public service did not suffer more in the years before 1920 was in part due to the fact that, after all, the Wilsonian program was hardly a revolutionary one. Moreover, the impact of the spate of legislation between 1913 and 1915, as well as the demands of global warfare, brought the greatest expansion of the federal service up to that time. With the patronage system and other types of informal recruitment completely inadequate to meet the wartime personnel requirements, the Civil Service Commission served for the first time as a central recruiting agency for the great bulk of the federal mechanism. As a result of its wartime endeavors, the Commission significantly influenced—also for the first time—the personnel procedures of private industry. In the technical aspects of examination and recruitment the federal government was by 1920 considerably ahead of business and industry, and in the years to follow many private employers were quick to apply these aspects of the merit system to their own affairs.

Far more important, however, was the explosive suggestion, implicit in the wartime expansion of governmental authority, that there might be some merit in the radical idea that government could be a positive good. For the experience of the war years had clearly demonstrated that, when the nation so desired, almost any scale of collective endeavor was feasible. The positive potential of a coordinated supervision of the American productive machine was, to be sure, only briefly and imperfectly illustrated at this time. But the idea remained, and the slowly but surely increasing prestige of the federal public service in recent decades may best be dated from this point. So also may we date from this time the beginning of the effective decline of the nineteenth century version of the Protestant Ethic which had for so long tended to estop the growth of the positive state.

Even so, when the dangers of war were over and the twenties commenced to prosper, the American public, as if in penance for its brief aberration, turned to the past. The old voluntaristic ethic seemed valid once more. But it was not quite the same. There could be no return to unbridled competition. Rather, a version of the New Nationalism first asserted by Theodore Roosevelt came to the fore. Under this doctrine the new Progressive State which the Republicans had inherited was turned to the positive support of private enterprise as opposed to its limitation and control. The business of government was now explicitly business, and the great new granite structure housing Hoover's cherished Department of Commerce symbolized the new conception of government.

While the great growth of the public service under Woodrow Wilson was quickly arrested, the number of civil employees was never reduced to within 100,000 of its prewar total. The federal service was by no means placed on a pedestal during the twenties, but neither was it seriously challenged. Indeed, under the business orientation of the Republican party the economy and efficiency of President Taft flowered again, with considerable benefit to the service. The Budget and Accounting Act of 1921 provided a much-needed governmental control mechanism, with the President's hand in fiscal affairs greatly strengthened. By 1923 both a new retirement system and a new position-classification scheme had been put into effect, and shortly thereafter the first personnel director for a major federal department was appointed. Under Coolidge, the Harding scandals were quickly brought under control, and with President Hoover came the first of a long series of executive reorganizations. By 1932 the merit system encompassed 80 percent of the offices and the Civil Service Commission was close to becoming the central public personnel agency which had been envisioned twenty years earlier.

Meanwhile, however, Calvin Coolidge had reportedly predicted to his Secret Service bodyguard, Colonel Edmund Starling, "They're going to elect that superman Hoover, and he's going to have some trouble. He's going to have to spend money. But he won't spend enough."* Those in political power during the early thirties could not reach past their ethical views of the proper function of government for the political invention necessary to meet the economic crisis. Their answer to depression was, as it had always been, economy and charity; and civil servants suffered with everyone else.

The civil service and the positive state: the second phase.   In 1932 the Democrats also suggested economy. But when Franklin D. Roosevelt came into office the unprecedented necessities of immediate events swept the administration far past its campaign promises into the famous Hundred Days. It took no revolution to transfer almost overnight to the national government more power over persons and property than any government in this country had ever effectively possessed except during the First World War. The American social system had always been capable of cooperation when the need was great enough, and the collectivist effort under the auspices of the Blue Eagle was marked with a sort of religious fervor. Government assumed an importance it had never before enjoyed during peacetime. Stimulated both by a sincere desire to be of service during a crisis as well as by a lack of employment opportunities in private enterprise, an unusually large number of the more socially inventive graduates from the nation's educational system entered the public service during the years before the Second World War. The administration, somewhat fearful of the traditional practice of calling upon the business community for emergency assistance, encouraged this trend. For the first time the federal service ranked high as an occupational goal among the youth of the nation. In turn, under the aegis of the New Deal and its truly powerful concept of positive political action, the civil bureaucracy reached the apex of its prestige and power during the first half of the twentieth century.

This was by no means a neutral and nonpartisan civil bureaucracy recruited entirely through staid merit system procedures. Indeed, throughout the first term of Franklin D. Roosevelt, the merit system was hard put to maintain itself. The public service had always felt the impact of a change in party control; and under F. D. R. and the unprecedented problems of the thirties, all things, including the offices, were subordinated to the politics of profound social change. Fortunately for those in the competitive service in 1933, enough new offices were created to forestall a patronage raid of the McKinley variety, but civil service reform was shelved for nearly five years. Nor was it revived until the merit system and the administrative machinery of the government became so neglected and their state of disrepair so shocking that it was realized something would have to be done or the entire social program might be endangered. The President's Committee on Administrative Management pointed the way to reform in 1937. At the same time, the gradually improving economic conditions gave the American public a breathing spell in which to consider the possible dangers inherent in placing almost unlimited

*Thomas Sugrue, *Starling of the White House* (New York: Simon and Schuster, 1946), p. 263.

powers at the disposal of the executive branch. Only then did civil service reform again, for the first time since the eighteen eighties, become an important political issue on which even F. D. R. felt he was vulnerable.

From 1938 through 1940 social politics stood aside while a renewed concern over the state of the public service manifested itself. As the whole civil establishment was tightened and centralized, so also with public personnel management. The Civil Service Commission at long last found itself at the helm of a consolidated system of public employment. Meanwhile, the loose employment procedures of the thirties had brought into the service a multitude of persons from private enterprise, the universities, and elsewhere, with the result that both the service in general and personnel management in particular were fairly bubbling with new procedures and concepts, many of them imported from the nongovernmental world. This meant the end of the traditional isolation of public and private personnel management into separate and almost watertight compartments. Cross-fertilization between the two was henceforth to become more and more the norm rather than the exception. This presaged another type of struggle, however, between those who saw the prime function of the merit system as control of the patronage and those who looked forward to the elimination of rigid controls in favor of the industrial concept of personnel work as a positive aid to line management.

Almost immediately, however, it was necessary rapidly to readjust the federal service to the requirements of another world war. Centralization of personnel management became of necessity an extremely loose decentralization. Examinations were reduced to interviews, and the old procedural controls of the merit system were greatly relaxed. With the tremendous demand for civil and military personnel and the virtual disappearance of unemployment, the problem of manpower allocation and control arose for the first time. The spirit of our second great wartime cooperative effort was still voluntaristic. But it was an intensely felt voluntarism, verging almost on submission and carrying with it an extraordinary concentration of governmental authority. By 1945 the nation seemed almost one vast public service, with the executive branch of the government at the helm and at the height of its power under F. D. R.'s astute political guidance.

But, with Roosevelt's death and the end of the war, both the spirit and the framework of the voluntaristic house of cards began to collapse. Yet it left behind it a vastly strengthened sense of the potentialities of collective effort and a heightened desire to fulfill more completely than after World War I some of the alleged goals of the war. A renewed fear of depression and the continuation of Cold War on the international scene somewhat bolstered the political forces in favor of maintaining a government of positive powers through a time of peace and relative prosperity. However, the sedative effects of continued prosperity, the evident power of communism, and a reaction against the overwhelming power of an executive branch which had often generated as much controversy as it had settled, combined to produce an almost schizophrenic attitude toward government during the late forties. The fact that, while we had won the war, almost nothing seemed settled, only built up the tension. Typically, a scapegoat was sought and for many it became the federal service, which for a decade had loomed so large on the political scene.

Underneath, two fundamental ethical imperatives were clashing. By 1945 the old Jacksonian combination of liberty and equality had split, with business enterprise emphasizing the former, labor the latter, and agriculture somewhere in between. Many saw in the New Deal a slow but sure drift to socialism and sought refuge again in the individualism of the old Protestant Ethic. Others, seeing the ameliorating effects of New Deal social legislation in terms of equality and security, sought to build even further on the newer Social Ethic. Further complicating the issue and effectively blocking any solution in fully traditional terms were the exasperating requirements of foreign policy. From 1945 through 1952 American politics was fought more along ideological lines than during any period since the late nineteenth century and, before that, just prior to the Civil War. Once again the struggle was to a great extent focused on the civil service as not only a prime symbol but also an effective center of political power.

Under the combined impact of the post-World War II reduction-in-force, the expansion and contraction stimulated by the Korean affair, the struggle of Congress to regain something of its former political status at the expense of the executive branch, a new and trying loyalty program, and a series of scandals, the service was hard put to maintain itself. Basically, three major forces were at play on the civil bureaucracy during the Truman administration. While the Civil Service Commission struggled valiantly to rebuild the merit system, others, with their power largely centered in Congress, were attempting to bring the civil service to heel. In addition, the new concepts of employment security which had been focused on private industry during the thirties were turned toward the federal service, with the encouragement of veterans organizations, the public employee unions, and the many others who simply sought to control the discretion of the executive branch through any means at command. This meant that, while the Civil Service Commission, the First Hoover Commission, and most administrators sought a new decentralization in personnel management, much postwar legislation, particularly that concerning veteran preference, more or less explicitly worked in favor of centralization.

Not only was the political system operating at cross purposes, but the merit system of the Pendleton Act was being used as a control mechanism in a manner which had never been intended by Curtis, Eaton, and Schurz in 1883. All this generated, in turn, still further inequities and insecurities, for the service was simply too great and complex to be efficiently governed through relatively rigid rules administered from the top of a hierarchy. If the Social Ethic was producing peculiar results within industry by the postwar decade, so it was also within the civil bureaucracy. Despite the warnings of the first civil service reformers, both the front and back doors to their merit system were largely closed by 1950. This resulted in considerable confusion within the federal establishment and contributed to the steady decline in public employee morale.

Meanwhile, a strengthened if somewhat discordant Republicanism approached the election of 1952 determined to make the pruning and cleansing of the federal service a major issue of the campaign. Thus President Eisenhower came into office with a popular mandate to do something about the "mess in Washing-ton." Once again, for the third time, there was a widespread feeling that the federal service was unrepresentative. In a limited sense the charge was true. The temper of the service as a whole was unquestionably more in tune with a positive state than with a concept of a national government with strictly limited powers. The new administration's distrust of the civil bureaucracy became almost immediately apparent through a simultaneous stepping up of economy moves, security efforts, and patronage manipulations along with congressional investigations. Again employee morale plummeted, to reach in 1954 a new low for the last thirty years. That the Republicans moved more slowly in reorienting the civil establishment than many of its partisans had hoped, was a tribute both to the President's unwillingness to permit a full scale spoils raid and to the fact that most of the service was by this time sufficiently indoctrinated with the concept of political neutrality to be able to serve a new master effectively. Prosperity and full employment further relieved some of the pressure.

At the same time, however, the business orientation of the new administration supported a major attack, reminiscent in tenor of the twenties, upon many fundamental personnel problems. In this effort even Congress finally acquiesced with a good deal of grace, largely ceasing its negative and restrictive approach to personnel matters in favor of more positive legislation in support of the President's program. With almost textbook attention to the views of the President's Committee on Administrative Management of 1937 and the First Hoover Commission, the Civil Service Commission was reorganized and strengthened as an arm of the executive branch, the line between the patronage and the permanent service was sharpened, the service was for the first time cushioned against the impact of emergencies, pay and fringe benefits were increased to more competitive levels, training and employee development programs were promoted on an increasingly effective scale, some dents were made in the traditional departmentalization of the service, civil-military personnel relations were given long overdue attention, and decentralization in public personnel management was again greatly stressed. In sum total this was perhaps the most impressive set of accomplishments ever realized on the federal personnel scene during any equivalent period. Even the Second Hoover Commission found little fault with this program in main outline. As a result of these actions as well as a growing understanding of the requirements of governmental administration on the part of the new political executives, morale was clearly on the upturn in 1955 for the first time in a decade. If at the end of Eisenhower's first term the administration and the civil bureaucracy were hardly the bosom friends they had been under Roosevelt, they were at least mutually respectful of each other's position, a state of affairs which in the long run is probably more desirable.

The election of 1956 confirmed Eisenhower's popularity. It also confirmed the positive state and the civil bureaucracy which it implies. However, this was not a New Deal confirmation on ideological grounds. Rather, the election signified a relatively rational acceptance of the fact that most of what the federal government was doing needed doing in light of the times. In a sense, the Eisenhower administration's chief claim to fame will probably lie in its very considerable success in stimulating a return to a pragmatic conception of politics. Such a concept, which lies at the heart of the New Republicanism, means the assessment of the relative merits of individualism and equality, and the legislation relating to them, more in terms of everyday workability and practice than of theory. Compared to the New Deal, this is conservatism, but a conservatism more like that of Andrew Jackson and Abraham Lincoln than that of Mark Hanna and William McKinley.

What was happening underneath was, of course, that the Protestant Ethic had been generating its own purgative in the form of political rules controlling the distribution of goods, services, and income. The immediate success of these rules had somewhat undermined the surface validity of the old Protestant Ethic in favor of a new Social Ethic. But by mid-century the Social Ethic and the regulations it brought with it had produced so many unanticipated consequences that it, too, was being challenged. In effect, the Protestant and Social Ethics were to some extent cancelling each other out, with a new amalgam beginning to form. This synthesis, while modifying the Social Ethic's Weberian concept of a hierarchic organization with rigid controls in favor of pluralism and decentralization, also sought to conserve much of the Protestant Ethic's individualism through a new human relations emphasis on the recognition of individual dignity and potential creativity.

Into the future.   . . . Finally, there is the possibility of a new theory of public administration, including public personnel management, in which the emphasis may lie more on what is now being called "democracy in administration" and less on centralization and all-embracing control systems designed more to prevent than to produce.

Lest these conclusions seem too optimistic, we must recognize, of course, that politics can never be placid. The form and functions of the civil bureaucracy of the national government will never cease to be of great and legitimate concern to the body politic. This is likely to be especially true when the bureaucracy is so close to the center of political power. However, it seems clear that by the beginning of Eisenhower's second term in the White House another great watershed in American political development had been reached, this time signifying that at long last the need for an intelligent, flexible, and well organized civil service had been accepted by the great majority of the nation.

5
The Impact of Bureaucracy on Society

Bureaucracy is a part of the American heritage, as we have seen. It is likely to follow us all the days of our lives. Therefore it is proper to inquire, with historical perspective, about bureaucracy's impact on our society and the effects it may have in the future.

Why is bureaucracy so clearly here to stay? Max Weber, in our second selection from *From Max Weber: Essays in Sociology*, suggests that most power holders have simply found that bureaucracy is indispensable if the enormous tasks facing society are to be attempted at all. The alternatives are grim. "If the official stops working, or if his work is forcefully interrupted, chaos results, and it is difficult to improvise replacements from among the governed who are fit to master such chaos." The same principles hold true, *mutatis mutandis*, in private bureaucracies like large corporations. Bureaucracy is not totally unassailable, Weber concedes, but as a practical matter he argues that "the idea of eliminating these organizations becomes more and more utopian."

If bureaucracy indeed has great power, there are, inevitably, both practical and theoretical problems in its relation to the power of the people in a democracy. In the selection from *Inside Bureaucracy*, Anthony Downs contends that as bureaucratization proliferates, social efficiency increases, and individual freedom of choice is maximized. Hyman Rickover, famous for his role as the father of the atomic submarine, is not as optimistically trusting and asks in his article whether bureaucracy "can smoothly be integrated into democracy." In practical terms, the great expansion of bureaucracy caused by technology, urbanization, the population explosion, and American "giantism," has made a smooth integration absolutely necessary in Rickover's opinion. We are ill equipped to deal with this theoretically, he says, because the institutionalization of bureaucracy was not anticipated by the architects of our system. Instead, we have been saddled with the effects of uncoordinated *ad hoc* decisions about the place of bureaucracy. We suffer from the politicization of the higher levels of the civil service. Worst of all, the pure administrator, a man who directs organizations for a living, has emerged into prominence; he has neither the popular mandate of the politician nor the technical qualifications of the people who actually do the work. This kind of man, given access to the power of bureaucracy, can pose a grave threat to democracy, according to Rickover. His solution for this is the adaptation of professionalized European bureaucratic standards. "The more we professionalize bureaucracy," Rickover avers, "the more democratic it will become. A hierarchy based purely on merit diminishes no man."

Thus we return to the merit concept, which in Admiral Rickover's prescription will convert the impact of bureaucracy on democracy into a positive force. Michael Young has explored the implications of this more thoroughly, however, in his brilliant social satire, *The Rise of the Meritocracy 1870-2033*. The narrator of this book is a British sociologist of the twenty-first century who assesses the state of his country on the eve of a great rally of social protest. England has been greatly changed in the preceding sixty years by the application of the civil service merit model to all of education and society. The upper class in 2033 is composed solely of the very able and intelligent. They are selected at an early age by means of psychological I.Q. tests, given the best education, and placed in control of society. They are of course compensated for their work extremely well, and given "books to inform, music to stimulate, wines to soothe." Meanwhile the lower class is composed solely of the stupid. They do the manual work. They get far less money. They don't need books, their music is raucous, and their drink is beer, which they must pay for. They have been given every chance to demonstrate hidden intelligence and so rise in society, but the lower class by definition has been found wanting and its members know it. Now, if it is true that "a hierarchy based on merit diminishes no man," the lower class so envisioned ought to be content with its position, in the manner of Huxley's lowly Deltas and Epsilon morons in *Brave New World*. But alas! "For the first time in human history the inferior man has no redress to buttress his self-regard. . . . Men who have lost their self-respect are liable to lose their inner vitality . . . and may only too easily cease to be either good citizens or good technicians. The common man is liable to sulk for his fig-leaf." Young's chapter on "The Status of the Worker," an excerpt of which is included in our selection, leaves the reader to draw his own conclusions. But it is at least clear that the mating of democracy and bureaucracy will require the two institutions to be more mature than they presently are.

It is instructive to compare Young's vision with the nature of contemporary Communism. Presumably, bureaucracy attains its ultimate impact when bureaucrats fashion a state in their image, and run it to serve their own interests. This is the thesis of the one-time high Yugoslav government official Milovan Djilas in *The*

New Class, a book that has provoked great antagonism in the Communist world it analyzes. In the Russian Revolution of 1917, professional revolutionaries led by the Bolshevik faction of the Communist party established a new state, the U.S.S.R. When the revolutionaries turned to the tasks of administering the state, the Party became the core of the new ruling class. According to Djilas, the new class consists of the political bureaucracy, in the U.S.S.R. and in other Communist countries. The new class completely controls society and ultimately owns it. Unlike the meritocracy of intelligence described by Young, anyone who wants to join the new class under Communism must prove his merit as a future bureaucrat by demonstrating loyalty to the Party. The impact of bureaucracy, following this analysis, is as close to total as possible. Although "all changes initiated by the Communist chiefs are dictated first of all by the interests and aspirations of the new class . . . this does not mean, however, that such changes may not be important for the rest of the people as well." Even a Communist bureaucracy in full control must at length make at least minimal adjustments of bureaucratic interests and procedures to the requirements of society. Some small comfort may be taken as a result.

In conclusion, it is ironic that in cases when bureaucrats as a class have the most power, they turn it on themselves as well as on society. As Djilas says, "On the one hand, Communism is open and kind to all; on the other hand, it is exclusive and intolerant even of its own adherents." Djilas ought to know. He has spent years in Yugoslav jails.

Max Weber

The Durability of Bureaucracy

THE PERMANENT CHARACTER OF THE BUREAUCRATIC MACHINE

Once it is fully established, bureaucracy is among those social structures which are the hardest to destroy. Bureaucracy is *the* means of carrying "community action" over into rationally ordered "societal action." Therefore, as an instrument for "societalizing" relations of power, bureaucracy has been and is a power instrument of the first order—for the one who controls the bureaucratic apparatus.

Under otherwise equal conditions, a "societal action," which is methodically

Abridged from *From Max Weber: Essays in Sociology*, edited and translated by H. H. Gerth and C. Wright Mills, pp. 228-232. Copyright 1946 by Oxford University Press, Inc. Reprinted by permission.

ordered and led, is superior to every resistance of "mass" or even of "communal action." And where the bureaucratization of administration has been completely carried through, a form of power relation is established that is practically unshatterable.

The individual bureaucrat cannot squirm out of the apparatus in which he is harnessed. In contrast to the honorific or avocational "notable," the professional bureaucrat is chained to his activity by his entire material and ideal existence. In the great majority of cases, he is only a single cog in an ever-moving mechanism which prescribes to him an essentially fixed route of march. The official is entrusted with specialized tasks and normally the mechanism cannot be put into motion or arrested by him, but only from the very top. The individual bureaucrat is thus forged to the community of all the functionaries who are integrated into the mechanism. They have a common interest in seeing that the mechanism continues its functions and that the societally exercised authority carries on.

The ruled, for their part, cannot dispense with or replace the bureaucratic apparatus of authority once it exists. For this bureaucracy rests upon expert training, a functional specialization of work, and an attitude set for habitual and virtuoso-like mastery of single yet methodically integrated functions. If the official stops working, or if his work is forcefully interrupted, chaos results, and it is difficult to improvise replacements from among the governed who are fit to master such chaos. This holds for public administration as well as for private economic management. More and more the material fate of the masses depends upon the steady and correct functioning of the increasingly bureaucratic organizations of private capitalism. The idea of eliminating these organizations becomes more and more utopian.

The discipline of officialdom refers to the attitude-set of the official for precise obedience within his *habitual* activity, in public as well as in private organizations. This discipline increasingly becomes the basis of all order, however great the practical importance of administration on the basis of the filed documents may be. The naive idea of Bakuninism of destroying the basis of "acquired rights" and "domination" by destroying public documents overlooks the settled orientation of *man* for keeping to the habitual rules and regulations that continue to exist independently of the documents. Every reorganization of beaten or dissolved troops, as well as the restoration of administrative orders destroyed by revolt, panic, or other catastrophes, is realized by appealing to the trained orientation of obedient compliance to such orders. Such compliance has been conditioned into the officials, on the one hand, and, on the other hand, into the governed. If such an appeal is successful it brings, as it were, the disturbed mechanism into gear again.

The objective indispensability of the once-existing apparatus, with its peculiar, "impersonal" character, means that the mechanism—in contrast to feudal orders based upon personal piety—is easily made to work for anybody who knows how to gain control over it. A rationally ordered system of officials continues to function smoothly after the enemy has occupied the area; he merely needs to change the top officials. This body of officials continues to operate because it is to the vital interest of everyone concerned, including above all the enemy.

During the course of his long years in power, Bismarck brought his ministerial colleagues into unconditional bureaucratic dependence by eliminating all independent statesmen. Upon his retirement, he saw to his surprise that they continued to manage their offices unconcerned and undismayed, as if he had not been the master mind and creator of these creatures, but rather as if some single figure had been exchanged for some other figure in the bureaucratic machine. With all the changes of masters in France since the time of the First Empire, the power machine has remained essentially the same. Such a machine makes "revolution," in the sense of the forceful creation of entirely new formations of authority, technically more and more impossible, especially when the apparatus controls the modern means of communication (telegraph, etc.) and also by virtue of its internal rationalized structure. In classic fashion, France has demonstrated how this process has substituted *coups d'état* for "revolutions": all successful transformations in France have amounted to *coups d'état*.

ECONOMIC AND SOCIAL CONSEQUENCES OF BUREAUCRACY

It is clear that the bureaucratic organization of a social structure, and especially of a political one, can and regularly does have far-reaching economic consequences. But what sort of consequences? Of course in any individual case it depends upon the distribution of economic and social power, and especially upon the sphere that is occupied by the emerging bureaucratic mechanism. The consequences of bureaucracy depend therefore upon the direction which the powers using the apparatus give to it. And very frequently a crypto-plutocratic distribution of power has been the result.

In England, but especially in the United States, party donors regularly stand behind the bureaucratic party organizations. They have financed these parties and have been able to influence them to a large extent. The breweries in England, the so-called "heavy industry," and in Germany the Hansa League with their voting funds are well enough known as political donors to parties. In modern times bureaucratization and social leveling within political, and particularly within state organizations in connection with the destruction of feudal and local privileges, have very frequently benefited the interests of capitalism. Often bureaucratization has been carried out in direct alliance with capitalist interests, for example, the great historical alliance of the power of the absolute prince with capitalist interests. In general, a legal leveling and destruction of firmly established local structures ruled by notables has usually made for a wider range of capitalist activity. Yet one may expect as an effect of bureaucratization, a policy that meets the petty bourgeois interest in a secured traditional "subsistence," or even a state socialist policy that strangles opportunities for private profit. This has occurred in several cases of historical and far-reaching importance, specifically during antiquity; it is undoubtedly to be expected as a future development. Perhaps it will occur in Germany.

The very different effects of political organizations which were, at least in principle, quite similar—in Egypt under the Pharaohs and in Hellenic and Roman times—show the very different economic significances of bureaucratization which are possible according to the direction of other factors. The mere fact of bureaucratic organization does not unambiguously tell us about the concrete direction of its economic effects, which are always in some manner present. At least it does not tell us as much as can be told about its relatively leveling effect socially. In this respect, one has to remember that bureaucracy as such is a precision instrument which can put itself at the disposal of quite varied—purely political as well as purely economic, or any other sort—of interests in domination. Therefore, the measure of its parallelism with democratization must not be exaggerated, however typical it may be. Under certain conditions, strata of feudal lords have also put bureaucracy into their service. There is also the possibility—and often it has become a fact, for instance, in the Roman principate and in some forms of absolutist state structures—that a bureaucratization of administration is deliberately connected with the formation of *estates*, or is entangled with them by the force of the existing groupings of social power. The express reservation of offices for certain status groups is very frequent, and actual reservations are even more frequent. The democratization of society in its totality, and in the *modern* sense of the term, whether actual or perhaps merely formal, is an especially favorable basis of bureaucratization, but by no means the only possible one. After all, bureaucracy strives merely to level those powers that stand in its way and in those areas that, in the individual case, it seeks to occupy. We must remember this fact—which we have encountered several times and which we shall have to discuss repeatedly: that "democracy" as such is opposed to the "rule" of bureaucracy, in spite and perhaps because of its unavoidable yet unintended promotion of bureaucratization. Under certain conditions, democracy creates obvious ruptures and blockages to bureaucratic organization. Hence, in every individual historical case, one must observe in what special direction bureaucratization has developed.

Anthony Downs

Social Efficiency
and Individual Freedom

There is a widespread belief that U.S. society is becoming more and more "bureaucratized" because of the rising prominence of large organizations in American life.

A RAND Corporation research study. Copyright © 1967 by The RAND Corporation. Reprinted from *Inside Bureaucracy*, pp. 253-260, by permission of the author, publisher Little, Brown and Company, Inc., and The RAND Corporation.

This trend is universally regarded as undesirable. Its stronger critics think that the average individual will become enmeshed in a tightening net of rules and regulations formulated by huge, "faceless" organizations. They also fear that society will become dominated by empire building, wasteful spending, egregious blunders, miles of red tape, frustrating delays, "buck-passing," and other horrors they attribute to bureaucracy.

This article will discuss whether or not bureaucratization is really increasing, what might be causing its prevailing trends, and what their likely impact will be upon individual freedom and the efficiency of social action.

IS SOCIETY BECOMING MORE BUREAUCRATIC?

The following phenomena could be interpreted as evidence that a given society is becoming more bureaucratic:

—A rising proportion of the labor force employed by large, nonmarket organizations (such as government agencies).

—Increasing regulation of political, economic, social, and cultural life by such organizations.

—A rising proportion of the labor force consisting of persons who work for large, market-oriented firms but who produce outputs that cannot be evaluated in markets. This could occur in one or both of the following ways:

1. A rising proportion of the labor force employed in large firms, but without any accompanying change in the proportion of employees within those firms who produce no directly marketable products.

2. A shift of employment distribution within large firms that increases the proportion of workers therein who produce no directly marketable products.

Since this is primarily a theoretical study, we will not try to make a thorough examination of the facts concerning these potential indicators. Rather, we will merely cite a few relevant statistics.

First, the proportion of the total labor force in the United States employed by all governments is rising at an impressive rate. This is shown in Table 4.

Since most government employees work in bureaus, this is significant evidence that the government bureaucracy of the United States is growing both absolutely and relatively. Moreover, it has grown considerably faster since World War II than it did before.

Second, we cannot formulate any measures that would reliably indicate whether the degree of regulation by bureaus is rising or falling. However, there is a widespread informal consensus that the absolute level of government regulation over a wide spectrum of activities has markedly increased since World War II. This conclusion is supported by the fact that governments employ a higher proportion of the labor force and absorb a higher proportion of the total national output than ever before in peacetime.

Third, there is some evidence that large firms in the private sector of the U.S.

economy have recently grown faster than small ones. From 1947 to 1961, the number of corporations rose 115.6 percent, whereas the total number of firms rose only 41.0 percent. Although not all corporations are large, average total receipts per corporation in 1961 were $692,389. This is 37 times greater than the analogous average for sole proprietorships ($18,500), and almost nine times greater than the average for active partnerships ($78,182). Moreover, although corporations comprised only 10.5 percent of all private firms in 1961, they took in 77.1 percent of all private business receipts. These data also indicate that corporations have grown in relative importance, since in 1947 they comprised 6.8 percent of all firms and took in 68.8 percent of all private business receipts.

Table 4
Total Government Employment Including Military

Year	Number (thousands)	Percentage of Total Employed Labor Force
1900	1,110	4.1
1910	1,736	4.9
1920	2,529	6.3
1930	3,310	7.3
1940	3,762	8.3
1950	7,245	12.3
1960	10,867	15.7
1965	12,534	16.8

Sources: U.S. Bureau of the Census, *Statistical Abstract of the United States: 1965*, 86th Edition (Washington, D.C., 1965), pp. 216, 440; Council of Economic Advisers, *Economic Indicators: November 1965,* (Washington, D.C., 1965), pp. 10-13; Solomon Fabricant, *The Trend of Government Activity in the United States Since 1900* (New York: National Bureau of Economic Research, 1952).

These figures do not prove that large private firms employ a higher proportion of the total labor force than they did right after World War II. However, the data do indicate that they account for a growing proportion of total employment by all private firms, thereby increasing the possibility that a person working for a private firm will be a bureaucrat since bureaucrats can exist only in large organizations.

Finally, within large private firms there has been a significant shift from production jobs to administrative jobs. By 1964 this percentage had risen to 26.0. Production jobs are much easier to relate to market prices through cost accounting methods than administrative jobs. Hence this rise in the relative significance of administration in manufacturing firms indicates at least a strong possibility that bureaucracy in such firms has increased.

Admittedly, the above evidence is hardly conclusive. Nevertheless, it tends to provide some confirmation for the impression that bureaucratization in the United States is on the increase.

SOME POSSIBLE CAUSES OF INCREASING BUREAUCRATIZATION

Four possible causes of such increasing bureaucratization are all connected with the tendencies of modern societies to grow larger in total population, more complex in specialization, more sophisticated in technology, more urbanized, and wealthier per capita as time passes.

First, as societies become more complex, they generate more conflicts requiring settlement through nonmarket action, particularly government action. The economic growth of modern societies has occurred through more intensive division of labor, as well as greater extension of given techniques and organization. Intensive specialization generates an extremely complicated web of relationships among individuals. Many of these relationships involve externalities, that is, actions of one individual that directly affect the welfare of others without passing through a market. Moreover, because urbanization groups people close together, increasing urbanization plus more intensive specialization are likely to cause a continuous rise in the proportion of all relationships that have such external effects. These effects frequently lead to regulation by nonmarket organizations.

Second, the growing population and wealth of modern societies tend to increase the average size of many organizations therein, and large size is a necessary characteristic of bureaucracy. Private firms become larger because the possibilities of mass producing specialized goods create economies of scale, making big firms more efficient. Governmental agencies become larger because they must deal with bigger constituencies, or handle more complex interdependencies with other agencies (including other bureaus). The larger an organization becomes, the higher the probability that jobs therein will meet [the] criteria for bureaucratic positions.

Third, technological change has encouraged mechanization of market-oriented jobs. These jobs have two characteristics conducive to mechanization. The processes they involve and the outputs they produce are more clearly definable, and any operation must be precisely defined before it can be mechanized. It is also easier to make economic calculations involving such jobs, since the costs and revenues involved can also be clearly identified. This makes it simpler to decide whether substitution of machinery for labor will pay off. Faster mechanization of nonbureaucratic jobs tends to increase the proportion of bureaucrats in the employed labor force (though not necessarily the proportion of their outputs in the total output volume).

Fourth, as societies grow wealthier, their members prefer more of those goods best furnished by nonmarket-oriented organizations. Economists have long noted systematic shifts in the composition of a nation's labor force as its per capita income rises. At first the proportion of workers in the primary occupations (mining, fishing, agriculture) declines, and that in secondary occupations (manufacturing and material processing) rises. Then secondary employment begins to decline relative to that in tertiary occupations (distribution and services), perhaps even in absolute terms. The latter shift may include an increased emphasis on certain services that must be (or have traditionally been) furnished by nonmarket-oriented organizations. One example is education; another is public subsidization of non-self-supporting aesthetic or recreational facilities, such as art museums, music centers, sports stadia, and large parks.

HAS THERE BEEN AN EXCESSIVE EXPANSION OF BUREAUS?

These reasons for expecting increased bureaucratization do not provide any indication of whether the actual expansion of bureaus is likely to correspond to their theoretically optimal growth. This problem can be restated as follows:

1.   Is there any inherent tendency for an excessive number of bureaus to exist, either because too many are created or because obsolete bureaus fail to disappear?
2.   Is there any inherent tendency for each individual bureau to expand excessively in total output, in units of input per unit of output, or in total scope of activities?
3.   Is there any inherent tendency for all bureaus considered as a whole to expand excessively in total output, in units of input per unit of output, or in total scope of activities?

Clearly, the concept of "excessiveness" must be defined unequivocally before these questions can be answered. Yet this is impossible. Since the value of a bureau's output cannot be determined in a free market, it must be determined some other way, often through political choice mechanisms. With different values existing in society, bureau outputs worthless to some people may be extremely beneficial to others. This makes it almost impossible to determine their true value. The above questions then are essentially ethical or political in nature, and cannot be answered scientifically.

This does not mean that no scientific measures of efficiency can ever be applied to the operations of individual bureaus. In many cases, certain ways of doing things can definitely be proved superior to others. Also, scientific analysis can be an extremely valuable aid to bureau decisionmaking even when the ultimate choices depend upon values or opinions. Furthermore, we can intuitively postulate that the total amount of waste and inefficiency in society is likely to rise as bureaucracy becomes more prominent. This seems probable because true waste is so much harder to define and detect in bureaus than in private firms. Also, there are no automatic mechanisms for limiting it in the former as there are in the latter. This admittedly untestable conclusion implies that society should arrange to have services produced by market-oriented firms rather than bureaus when possible, other things being equal. However, it does not imply that recent trends toward bureaucratization of society are excessive or will become so in the future.

Even though our theory does not enable us to judge whether bureaucratization has become excessive, it does provide an important conclusion relevant to this issue. Critics of bureaus often claim that their growth has been excessive because it results from inherent tendencies to expand rather than from any true social needs for the service. However, bureaus cannot expand without additional resources, which they must obtain either through voluntary contributions or from some government allocation agency. But . . . in a democratic society these external agents will not give a bureau such resources unless it produces outputs of commensurate value to them (assuming the bureau is not a military organization willing to coerce them). Hence, in a gross sense, bureaus do engage in voluntary *quid pro quo* transactions with the agents that support them. Therefore, the recent expansion of bureaus in democracies has occurred largely in accordance with the desires of major nonbureaucratic institutions therein. Consequently, we may presume that these institutions do not believe the overall bureaucratization of society has been excessive, or they would not continue to support them.

This conclusion is valid even if every citizen believes that a majority of all government bureaucratic effort is wasteful. Each citizen can easily identify many government bureaus whose costs to him outweigh the benefits they provide him. But certain other bureaus provide a surplus of benefits to a minority of citizens, including him. These beneficiaries must form coalitions with the supporters of other minority-serving bureaus in order to obtain such large benefits. As long as the total utility received by most citizens in this logrolling process exceeds the total cost they pay, they tacitly support the resulting expansion of bureaucracy, even though they may overtly complain loudly about waste in those bureaus that do not benefit them directly.

If the bureaucracy as a whole were really excessive in size, some political party would advocate drastic reductions affecting a whole spectrum of minority-serving bureaus. This party would receive the vote of every citizen who believed he was paying more to support wasteful bureaus than he was receiving from those minority-serving bureaus that benefited him directly. If such citizens were in the majority, the bureau-wrecking party would be elected, and would presumably slash the size of the bureaucracy as a whole. Until this occurs, we are forced to conclude that the overall size of the bureaucracy is not excessive in relation to the services it is providing for society.

This conclusion does not apply in nondemocratic societies. Since genuine opposition parties are not allowed to exist, the citizenry is never given a chance to vote on whether to accept the *status quo* or to engage in wholesale bureau reduction. Moreover, the reigning group controls the government, and probably indulges in the inherent tendency of government bureaus to expand. Hence it is likely that the government bureaucracy is actually excessive in all nondemocratic societies.

INDIVIDUAL FREEDOM AND THE GROWTH OF BUREAUCRACY

Comparing present life in the United States with that of past decades, we can hardly doubt that bureaus exert a growing absolute level of control over individuals. Everyone finds himself forced to fill out more forms, pay more taxes to support bureaus, obey more bureaucratic rules, and otherwise interact with more officials than ever before. Nevertheless, it would be a gross error to conclude from this that bureaus have reduced individual freedom of choice. The word *freedom* has two very different meanings: power of choice, and absence of restraint. It is true that bureaus place far more restraints on the average man today than they did formerly. However, today's citizen also enjoys a much greater range in choice of possible behavior than his predecessors did. Moreover, the number of behavioral options open to him is growing every year through such changes as supersonic aircraft, new medicines, rising real income, increased foreign trade, better highways, longer vacations, higher retirement pensions, and a host of others.

This analysis suggests four significant conclusions. First, the average individual's overall freedom is actually expanding rapidly. Even though the regulations imposed upon him by bureaus continue to multiply, his action alternatives multiply even faster.

Second, increased bureaucratic regulations are actually one of the causes of his greater freedom. The forces generating ever wider options are the same ones that generate the need for more bureaucratic rules. Without increased bureaucratic regulation, such forces as technological change, urbanization, and more intensive division of labor would either be impossible, or would lead to greater social disorganization and a narrower range of choice for the individual. Thus, greater bureaucratization is one of the inherent costs of greater freedom of choice, and could not be abolished without reducing that freedom.

Third, it is true that bureaus often place more restraints upon individuals than are necessary to accomplish their social functions. Thus, even though the total effect of increased bureaucratization is an expansion of individual choice, the marginal effect of some regulations is an unnecessary restriction of choice designed mainly to benefit the bureau's members.

Fourth, it is conceivable that bureaucratization might someday become so extensive as to result in an overall reduction of freedom of choice. This could happen if bureaus took over nearly all economic production and operated it without any market orientation. They might reduce total output significantly below what it would be under private market-oriented management. Or they might alter the composition of final output so that it did not correspond very closely to what consumers really desired (as has happened in the Soviet Union). Government bureaus might also control most of the country's activity and use a centralized personnel control system. Then occupational choices might be severely restricted for individuals considered undesirable by any one bureau. Even if no such system existed, persons with certain technical specialties might find their job choices limited if a single government bureau controlled all positions requiring their skills. This is true now regarding customs inspectors and supersonic bomber pilots. Whenever men know their livelihood is permanently dependent on a single employer, their willingness to voice opinions or undertake acts disapproved by that employer drops sharply. Hence the myriad-firm private economic sector plays a crucial political role as a source of market-oriented production jobs.

These freedom-reducing results of over-bureaucratization already exist in some nations. However, we do not believe they are very probable in the United States in the near future, except in a few occupations monopolized by individual bureaus. In the foreseeable future, then, the growth of bureaus in the United States will continue to represent the interaction of a long-run trend toward increasing individual choice, and short-run maneuvers by individual bureaucrats producing unnecessary restraints and inefficiencies.

Hyman G. Rickover

Bureaucracy in a Democratic Society

I have spent my adult life in a public bureaucracy, and I have worked closely with other public agencies and with the bureaucratic organizations through which large-scale private enterprise functions. This practical experience, augmented by much relevant reading and reflection, has led me to certain conclusions. These I will submit here, but I point out what they are: personal opinions, not expert testimony.

The juxtaposition of democracy and bureaucracy calls attention to their antithetical characteristics, and raises the question whether they *can* coexist without adversely affecting each other; or rather, since we are committed to a free and democratic society, whether bureaucracy can be smoothly integrated into democracy. . . .

Bureaucracy antedates modern democracy by centuries. It persists in our society because no one has yet invented an instrument equally efficient in performing tasks—on a continuing basis—that require coordination of the efforts of large numbers of people, with different kinds and degrees of professional expertise relevant to the job at hand, especially when their work must be closely intermeshed. Able administrators have shaped bureaucracy for the intricate business of public administration. In so doing, they have also made it a most effective instrument for the management of large affairs and enterprises in general.

Reprinted by permission from "The Bureaucracy" by Hyman G. Rickover in *The Mazes of Modern Government*, an Occasional Paper published by the Center for the Study of Democratic Institutions in Santa Barbara, California, 1964, pp. 26, 28-33.

In popular usage the word bureaucracy has a pejorative implication, but only when applied to government agencies. Most Americans dislike and fear huge, bureaucratically organized power-conglomerates in government but are not even aware of similar conglomerates outside government. This gives them a lopsided picture of American society as a vast market-place where individuals compete with each other in a free and fair fashion, the best man wins, and the consumer is sovereign. Upon this free market descends a huge and menacing government bureaucracy intent on imposing its will on the hapless traders. There is a widespread and assiduously promoted belief that bureaucracy is synonymous with government. What gives this plausibility is that at one time—some two centuries ago—in the mercantilist age, when monarchical absolutism reached its height, this was largely true.

Men like Louis XIV should have amended their boast to read "the State is I and my bureaucracy," because it was through his bureaucracy that an absolute king ruled. The hatred of the people against this instrument of royal government was justified, for the monarch used it chiefly for his own purposes, with little regard for the interests of his subjects. Thus the bureaucracy administered the monarch's mercantilist policies which served no purpose other than to provide him with the wherewithal for waging dynastic wars. It was said of eighteenth-century Prussia that it "was not a country with an army, but an army with a country which served as headquarters and food magazine." The king's bureaucracy managed the country to this end. Much the same was true of every other absolute monarchy of the time.

Most Americans have a picture of this absolutist bureaucracy in their minds when they speak unfavorably of "*the* bureaucracy." But in a modern democracy the administrative apparatus of government is something quite different. With all its faults, it has been set up and carries out the tasks assigned to it by the general government, itself chosen by and accountable to the people. Apart from this vital difference, there is the equally important difference that a democratic government does not normally expand the bureaucracy *in order to make itself more powerful vis-à-vis the people.* Bureaucracy in government expands for the same reasons that bureaucracy in private life expands: explosion of population and technology.

When the term is used in too narrow a sense, this reason for expansion tends to be overlooked. The word bureaucracy now has a broader meaning because the phenomenon it describes is to be found in a wider range of circumstances. Any organization that in structure and *modus operandi* resembles the classical pattern of bureaucracy is properly termed a bureaucracy. These characteristics, rather than the particular area—public versus private—in which it operates, convey the bureaucratic cognomen to a given organization.

Bureaucratic organizations are today as numerous in the private as in the public sphere. They proliferate because every area of national life is now dominated by giant organizations, and bureaucracy is the inevitable concomitant of giantism. In no other democratic country has bureaucratization of life gone as far as with us.

Not all our giantism is necessary. If we wished, we could eliminate some of it, as in education, where enormous factory-like institutions are neither beneficial to students nor even particularly efficient—in terms of education if not of expenditure. In other Western nations schools are kept small, there is virtually no bureaucracy, and the results surpass our own. There are other areas where size serves no useful purpose or where its advantages are outweighed by the undesirable side-effects of bureaucratization. However, most American giantism is ineluctable, given the size of our population and the imperatives of modern technoscience.

The world has never seen a population growth to equal our own. In the last two centuries we have multiplied a hundredfold while in most of Western Europe growth has been on the order of three to five fold. Immigration accounts for this only in part. Despite its virtual cessation some fifty years ago, we continue to increase at a faster rate than other industrial nations. We should reach the billion mark in a century.

Urbanization, too, proceeds faster here. A generation ago we were predominantly rural; now two thirds live in huge urban and suburban conglomerations. There is no sign of an end to this mass movement into the cities, for the same pressures that destroy small-owner enterprise in industry appear to be working on the family farm. It is now threatened by a new type of large landed estate—the commercial factory farm. As always, technology produces a surplus of goods and a scarcity of jobs. This is happening faster here than abroad where the social value of family farming appears to be rated higher than maximum productivity.

In a sparsely populated country, where most people live on farms and in small towns, few government services are needed. But when space around a man contracts, more rules are needed to discipline his behavior toward others. The restraints that knowing one's neighbors imposes are lost in the anonymity of city life. It takes a big bureaucracy merely to maintain peace among the multitudes and keep their cars circulating freely, not to mention supplying them with pure water, public health services, sewage disposal facilities, and so on.

Modern technology has placed in the hands of man the means to do much greater harm than was ever before possible, both to fellow-citizens and to society at large. The individual is helpless to protect himself against consequences of misuse of technology that result in soil erosion, air and water pollution, or against substances harmful to him in "miracle" foods, drugs, pesticides, and weed-killers—to name but a few things. He *must* call on his government for assistance.

Even as misuse of technology leads to growth of the *public* bureaucracy, so the desire to extract from technology the ultimate in material affluence leads to growth of *private* bureaucracies. Maximum utilization of modern technology requires large organizations and these, as I said before, cannot be managed efficiently except in a bureaucratic manner.

The changes wrought by explosion of population and technology have happened so fast that we do not yet fully grasp their consequences. Still cherishing our traditional ideal of a government that is small, costs little, and hardly touches us in our private lives, we put the blame for bureaucracy and big government everywhere except where it belongs—on ourselves. It is we who have created the conditions that make it indispensable; we with our heedless passion for change, for instant scientific "miracles," for bigness *per se*, for endlessly increasing material affluence.

We have created a way of life that is dominated by large bureaucratic organizations. Most of us work for such organizations—only 15 percent are now self-employed—all of us consume their products and are subject to the rules they impose on us. We must learn to live *with* them rather than *under* them. This means we must constantly be on the alert that they do not dwarf man—the individual unorganized citizen in whom is grounded our free society.

It is our misfortune that the founding fathers left us no guidance on how to deal with bureaucracy. We have never since had men their equal—men who were both first-rate political thinkers and outstandingly capable practical politicians, besides possessing great civic courage. This rare combination of qualities accounts for the straightforward manner in which they went to the root of any given problem, found a practical way to solve it, and did not hesitate to advocate the solution they came up with, no matter how startlingly revolutionary or "controversial" it might have appeared to their countrymen. All our later efforts to adapt government to the changing needs of our society have been less successful than the initial act of creation, chiefly, I believe, because we have been content with *ad hoc* measures.

The veneration we rightly feel for the Constitution makes exploration in depth of our political system seem almost sacrilegious. Yet if the makers of the Constitution lived today, they would not hesitate to question our ways of managing democracy if these appeared to them unsatisfactory. Unlike ourselves, who constantly confuse principle with procedure and tenet with technique, they would proceed forthwith to reassess our procedures and techniques in order to discover whether—under present-day conditions—these still serve to realize the basic principles and tenets of democracy.

I presume this is what Jefferson meant when he spoke of the need of "permanent revolution." Technological changes may so alter the consequences of established democratic processes as to produce results that are the very opposite of what democracy seeks to attain: preservation of the individual as an autonomous human being, and government chosen by and accountable to the people. Bureaucracy is a case in point. Present practices have no sanctity except insofar as they conform to the tenets of democracy.

The Constitution mentions neither bureaucracy nor public administration. There are references to "officers" of the United States and "office" under the United States; provision is made for the President by and with the advice and consent of the Senate to appoint all officers of the United States. Also, Congress "may by law vest the appointment of such inferior officers, as they think proper, in the President alone, in the courts of law, or in the heads of departments," and the "principal officers in the executive departments" must, on request by the President, "submit opinions, in writing, upon any subject relating to the duties of their respective offices." On this slender basis rests the vast bureaucracy which by sheer numbers now all but dwarfs Congress and the judiciary (the only part of government that remains free from bureaucratic accretions). The federal bureaucracy accounts in large part for the enormously enhanced power of the President *vis-à-vis* the other two coordinate branches of government. This imbalance was neither foreseen nor desired by the framers of the Constitution.

In the absence of constitutional rules, we might with profit examine how the nations of Western Europe have gone about fitting bureaucracy into their political systems. These, no less than our own, are fruits of the Enlightenment. Throughout the Western world democracy has a common intellectual origin. We tend to look askance at the democratic procedures of others, asserting that we alone are a true democracy. Besides irritating our allies, this attitude cuts us off from a valuable source of information.

The bureaucratic apparatus of modern West European democracies traces back across centuries to the permanent corps of officials employed by feudal kings to administer the royal household. It has a consecutive history; there has been no sharp break and new start as with us. Bureaucracy has in turn been adapted to feudal, absolute, and constitutional monarchy and to parliamentary democracy (with or without a king). Europeans have had much experience fitting bureaucracy into different kinds of government.

Over the years they have made many improvements in the structure of bureaucracy in order to insure that it will offer efficient, incorruptible, technically competent service. These are worth our attention. We may find that some practices we think of as uniquely American and sacrosanct have long since been dropped abroad and replaced by practices deemed preferable.

For brevity's sake, I shall call the earlier bureaucracy under feudal and absolute monarchy a *proprietary bureaucracy*, the modern form a *public bureaucracy*. The first was essentially a private service, for it administered what the king considered his personal affairs. Under feudalism this included, besides the royal household, his private estates and such few public matters as fell within his jurisdiction. Under absolutism the national realm had become virtually indistinguishable from the royal domain, other power centers in the nation having been reduced to near-impotence; the bureaucracy was in effect the national government.

The four characteristics of *public bureaucracy* are hierarchy, professionalism, permanence, and impersonal rules for entry and promotion (as well as other interpersonal relations). Traditional to feudalism and absolutism, hierarchy is today based entirely on competence and experience. The bureaucracy is staffed top to bottom by a career civil service. Entry is by competitive examinations open to all. Permanence—that is, tenure—is an essential part of the service. The rules of the bureaucracy are its legal system, so to speak. They were originally introduced to prevent arbitrary misuse of power by superiors over subordinates. As with us, the rules tend to deteriorate into a rigid routine that stifles innovations and slows action, but the high-level professional qualifications in the best West European bureaucracies counteract this to some extent.

Left behind forever are such aspects of the *proprietary bureaucracy* as meddling in the internal affairs of the bureaucracy by the ruler or awarding high positions on grounds other than merit; for instance, upon receipt of a money gift to the ruler or the top bureaucrat, or as a favor to an individual for personal reasons, or to a special class—as when, contrary to the wishes of the ruler, noblemen were given preference over better qualified commoners, in order that the "image" of the bureaucracy as an aristocratic corps might be preserved. Some vestiges of these earlier practices still exist with us.

Bureaucracy is fitted into parliamentary democracy by placing each major administrative department under a political leader appointed by the party in power. He makes certain that the incoming party's policy is carried out but does not demote or dismiss a bureau head for having carried out a contrary policy of the preceding party. Still less would he demote or dismiss the bureau head because of displeasure over previous technical actions of the bureau—as can happen here because we do not allow bureaucracy the technical autonomy it enjoys abroad and also because we confuse the functions of the technical career head of a bureaucracy and those of the political officer set above him. On this point the Europeans have a better policy.

The career civil service staffs the entire bureaucracy; hence, the job of career head is not affected by party changes. He is permanent and technically expert. The political superior—a minister, corresponding to our department secretary—is temporary, technically amateur but politically proficient. His job is political, not administrative. To qualify he must have had experience as a politician. In his own field he is as expert as the career head in the technical field.

Thus, bureaucracy is professionalized throughout. Because a career to the top is open to them, first-rate professional men will enter and remain in civil service. Absence of political meddling with technical problems allows them to act and feel as true professionals. One cannot be a professional if he must submit to orders in technical matters from persons who have no technical qualifications, merely raw power.

The Hoover Commission's Task Force on Personnel and Civil Service, in its 1955 report, comments on the absence in the government bureaucracy of a "system to provide top management personnel." It notes that "functions of political executives, who serve at the pleasure of the Chief Executive, and of career administrators, who continue unless removed for cause, have been confused. Their respective functions and complementary relationships have not been clearly recognized. Policies and procedures have not been developed to meet the Government's needs, for either of these essential types of talent." The detailed recommendations of the Commission would bring our practice closer to the West European formula. They have not been adopted.

Among advanced democracies, we alone have no professional career civil service. Top jobs in the bureaucracy seldom go to experienced civil servants who have risen in the ranks; they go to outsiders. Jacksonian democracy first made it official dogma that patronage and rotation in office were democratic, while permanence or tenure and professionalism were elitist and smacked of European aristocracy. Jackson felt that government jobs were something anybody could fill; to set educational qualifications that average citizens could not meet was intolerable in a democracy. From this extreme position we have gradually been forced to retreat, as the right of the public to competent professional service took precedence over the right of every citizen to get his share of the spoils of victory. The lower echelons in government service are now under civil service. The top ones are not, or only rarely.

Both technical heads and political heads of bureaucracies are patronage jobs, though this uncouth word is not used at this high level. The criteria that govern appointments seldom relate to true fitness for the job. Common sense would suggest that the technical headship of a bureaucracy ought to go to a person with long and distinguished public service who possesses the specific technical competence required to administer the organization; and that the political headship ought to go to a person with political experience. But we are bemused by the myth of the "pure" administrator.

He is a uniquely American phenomenon: a man who makes a career of administering organizations. As Mirabeau noted, "to administer is to rule." The "pure" administrator is a special sort of ruler; that is his métier. In the past, noble blood was thought, in a mysterious way, to confer skill in the craft of ruling. We believe that courses in leadership, administration, and handling people will do it. We organize almost any large enterprise—private or public—so as to put the technical people *under* the "pure" administrators. By technical people I mean the persons who do the work for which the organization exists: teachers in education, for instance; production men in industry.

Abroad, an administrator in any large organization is expected to be professionally qualified; he learns management on the job, not from college courses. In government, great emphasis is laid on in-service training over a long period before a bureaucrat begins to make decisions. In this country it may happen that a first-rate technical man is overruled on technical matters or meddled with in his work by some boy fresh from college who, on the strength of leadership and suchlike courses, rates as an administrator, and therefore is automatically superior to the technical man who may have had years of experience. That doesn't count; he isn't a "ruler."

It is odd that we should have this veneration for professional rulers of organizations. There is some justification for it when an organization performs routine jobs or technical work that is not too complicated to be understood by the top man, even though his special training—like that of the court officials of feudal kings—has prepared him only for organizational housekeeping, with perhaps some ceremonial chores thrown in. But when the technical work of a bureaucracy is complicated and the staff is professionally competent, superimposing these "pure" administrators leads to friction, poor work, and the loss of capable men who will not work under such conditions. It is no hardship to serve a man who is superior to you in the competence that really counts on the job, but it is galling to have to let a man overrule you in matters in which you are expert and he is ignorant.

Just as in days gone by noblemen were thought to be endowed with the ability of managing any enterprise, so we consider the "pure" administrator who has risen to the top in one kind of bureaucracy capable of stepping into a top job in any other—from heading a large private bureaucracy into the headship of a federal department.

The work experience of such a top administrator qualifies him no more for the political leadership job than it qualifies him to administer a bureau with whose technical work he is unacquainted. He may, of course, on his own have acquired the knowledge, breadth of thinking, and concern for the public interest that is needed in the political headship job. We have been lucky to have such men, but they are rare. To base our system on finding men of this caliber does not recommend itself.

The bureaucracy manages reasonably well when it does more or less established administrative work. But when we require it to work in high-level technology, we pay an exorbitant price for our poorly devised system. Our leadtimes are overlong; part of the reason must be ascribed to the structure and *opus operandi* of bureaucracy. The higher our technology, the less important is the "pure" administrator. He has his functions, but properly he should be working under a top technical man; for instance, school administrators ought to do their housekeeping chores under a teacher principal.

Not all Western European countries successfully apply the formula I have described, but all subscribe to it. I believe we might do well to examine and possibly adapt it to our own needs. Nothing in the formula would make it unacceptable to us. Like operating-room procedure it has universal validity—it best serves the purpose for which it is intended.

A final word on the effect of bureaucracy on the individual who works in it: Democracy is not merely a political system; it partakes of the elements of a faith. Its first commandment may be expressed in the Kantian imperative: "Every man is to be respected as an absolute end in himself; and it is a crime against the dignity that belongs to him as a human being, to use him as a mere means for some external purpose."

As it is structured, bureaucracy all too easily permits men to be used for the ends of the organization in ways that diminish the liberties they are supposed to enjoy in our free society. Not infrequently, these ends may in fact be merely the personal predilection of the men at the top who come to think of the organization as their property. This is the crime *par excellence* of pure administrators whose sense of worth comes from their position in the hierarchy alone. It is less prevalent among men who are true professionals, who are allowed to function as professionals, and who owe their status to their own merit. The more we professionalize bureaucracy, the more democratic it will become. A hierarchy based purely on merit diminishes no man.

The right to be judged only by one's own peers is or should be "inalienable."

This could be our own distinctive contribution to the problem of fitting bureaucracy into democracy.

Michael Young

The Meritocracy of the Future

What was the connection between the gutting of the Ministry of Education and the attempt on the life of the Chairman of the T.U.C.? Between the unofficial transport strike and the equally unofficial walk-out of domestic servants? All these questions are rendered doubly topical by the general strike which the Populists have called for the coming May, on the first anniversary of the troubles. Will there be a response? Will 2034 repeat 1789 or merely 1848? I would submit that more topical, and more important, a subject could hardly be discussed. It touches on a clear and present danger to the state.

The Prime Minister, in his frank report to the House of Lords, put part of the responsibility for the May Affair upon administrative failings. The wrecking of Wren's store at Stevenage the Prime Minister regards as a local disturbance; its 2000 shop assistants were undoubtedly incensed by the management's unexpected rejection of the four-day week. Destruction of the atomic station at South Shields might never have happened with a less provocative director. The walk-out of domestic servants was precipitated by the slowness of the Price Review, similar trouble in the other Provinces of Europe being evidence enough for that. Feeling against the Education Ministry was stimulated by the publication in April of the last report of the Standing Commission on the National Intelligence, and so on. All this I readily accept, yet it is not the whole story. We also have to explain why administrative miscalculations, that in an ordinary year would have passed almost unnoticed, should on this occasion have provoked such fierce and concerted protest. To understand what happened, and so be prepared for what is going to happen, we have to take the measure of the Populist movement, with its strange blend of women in the lead and men in the rank and file.

The women's circles have produced evangelists before; their eclipse has usually been as sudden as their rising. Not so the leaders by whom we are now plagued. They have consolidated their strength. The Convention they organized at Leicester shortly before Christmas 2032 was their decisive moment. The women's circles would be mustered—that was well known; the women's sections of the Technicians' Party would be there—that was half allowed for. What was not expected was the attendance of so many representatives, men as well as women, from local branches of the Party and the Unions. In defiance of their leaders, they came from all over the country, and particularly from the North of England and Scotland—this hostility to London and the South is a sinister aspect of the agitation too much played down by government sociologists. Even the Association of Scientific Benefactors was represented. From Leicester sprang the ill-assorted conglomeration which has come to be known as the Populist Movement, with its strange charter. For the only time within living memory a dissident minority from the élite has struck up an alliance with the lower orders, hitherto so isolated and so docile. Their union fomented the local incidents in Kirkcaldy and Stevenage, South Shields and Whitehall, into the national crisis of last May.

What does it all mean? Only the historians of the future will know, perhaps even they will not agree. Close as we are to the crisis, with every day bringing fresh news, it is impossible for anyone to be more than tentative in his opinions. No consensus has yet formed. The official view is that such an alliance across class-lines is a misalliance, the background of leaders and led so different, and the common interest between them so slight, that the movement cannot last. The *Sunday Scientist* has in a much-quoted, if scurrilous, phrase likened some of the leaders to "Rimsky-Korsakov in a Lyons Corner House." Has Somerville vulgarized itself without finding any deep response? I think not, at least I do not agree about the response. The Populists could not have gathered such momentum, the May Affair reached such dimensions, unless there were more than passing resentments to feed on. My reading is that these resentments have their roots deep in history....

GOLDEN AGE OF EQUALITY

I have in the first part of this book reviewed the means by which our modern élite has been established, and what a splendid result it is! No longer is it just the brilliant individual who shines forth; the world beholds for the first time the spectacle of a brilliant class, the five percent of the nation who know what five percent means. Every member is a tried specialist in his own sphere. Mounting at a faster and faster rate, our knowledge has been cumulative from generation to generation. In the course of a mere hundred years we have come close to realizing at one stroke the ideal of Plato, Erasmus, and Shaw. But, if sociology teaches anything, it teaches that no society is completely stable; always there are strains and conflicts. In the first part of this essay I have mentioned some of the tensions—between family and community, between different parts of the educational structure, between young and old, between the *déclassé* and the other members of the proletariat—incident to the rise of the meritocracy. Now I turn, in this second part, to consider from the same point of view, the consequences of progress for the lower class, and, as I have said, particularly for those born into it.

My method of analysis is historical; the comparison I draw once more with a century ago. Taylor has called that time the golden age of equality.* A sort of egalitarianism flourished then because two contradictory principles for legitimizing power were struggling for mastery—the principle of kinship and the principle of merit—and nearly everyone, in his heart of hearts, believed in both. Everyone thought it proper to advance his son and honor his father; everyone thought it proper to seek out ability and honor achievement. Individuals were riven as much as society. The consequence was that anyone who had reached privilege behind the shield of only one of these principles could be attacked with the sword of the other—the man born great was criticized because, by another reckoning, he did not deserve his fortune; and the base-born achieving greatness could be charged half impostor. The powerful were, by this whirligig, unfailingly unseated.

Many people were catapulted forward by their parents' riches and influence; not only did they benefit from the culture festooning their homes, they were sent to the best schools and colleges, dispatched on trips abroad and given expensive training for Bar, countinghouse, or surgery—all the advantages, in short, which we in our day try to keep for the deserving. But since such treatment was sanctioned by only half the moral code, the beneficiaries were only half at home in their station in life. They could not say to themselves with complete conviction "I am the best man for the job" because they knew that they had not won their place in open competition and, if they were honest, had to recognize that a dozen of their subordinates would have been as good, or perhaps better. Although they some-times sought to deny self-doubt by too brassy an assertion of self-confidence, such denial was hard to sustain when it plainly ran against the facts. The upper-class man had to be insensitive indeed not to have noticed, at some time in his life, that a private in his regiment, a butler or "charlady" in his home, a driver of taxi or bus, or the humble workman with lined face and sharp eyes in the railway carriage or country pub—not to have noticed that amongst such people was intelligence, wit, and wisdom at least equal to his own, not to have noticed that every village had its Jude the Obscure. If he had so observed, if he had so recognized that his social inferiors were sometimes his biological superiors, if the great variety of people in all social classes had made him think in some dim way that "a man's a man for a' that," was he not likely to respond by treating them with a kind of respect?**

Even if the superiors deceived themselves, they could not their subordinates. These knew that many bosses were there not so much because of what they knew, as who they knew, and who their parents were, and went on, with wanton exagger-ation, to denounce all bosses on like account. Some men of talent took pains (if contemporary novels are to be relied on) to make it known in the factory, if not in the golf club, that they had "come up the hard way." But who could tell for

---

*Taylor, F. G. *The Role of Egalitarianism in Twentieth-century England*. 2004.

**In an earlier age the sumptuary laws passed by Henry VII to force lords to eat in the same great hall as their retainers were not only for the benefit of the retainers. In modern times there is nothing to be gained from social mixing, in school, in residence, or at work, because the upper class now have little or nothing to learn from the lower.

certain how far success had been accident, or lack of scruples offset lack of brains? The workmen had their doubts. They let fly with their criticism of the powers-that-be, and so kept even the able under restraint. The energy wasted on criticism and counter-criticism was colossal.

An even more important consequence of the conflict in values was that the workers could altogether dissociate their own judgments of themselves from the judgment of society. Subjective and objective status were often poles apart. The worker said to himself: "Here I am, a workman. Why am I a workman? Am I fit for nothing else? Of course not. Had I had a proper chance I would have shown the world. A doctor? A brewer? A minister? I could have done anything. I never had the chance. And so I am a worker. But don't think that at bottom I am any worse than anyone else. I'm better." Educational injustice enabled people to preserve their illusions, inequality of opportunity fostered the myth of human equality. Myth we know it to be; not so our ancestors.

GULF BETWEEN THE CLASSES

This evocation of the past shows how great the change has been. In those days no class was homogeneous in brains: clever members of the upper classes had as much in common with clever members of the lower classes as they did with stupid members of their own. Now that people are classified by ability, the gap between the classes has inevitably become wider. The upper classes are, on the one hand, no longer weakened by self-doubt and self-criticism. Today the eminent know that success is just reward for their own capacity, for their own efforts, and for their own undeniable achievement. They deserve to belong to a superior class. They know, too, that not only are they of higher caliber to start with, but that a first-class education has been built upon their native gifts. As a result, they can come as close as anyone to understanding the full and ever-growing complexity of our technical civilization. They are trained in science, and it is scientists who have inherited the earth. What can they have in common with people whose education stopped at sixteen or seventeen, leaving them with the merest smattering of dog-science? How can they carry on a two-sided conversation with the lower classes when they speak another, richer, and more exact language? Today, the élite know that, except for a grave error in administration, which should at once be corrected if brought to light, their social inferiors are inferiors in other ways as well—that is, in the two vital qualities, of intelligence and education, which are given pride of place in the more consistent value system of the twenty-first century. Hence one of our characteristic modern problems: some members of the meritocracy, as most moderate reformers admit, have become so impressed with their own importance as to lose sympathy with people whom they govern, and so tactless that even people of low caliber have been quite unnecessarily offended. The schools and universities are endeavoring to instill a more proper sense of humility—what does even modern man count beside the wonders which Nature has wrought in the universe?—but for the moment the efficiency of public relations with the lower class is not all that it might be.

As for the lower classes, their situation is different too. Today all persons, however humble, know they have had every chance. They are tested again and again. If on one occasion they are off-color, they have a second, a third, and fourth opportunity to demonstrate their ability. But if they have been labeled "dunce" repeatedly they cannot any longer pretend; their image of themselves is more nearly a true, unflattering, reflection. Are they not bound to recognize that they have an inferior status—not as in the past because they were denied opportunity; but because they *are* inferior?* For the first time in human history the inferior man has no ready buttress for his self-regard. This has presented contemporary psychology with its gravest problem. Men who have lost their self-respect are liable to lose their inner vitality (especially if they are inferior to their own parents and fall correspondingly in the social scale) and may only too easily cease to be either good citizens or good technicians. The common man is liable to sulk for his fig-leaf.

The consequences of so depressing the status of the inferior and elevating that of the superior have naturally engaged the full attention of social science. We cannot pretend that its path has always been smooth. Dr. Jason's "tadpole" argument which amounted, when stripped of verbiage, to saying that on the whole all tadpoles were happier because they knew that some of them would turn into frogs, was at best a half-truth. The young might be happier; but what of the many older tadpoles who knew they would never become frogs? The tadpoles only confused counsel. Since Lord Jason himself became a "frog," research has proceeded more steadily.

The situation has been saved by five things. First, by the philosophy underlying teaching in secondary modern schools. When these were started, no one quite knew what to do about the content of education for the lower classes. Children were taught the three R's as well as how to use simple tools and to measure with gauges and even micrometers. But this was only the formal skeleton of a course without an ideology to guide it. The schools had a far more important function than to equip their pupils with a few elementary skills; they also had to instil an attitude of mind which would be conducive to effective performance of their future tasks in life. The lower classes needed a *Mythos*, and they got what they needed, the Mythos of Muscularity. Luckily they already had this in a rudimentary form, which the modern schools have been able to promote into the modern cult of physical (as distinct from mental) prowess. The English love of sport was traditional, and nowhere stronger than in the lower classes. The modern schools were not breaking with the past, they were building on it, when they encouraged their pupils to value physical strength, bodily discipline, and manual dexterity. Handicrafts, gymnastics, and games have become the core of the curriculum. This enlightened approach has achieved a double purpose. Appreciation of manual work has

---

*This is not entirely a new realization. My colleague, Mr. Fallon, has drawn my attention to an old cartoon in the *New Yorker*, an ostensibly humorous American periodical, *circa* 1954. It showed a large psychiatrist confronting a small patient, saying, "You haven't got an inferiority complex. You *are* inferior."

been cultivated, and leisure made more enjoyable. Of the two, education for leisure has been the most important. More capable pupils have been trained to participate in active games which they can continue to play when they leave school; and the others who form the great majority have been given heightened appreciation of boxing, football, and other sports displayed before them nightly on the screens in their own homes. They esteem physical achievement almost as highly as we of the upper classes esteem mental.

Secondly, the adult education movement has, in its maturity, not only maintained and enlarged the regional centers but has arranged for everyone, irrespective of previous results, to attend there for a periodic intelligence check at intervals of five years. Tests can be even more frequent at the behest of the individual. A few remarkable changes of I.Q. both up and down, have occurred in middle life. Widely publicized in the popular newspapers, the reports have given new heart to many an ambitious technician. Now that psychiatric treatment is freely available in every workplace, many people with emotional blocks to the realization of their potential have been fully cured.

Thirdly, even when they have abandoned hope themselves, all parents have been solaced by the knowledge that, however low their own I.Q., their child (or grandchild) will have the chance to enter the meritocracy. The solace is a real one. Psychologists have shown that parents, whose own ambitions are thwarted, invariably displace those ambitions on to their children. They are satisfied if they think that their own child may achieve what they could not achieve themselves. "Do as I wish, not as I do," they say. The relationship can even be expressed in quantitative terms: according to the well-known principle of compensating aspirations, the greater the frustrations parents experience in their own lives, the greater their aspirations for their children. Almost from the moment when they fail their first intelligence tests at school, children can comfort themselves that one day they will have offspring who will do better; and even when it is dismally clear from teachers' reports that the offspring too are dull, there are still the grandchildren.* Personal failings are not so painful if there is a vision of vicarious triumph. As long as all have opportunity to rise through the schools, people can believe in immortality: they have a second chance through the younger generation. Also, the more children, the more second chances, which helps to account for the higher birth-rate in the second half of last century, after the reforms.

The fourth saving feature has been the very stupidity which has assigned the lower classes to their present status. A common mistake of some sociologists is to impute to the lower orders the same capacity as themselves—a way of thinking akin to anthropomorphism. Sociologists would naturally be aggrieved were they to be denied their proper status. But the lower classes are the objects of study, not the students. The attitude of mind is quite different. People of low intelligence have

*Three-generation interlocking of aspirations in the extended family was discussed in an interesting way by Michael Young in "The Role of the Extended Family in Channeling Aspirations," *British Journal of Sociology*, March 1967. Note the earliness of the date.

sterling qualities: they go to work, they are conscientious, they are dutiful to their families. But they are unambitious, innocent, and incapable of grasping clearly enough the grand design of modern society to offer any effective protest. Some are sulkily discontented, without being too sure what to do about it, and find their way to the psychologist or the priest. Most are not, for they know not what is done to them.

PIONEERS OF DIRTY WORK

The fifth, and most important, saving feature has been the application of scientific selection to industry. Earlier, I showed how promotion by merit gradually replaced promotion by seniority—how the grammar school and university streams were eventually extended into working life. I will now deal with the treatment of the secondary modern stream.

The modern schools have been reproduced in industry just as surely as the grammar schools, and with consequences just as far-reaching. The starting point is again the Hitler war. In the early years of that war the methods of distributing recruits were almost as haphazard as in industry. Only after several disasters was a more sensible practice adopted, described as follows in the words of a leading Command Psychiatrist in one of the official histories of the war:

> In allocating personnel, the basic principle should be that no man is to be employed on work which is definitely above, or, on the other hand, definitely below his ability. Any other method of allotment is wasteful of ability, or destructive of unit efficiency.

What wise and far-sighted words!

By the end of the war the instruction was obeyed and very few men entering the Forces were assigned to any branch until their intelligence and aptitudes had been ascertained as accurately as the crude methods of the time allowed. Much greater efficiency was obtained in the utilization of manpower when the stupid were kept together, and the lesson was not lost on some of the better brains in civilian industry. This was long before advertisers began to include "State I.Q." (soon shortened to S.I.Q.) in their copy; and longer still before H.Q. (at Eugenics House) supplied I.Q. certificates to authorized inquirers by teleprinter. The flower of that experiment of the 1940's was the Pioneer Corps. When this indispensable body of hewers and drawers was confined to men with I.Q.'s below the line required to get them into the Intelligence Corps, the rise in efficiency was spectacular. The morale of these dull-witted men was better. They were no longer daunted by having superior people to compete with. They were amongst their equals—they had more equal opportunities since they had more limited ones—and they were happier, had fewer mental breakdowns, *and* were harder working. The Army had learnt the lesson of the schools: that people can be taught more easily, and get on better, when they are classed with people of more or less equal intelligence, or lack of it.

Not until the 1960's did this same lesson strike home in civil life. Intelligent people used to ask themselves what they thought was a profound poser: "Who," they asked, "will do the dirty work in the future commonwealth?" Those who knew the right answer apparently said: "Machines, of course; they will be the robots of the future." It was a good answer as far as it went, but, in view of the many jobs which can never be taken over by machinery, at best a partial one. Then as they became aware of the new and revolutionary developments in intelligence testing, aptitude testing, and vocational selection, managements realized that a permanent peace-time Pioneer Corps was a practical possibility. At first tentatively, they suggested the correct answer to the old question: "Who will do the dirty work?" The correct answer was: "Why, men who like doing it, of course."

They could see the need for a kind of permanent civilian Pioneer Corps, men with large muscles and small brains (selected by other men with small muscles and large brains) who were not only good at emptying dustbins and heaving loads but liked doing it. They were never to be asked to do more than they were proved to be fit for. They were never to be forced to mix with anyone who made them feel foolish by emptying dustbins more quickly or, what was worse at that time, by consigning all dustbins to the rubbish-heap—a sure sign either of mental deficiency or genius. As I say, progressive managements were very tentative and even a little shamefaced. They were easily put off by references to Mr. Huxley's gammas and Mr. Orwell's proles. The managers did not see that these two gentlemen had both been attacking not equal opportunity, but the effects of conditioning and propaganda. By these means even intelligent people were to be brought to accept their fate as manual workers. We know that in the long run this is impossible, and in the short run absurdly wasteful and frustrating. The only good manual workers, we know, are those who have not the ability for anything better. Enlightened modern methods have nothing in common with these brave new worlds. But at first not all managers realized that so signally to square efficiency with justice, and order with humanity, was nothing less than a new stage in the ascent of man, brought within his reach by the early advances in the social sciences.

The Pioneer Corps was the essential counterpart of the administrative class in the civil service; its historical significance is as great as that. The success of open competition in government employment established the principle that the most responsible posts should be filled by the most able people; the Pioneers that the least responsible jobs should be filled by the least able people. In other words, a society in which power and responsibility were as much proportioned to merit as education. The civil service won acceptance far more easily—no one wanted to be blown, up by hydrogen bombs or starved of foreign exchange because something less han the finest brains were ensconced in Whitehall. The Pioneers encountered far more opposition. The community of principle governing the civil service and the Pioneers was not at once recognized. The objectors, amongst them a growing number of socialists, complained of "indignity." A vague word, to conceal a vague concept. The brute fact is that the great majority of minds were still thinking in pre-merit terms.

In the dark England of the distant past it made the best of sense to plead for equality. In the main way that counts, in their brain-power, the industrial workers, or the peasantry, or whoever it might be, were as good as their masters. What the anti-Pioneers did not realize was that the gradual shift from inheritance to merit as the ground of social selection was making (and has finally made) nonsense of all their loose talk of the equality of man. Men, after all, are notable not for the equality, but for the inequality, of their endowment. Once all the geniuses are amongst the élite, and all the morons amongst the workers, what meaning can equality have? What ideal can be upheld except the principle of equal status for equal intelligence? What is the purpose of abolishing inequalities in nurture except to reveal and make more pronounced the inescapable inequalities of Nature?

The decisive fact was the happiness of the Pioneers, or hand-workers, as they were at first called to distinguish them from brain-workers. No one wanted to flood the chronic wards of the mental hospitals, yet that is just what industry had for many years been doing by setting substandard people to perform tasks beyond their reach. No one wanted, least of all the socialists, to cause unnecessary suffering. The principle—"From each according to his capacity, neither more nor less"— was empirically justified. The workers were more content, and so, for the same reason, were the large middle-classes with I.Q.'s broadly between 100 and 125. It was shown time and time again by the psychologists that to put a highly intelligent man on a routine job was as disastrous—reflected as it was in sickness, absenteeism, and neurosis*—as the obverse. Matching of intelligence and job in the various streams of society was everywhere demonstrated as the highest expression of both efficiency and humanity; as the very engine of productivity at the same time as the liberator of mankind. Without the scientific study of human relations in industry, resentment against the declining status of the lower classes, and the widening gap between them and the upper classes, would have disrupted society long ago. . . .

FROM HERE, WHERE?

It was not my purpose in this essay to predict the course of events next May, but rather to show that the movement of protest had deep roots in our history. If my view be accepted, opposition even to the greatest institutions of modern society is inevitable. The hostility now manifest has long been latent. For more than half a century, the lower classes have been harboring resentments which they could not make articulate, until the present day.

If I have succeeded in adding at all to understanding of this complex story and persuaded any of my fellows not to take present discontents *too* lightly, my

---

*An investigation made just after the Hitler war was, to judge from the press, given insufficient attention at the time. "The women, who were on jobs requiring skill that did not correspond with their intelligence, had a higher incidence of recent definite neurosis than those on jobs whose skill requirements did correspond: the incidence of neurosis was equally high, irrespective of whether the skill required by the job was too high or too low compared with the worker's intelligence." Russell Fraser. *The Incidence of Neurosis amongst Factory Workers.* Industrial Health Research Board Report, No. 90, H.M.S.O., 1947. An earlier report of the same Board said that "severe boredom is usually found associated with more than average intelligence." I.H.R.B., No. 77, H.M.S.O., 1937.

purpose has been well achieved. But I am mindful that I may be expected to say a word about what is likely to happen. It can, of course, be no more than a personal opinion on which any reader of these pages is as well-tutored as myself. Nevertheless, I hold firmly to the belief that May 2034 will be at best an 1848, on the English model at that. There will be stir enough. The universities may shake. There will be other disturbances later on as long as the Populists survive. But on this occasion anything more serious than a few days' strike and a week's disturbance, which it will be well within the capacity of the police (with their new weapons) to quell, I do not for one moment envisage.

The reason I have already referred to. The charter is too vague. The demands are, with one exception, not in any way a fundamental challenge to the government. This is no revolutionary movement but a caucus of disparate groups held together only by a few charismatic personalities and an atmosphere of crisis. There is no tradition of political organization on which to draw. There are, indeed, already signs of dissension within the camp, as the result of the wise concessions which have been made. Since I began to write this essay a fortnight ago, the Chairman of the Social Science Research Council has proffered his weighty recommendations to the government. The Prime Minister quickly acted on these counsels of moderation, instructed Weather Control to bring on autumn a month early and announced, in his speech on 25 September at Kirkcaldy itself, that his party was going to expel half a dozen of its right-wing members, that the adoption scheme would not be made mandatory for the present, that equality of opportunity would be maintained as official policy, and that there was no intention at present of tampering with the primary schools or with adult education. His speech has, as *The Times* put it, "stolen the girls' thunder."

Behind the shift and turn of current politics is the underlying fact with which I opened my essay. The last century has witnessed a far-reaching redistribution of ability between the classes in society, and the consequence is that the lower classes no longer have the power to make revolt effective. For a short moment they may prosper through an alliance with the odd and passing disillusion of a section of the upper classes. But such *déclassé* people can never be more than an eccentric minority—the Populists have never been more than that as a serious political force— because the élite is treated with all the wise distinction that any heart can desire. Without intelligence in their heads, the lower classes are never more menacing than a rabble, even if they are sometimes sullen, sometimes mercurial, not yet completely predictable. If the hopes of some earlier dissidents had been realized and the brilliant children from the lower classes remained there, to teach, to inspire, and to organize the masses, then I should have had a different story to tell. The few who now propose such a radical step are a hundred years too late. This is the prediction I shall expect to verify when I stand next May listening to the speeches from the great rostrum at Peterloo.*

---

*Since the author of this essay was himself killed at Peterloo, the publishers regret they were not able to submit to him the proofs of his manuscript, for the corrections he might have wished to make before publication. The text, even this last section, has been left exactly as he wrote it. The failings of sociology are as illuminating as its successes.

Milovan Djilas

Rule by Bureaucrats

Everything happened differently in the U.S.S.R. and other Communist countries from what the leaders—even such prominent ones as Lenin, Stalin, Trotsky, and Bukharin—anticipated. They expected that the state would rapidly wither away, that democracy would be strengthened. The reverse happened. They expected a rapid improvement in the standard of living—there has been scarcely any change in this respect and, in the subjugated East European countries, the standard has even declined. In every instance, the standard of living has failed to rise in proportion to the rate of industrialization, which was much more rapid. It was believed that the differences between cities and villages, between intellectual and physical labor, would slowly disappear; instead these differences have increased. Communist anticipations in other areas—including their expectations for developments in the non-Communist world—have also failed to materialize.

The greatest illusion was that industrialization and collectivization in the U.S.S.R., and destruction of capitalist ownership, would result in a classless society. In 1936, when the new Constitution was promulgated, Stalin announced that the "exploiting class" has ceased to exist. The capitalist and other classes of ancient origin had in fact been destroyed, but a new class, previously unknown to history, had been formed.

It is understandable that this class, like those before it, should believe that the establishment of its power would result in happiness and freedom for all men. The only difference between this and other classes was that it treated the delay in the realization of its illusions more crudely. It thus affirmed that its power was more complete than the power of any other class before in history, and its class illusions and prejudices were proportionally greater.

This new class, the bureaucracy, or more accurately the political bureaucracy, has all the characteristics of earlier ones as well as some new characteristics of its own. Its origin had its special characteristics also, even though in essence it was similar to the beginnings of other classes.

Other classes, too, obtained their strength and power by the revolutionary path, destroying the political, social, and other orders they met in their way. However, almost without exception, these classes attained power *after* new economic patterns had taken shape in the old society. The case was the reverse with new classes in the Communist systems. It did not come to power to *complete* a new economic order but to *establish* its own and, in so doing, to establish its power over society.

From *The New Class, An Analysis of the Communist System,* by Milovan Djilas, 1957, Frederick A. Praeger, Inc. and Thames and Hudson Ltd., pp. 37-42, 59-69. Reprinted by permission

In earlier epochs the coming to power of some class, some part of a class, or of some party, was the final event resulting from its formation and its development. The reverse was true in the U.S.S.R. There the new class was definitely formed after it attained power. Its consciousness had to develop before its economic and physical powers, because the class had not taken root in the life of the nation. This class viewed its role in relation to the world from an idealistic point of view. Its practical possibilities were not diminished by this. In spite of its illusions, it represented an objective tendency toward industrialization. Its practical bent emanated from this tendency. The promise of an ideal world increased the faith in the ranks of the new class and sowed illusions among the masses. At the same time it inspired gigantic physical undertakings.

Because this new class had not been formed as a part of the economic and social life before it came to power, it could only be created in an organization of a special type, distinguished by a special discipline based on identical philosophic and ideological views of its members. A unity of belief and iron discipline was necessary to overcome its weaknesses.

The roots of the new class were implanted in a special party, of the Bolshevik type. Lenin was right in his view that his party was an exception in the history of human society, although he did not suspect that it would be the beginning of a new class.

To be more precise, the initiators of the new class are not found in the party of the Bolshevik type as a whole but in that stratum of professional revolutionaries who made up its core even before it attained power. It was not by accident that Lenin asserted after the failure of the 1905 revolution that only professional revolutionaries—men whose sole profession was revolutionary work—could build a new party of the Bolshevik type. It was still less accidental that even Stalin, the future creator of a new class, was the most outstanding example of such a professional revolutionary. The new ruling class has been gradually developing from this very narrow stratum of revolutionaries. These revolutionaries composed its core for a long period. Trotsky noted that in prerevolutionary professional revolutionaries was the origin of the future Stalinist bureaucrat. What he did not detect was the beginning of a new class of owners and exploiters.

This is not to say that the new party and the new class are identical. The party, however, is the core of that class, and its base. It is very difficult, perhaps impossible, to define the limits of the new class and to identify its members. The new class may be said to be made up of those who have special privileges and economic preference because of the administrative monopoly they hold.

Since administration is unavoidable in society, necessary administrative functions may be coexistent with parasitic functions in the same person. Not every member of the party is a member of the new class, any more than every artisan or member of the city party was a bourgeois.

In loose terms, as the new class becomes stronger and attains a more perceptible physiognomy, the role of the party diminishes. The core and the basis of the new class is created in the party and at its top, as well as in the state political organs. The once live, compact party, full of initiative, is disappearing to become transformed into the traditional oligarchy of the new class, irresistibly drawing into its ranks those who aspire to join the new class and repressing those who have any ideals.

The party makes the class, but the class grows as a result and uses the party as a basis. The class grows stronger, while the party grows weaker; this is the inescapable fate of every Communist party in power.

If it were not materially interested in production or if it did not have within itself the potentialities for the creation of a new class, no party could act in so morally and ideologically foolhardy a fashion, let alone stay in power for long. Stalin declared, after the end of the First Five-Year Plan: "If we had not created the apparatus, we would have failed!" He should have substituted "new class" for the word "apparatus," and everything would have been clearer.

It seems unusual that a political party could be the beginning of a new class. Parties are generally the product of classes and strata which have become intellectually and economically strong. However, if one grasps the actual conditions in pre-revolutionary Russia and in other countries in which Communism prevailed over national forces, it will be clear that a party of this type is the product of specific opportunities and that there is nothing unusual or accidental in this being so. Although the roots of Bolshevism reach far back into Russian history, the party is partly the product of the unique pattern of international relationships in which Russia found itself at the end of the nineteenth and the beginning of the twentieth century. Russia was no longer able to live in the modern world as an absolute monarchy, and Russia's capitalism was too weak and too dependent on the interests of foreign powers to make it possible to have an industrial revolution. This revolution could only be implemented by a new class, or by a change in the social order. As yet, there was no such class.

In history, it is not important who implements a process, it is only important that the process be implemented. Such was the case in Russia and other countries in which Communist revolutions took place. The revolution created forces, leaders, organizations, and ideas which were necessary to it. The new class came into existence for objective reasons, and by the wish, wits, and action of its leaders.

The social origin of the new class lies in the proletariat just as the aristocracy arose in a peasant society, and the bourgeoisie in a commercial and artisans' society. There are exceptions, depending on national conditions, but the proletariat in economically underdeveloped countries, being backward, constitutes the raw material from which the new class arises.

There are other reasons why the new class always acts as the champion of the working class. The new class is anti-capitalistic and, consequently, logically dependent upon the working strata. The new class is supported by the proletarian struggle and the traditional faith of the proletariat in a socialist, Communist society where there is no brutal exploitation. It is vitally important for the new class to assure a normal flow of production, hence it cannot ever lose its connection with the proletariat. Most important of all, the new class cannot achieve industrialization and consolidate its power without the help of the working class. On the other hand, the working class sees in expanded industry the salvation from its poverty and despair. Over a long period of time, the interests, ideas, faith, and hope of the new class, and of parts of the working class and of the poor peasants, coincide and unite. Such mergers have occurred in the past among other widely different classes. Did not the bourgeoisie represent the peasantry in the struggle against the feudal lords?

The movement of the new class toward power comes as a result of the efforts of the proletariat and the poor. These are the masses upon which the party or the new class must lean and with which its interests are most closely allied. This is true until the new class finally establishes its power and authority. Over and above this, the new class is interested in the proletariat and the poor only to the extent necessary for developing production and for maintaining in subjugation the most aggressive and rebellious social forces.

The monopoly which the new class establishes in the name of the working class over the whole of society is, primarily, a monopoly over the working class itself. This monopoly is first intellectual, over the so-called *avant-garde* proletariat, and then over the whole proletariat. This is the biggest deception the class must accomplish, but it shows that the power and interests of the new class lie primarily in industry. Without industry the new class cannot consolidate its position or authority.

Former sons of the working class are the most steadfast members of the new class. It has always been the fate of slaves to provide for their masters the most clever and gifted representatives. In this case a new exploiting and governing class is born from the exploited class. . . .

No class is established by its own action, even though its ascent is organized and accompanied by a conscious struggle. This holds true for the new class in Communism.

The new class, because it had a weak relationship to the economy and social structure, and of necessity had its origin in a single party, was forced to establish the highest possible organizational structure. Finally it was forced to a deliberate and conscious withdrawal from its earlier tenets. Consequently the new class is more highly organized and more highly class-conscious than any class in recorded history.

This proposition is true only if it is taken relatively; consciousness and organizational structure being taken in relation to the outside world and to other classes, powers, and social forces. No other class in history has been as cohesive and single-minded in defending itself and in controlling that which it holds—collective and monopolistic ownership and totalitarian authority.

On the other hand, the new class is also the most deluded and least conscious of itself. Every private capitalist or feudal lord was conscious of the fact that he belonged to a special discernible social category. He usually believed that this category was destined to make the human race happy, and that without this category chaos and general ruin would ensue. A Communist member of the new class also believes that, without his party, society would regress and founder. But he is not conscious of the fact that he belongs to a new ownership class, for he does not consider himself an owner and does not take into account the special privileges he enjoys. He thinks that he belongs to a group with prescribed ideas, aims, attitudes, and roles. That is all he sees. He cannot see that at the same time he belongs to a special social category: the *ownership* class.

Collective ownership, which acts to reduce the class, at the same time makes it unconscious of its class substance, and each one of the collective owners is deluded in that he thinks he uniquely belongs to a movement which would abolish classes in society.

A comparison of other characteristics of the new class with those of other ownership classes reveals many similarities and many differences. The new class is voracious and insatiable, just as the bourgeoisie was. But it does not have the virtues of frugality and economy that the bourgeoisie had. The new class is as exclusive as the aristocracy but without aristocracy's refinement and proud chivalry.

The new class also has advantages over other classes. Because it is more compact it is better prepared for greater sacrifices and heroic exploits. The individual is completely and totally subordinated to the whole; at least, the prevailing ideal calls for such subordination even when he is out seeking to better himself. The new class is strong enough to carry out material and other ventures that no other class was ever able to do. Since it possesses the nation's goods, the new class is in a position to devote itself religiously to the aims it has set and to direct all the forces of the people to the furtherance of these aims.

The new ownership is not the same as the political government, but is created and aided by that government. The use, enjoyment, and distribution of property is the privilege of the party and the party's top men.

Party members feel that authority, that control over property, brings with it the privileges of this world. Consequently, unscrupulous ambition, duplicity, toadyism, and jealousy inevitably must increase. Careerism and an ever expanding bureaucracy are the incurable diseases of Communism. Because the Communists have transformed themselves into owners, and because the road to power and to material privileges is open only through "devotion" to the party—to the class, to "socialism"—unscrupulous ambition must become one of the main ways of life and one of the main methods for the development of Communism.

In non-Communist systems, the phenomena of careerism and unscrupulous ambition are a sign that it is profitable to be a bureaucrat, or that owners have become parasites, so that the administration of property is left in the hands of employees. In Communism, careerism and unscrupulous ambition testify to the fact that there is an irresistible drive toward ownership and the privileges that accompany the administration of material goods and men.

Membership in other ownership classes is not identical with the ownership of particular property. This is still less the case in the Communist system inasmuch as ownership is collective. To be an owner or a joint owner in the Communist system means that one enters the ranks of the ruling political bureaucracy and nothing else.

In the new class, just as in other classes, some individuals constantly fall by the wayside while others go up the ladder. In private-ownership classes an individual left his property to his descendants. In the new class no one inherits anything except the aspiration to raise himself to a higher rung of the ladder. The new class is actually being created from the lowest and broadest strata of the people, and is in constant motion. Although it is sociologically possible to prescribe who belongs to the new class, it is difficult to do so; for the new class melts into and spills over into the people, into other lower classes, and is constantly changing.

The road to the top is theoretically open to all, just as every one of Napoleon's soldiers carried a marshal's baton in his knapsack. The only thing that is required to get on the road is sincere and complete loyalty to the party or to the new class. Open at the bottom, the new class becomes increasingly and relentlessly narrower at the top. Not only is the desire necessary for the climb; also necessary is the ability to understand and develop doctrines, firmness in struggles against antagonists, exceptional dexterity and cleverness in intra-party struggles, and talent in strengthening the class. Many present themselves, but few are chosen. Although more open in some respects than other classes, the new class is also more exclusive than other classes. Since one of the new class's most important features is monopoly of authority, this exclusiveness is strengthened by bureaucratic hierarchical prejudices.

Nowhere, at any time, has the road been as wide open to the devoted and the loyal as it is in the Communist system. But the ascent to the heights has never at any time been so difficult or required so much sacrifice and so many victims. On the one hand, Communism is open and kind to all; on the other hand, it is exclusive and intolerant even of its own adherents.

The fact that there is a new ownership class in Communist countries does not explain everything, but it is the most important key to understanding the changes which are periodically taking place in these countries, especially in the U.S.S.R.

It goes without saying that every such change in each separate Communist country and in the Communist system as a whole must be examined separately, in order to determine the extent and significance of the change in the specific circumstances. To do this, however, the system should be understood as a whole to the fullest extent possible.

In connection with current changes in the U.S.S.R. it will be profitable to point out in passing what is occurring in the kolkhozes [collective farms]. The establishment of kolkhozes and the Soviet government policy toward them illustrates clearly the exploiting nature of the new class.

Stalin did not and Khrushchev does not consider kolkhozes as a "logical socialistic" form of ownership. In practice this means that the new class has not succeeded in completely taking over the management of the villages. Through the kolkhozes and the use of the compulsory crop-purchase system, the new class has succeeded in making vassals of the peasants and grabbing a lion's share of the peasants' income, but the new class has not become the only power of the land. Stalin was completely aware of this. Before his death, in *Economic Problems of Socialism in the U.S.S.R.*, Stalin foresaw that the kolkhozes should become state property, which is to say that the bureaucracy should become the real owner. Criticizing Stalin for his excess use of purges, Khrushchev did not however renounce Stalin's views on property in kolkhozes. The appointment by the new regime of 30,000 party workers, mostly to be presidents of kolkhozes, was only one of the measures in line with Stalin's policy.

Just as under Stalin, the new regime, in executing its so-called liberalization policy, is extending the "socialist" ownership of the new class. Decentralization in the economy does not mean a change in ownership, but only gives greater rights to the lower strata of the bureaucracy or of the new class. If the so-called liberalization and decentralization meant anything else, that would be manifest in the political right of at least part of the people to exercise some influence in the management of material goods. At least, the people would have the right to criticize the arbitrariness of the oligarchy. This would lead to the creation of a new political movement, even though it were only a loyal opposition. However, this is not even mentioned, just as democracy in the party is not mentioned. Liberalization and decentralization are in force only for Communists; first for the oligarchy, the leaders of the new class; and second, for those in the lower echelons. This is the new method, inevitable under changing conditions, for the further strengthening and consolidation of monopolistic ownership and totalitarian authority of the new class.

The fact that there is a new owning, monopolistic, and totalitarian class in Communist countries calls for the following conclusion: All changes initiated by the Communist chiefs are dictated first of all by the interests and aspirations of the new class, which, like every social group, lives and reacts, defends itself and advances, with the aim of increasing its power. This does not mean, however, that such changes may not be important for the rest of the people as well. Although the innovations introduced by the new class have not yet materially altered the Communist system, they must not be underestimated. It is necessary to gain insight into the substance of these changes in order to determine their range and significance.

The Communist regime, in common with others, must take into account the mood and movement of the masses. Because of the exclusiveness of the Communist Party and the absence of free public opinion in its ranks, the regime cannot discern the real status of the masses. However, their dissatisfaction does penetrate the consciousness of the top leaders. In spite of its totalitarian management, the new class is not immune to every type of opposition.

Once in power, the Communists have no difficulty in settling their accounts with the bourgeoisie and large-estate owners. The historical development is hostile to them and their property and it is easy to arouse the masses against them. Seizing property from the bourgeoisie and the large-estate owners is quite easy; difficulties arise when seizure of small properties is involved. Having acquired power in the course of earlier expropriations, the Communists can do even this. Relations are rapidly clarified: there are no more old classes and old owners, society is "classless," or on the road to being so, and men have started to live in a new manner.

Under such conditions, demands to return to the old prerevolutionary relations seem unrealistic, if not ridiculous. Material and social bases no longer exist for the maintenance of such relations. The Communists meet such demands as if they were jests.

The new class is most sensitive to demands on the part of the people for a special kind of freedom, not for freedom in general or political freedom. It is especially sensitive to demands for freedom of thought and criticism, within the limits of present conditions and within the limits of "socialism"; not for demands for a return to previous social and ownership relations. This sensitivity originates from the class's special position.

The new class instinctively feels that national goods are, in fact, its property, and that even the terms "socialist," "social," and "state" property denote a general legal fiction. The new class also thinks that any breach of its totalitarian authority might imperil its ownership. Consequently, the new class opposes *any* type of freedom, ostensibly for the purpose of preserving "socialist" ownership. Criticism of the new class's monopolistic administration of property generates the fear of a possible loss of power. The new class is sensitive to these criticisms and demands depending on the extent to which they expose the manner in which it rules and holds power.

This is an important contradiction. Property is legally considered social and national property. But, in actuality, a single group manages it in its own interest. The discrepancy between legal and actual conditions continuously results in obscure and abnormal social and economic relationships. It also means that the words of the leading group do not correspond to its actions; and that all actions result in strengthening its property holdings and its political position.

This contradiction cannot be resolved without jeopardizing the class's position. Other ruling, property-owning classes could not resolve this contradiction either, unless forcefully deprived of monopoly of power and ownership. Wherever there has been a higher degree of freedom for society as a whole, the ruling classes have been forced, in one way or another, to renounce monopoly of ownership. The reverse is true also: wherever monopoly of ownership has been impossible, freedom, to some degree, has become inevitable.

In Communism, power and ownership are almost always in the same hands, but this fact is concealed under a legal guise. In classical capitalism, the worker had equality with the capitalist before the law, even though the worker was being exploited and the capitalist was doing the exploiting. In Communism, legally, all are equal with respect to material goods. The formal owner is the nation. In reality, because of monopolistic administration, only the narrowest stratum of administrators enjoys the rights of ownership.

Every real demand for freedom in Communism, the kind of demand that hits at the substance of Communism, boils down to a demand for bringing material and property relations into accord with what the law provides.

A demand for freedom—based on the position that capital goods produced by the nation can be managed more efficiently by society than by private monopoly or a private owner, and consequently should actually be in the hands or under control of society exercised through its freely elected representatives—would force the new class either to make concessions to other forces, or to take off the mask and admit its ruling and exploiting characteristics. The type of ownership and exploitation which the new class creates by using its authority and its administrative privileges is such that even the class itself must deny it. Does not the new class emphasize that it uses its authority and administrative functions in the name of the nation as a whole to preserve national property?

This makes the legal position of the new class uncertain and is also the source of the new class's biggest internal difficulties. The contradiction discloses the disharmony between words and actions: While promising to abolish social differences, it must always increase them by acquiring the products of the nation's workshops and granting privileges to its adherents. It must proclaim loudly its dogma that it is fulfilling its historical mission of "final" liberation of mankind from every misery and calamity while it acts in exactly the opposite way.

The contradiction between the new class's real ownership position and its legal position can furnish the basic reason for criticism. This contradiction has within it the ability not only to incite others but also to corrode the class's own ranks, since privileges are actually being enjoyed by only a few. This contradiction, when intensified, holds prospects of real changes in the Communist system, whether the ruling class is in favor of the change or not. The fact that this contradiction is so obvious has been the reason for the changes made by the new class, especially in so-called liberalization and decentralization.

Forced to withdraw and surrender to individual strata, the new class aims at concealing this contradiction and strengthening its own position. Since ownership and authority continue intact, all measures taken by the new class—even those democratically inspired—show a tendency toward strengthening the management of the political bureaucracy. The system turns democratic measures into positive methods for consolidating the position of the ruling classes. Slavery in ancient times in the East inevitably permeated all of society's activities and components, including the family. In the same way, the monopolism and totalitarianism of the ruling class in the Communist system are imposed on all the aspects of social life, even though the political heads are not aiming at this.

Yugoslavia's so-called workers' management and autonomy, conceived at the time of the struggle against Soviet imperialism as a far-reaching democratic measure to deprive the party of the monopoly of administration, has been increasingly relegated to one of the areas of party work. Thus, it is hardly possible to change the present system. The aim of creating a new democracy through this type of administration will not be achieved. Besides, freedom cannot be extended to the largest piece of the pie. Workers' management has not brought about a sharing in profits by those who produce, either on a national level or in local enterprises. This type of administration has increasingly turned into a safe type for the regime. Through various taxes and other means, the regime has appropriated even the share of the profits which the workers believed would be given to them. Only crumbs from the tables and illusions have been left to the workers. Without universal freedom not even workers' management can become free. Clearly, in an unfree society nobody can freely decide anything. The givers have somehow obtained the most value from the gift of freedom they supposedly handed the workers.

This does not mean that the new class cannot make concessions to the people, even though it only considers its own interests. Workers' management, or decentralization, is a concession to the masses. Circumstances may drive the new class, no matter how monopolistic and totalitarian it may be, to retreat before the masses. In 1948, when the conflict took place between Yugoslavia and the U.S.S.R., the Yugoslav leaders were forced to execute some reforms. Even though it might mean a backward step, they set up reforms as soon as they saw themselves in jeopardy. Something similar is happening today in the eastern European countries.

In defending its authority the ruling class must execute reforms every time it becomes obvious to the people that the class is treating national property as its own. Such reforms are not proclaimed as being what they really are, but rather as part of the "further development of socialism" and "socialist democracy." The groundwork for reforms is laid when the discrepancy mentioned above becomes public. From the historical point of view the new class is forced to fortify its authority and ownership constantly, even though it is running away from the truth. It must constantly demonstrate how it is successfully creating a society of happy people, all of whom enjoy equal rights and have been freed of every type of exploitation. The new class cannot avoid falling continuously into profound internal contradictions; for in spite of its historical origin it is not able to make its ownership lawful, and it cannot renounce ownership without undermining itself. Consequently, it is forced to try to justify its increasing authority, invoking abstract and unreal purposes.

This is a class whose power over men is the most complete known to history. For this reason it is a class with very limited views, views which are false and unsafe. Closely ingrown, and in complete authority, the new class must unrealistically evaluate its own role and that of the people around it.

Having achieved industrialization, the new class can now do nothing more than strengthen its brute force and pillage the people. It ceases to create. Its spiritual heritage is overtaken by darkness.

While the new class accomplished one of its greatest successes in the revolution, its method of control is one of the most shameful pages in human history. Men will marvel at the grandiose ventures it accomplished, and will be ashamed of the means it used to accomplish them.

When the new class leaves the historical scene—and this must happen—there will be less sorrow over its passing than there was for any other class before it. Smothering everything except what suited its ego, it has condemned itself to failure and shameful ruin.